Bigfoot Evidence

A case for the existence of the Sasquatch

WILLIAM JEVNING

ISBN: 10:1543292356
ISBN:13:978-1543292350

DEDICATION

To my mother "Gerry"

CONTENTS

ACKNOWLEDGMENTS

I wish to thank everyone who shared their personal encounters and photographs, and to my friend Tony for his legal knowledge and perspectives.

1 FOUNDATIONS

Until the late 1950's the subject of Sasquatch was not widely known, since sightings were local curiosities, and word did not travel outside the area where the events took place. News was not shared except for big stories, right up to the outbreak of World War 2.

Sightings of the creatures had been happening literally for centuries, yet remained as local oddities, until stories began making it onto the national wire services, and people began investigating the phenomena.

To this day many often say there is no evidence to support the existence of the creatures; however this is always a statement based on nothing more than personal opinion.

At times people with scientific accreditation have become involved in the controversy surrounding the subject. They often have little more to offer than personal opinions based on their training. Many professionals fear destroying their career by becoming too involved in the subject of Bigfoot, but even those who choose to become involved have less to contribute than some non-professionals with no scientific credentials who have witnessed the creatures themselves, and have been researching the topic for decades. The result is the current murky condition of the subject that allows every "opinion" under the sun to govern the topic.

The issue of the creature's very existence has fallen into such controversy that no one in their right mind wants to touch it, let alone consider launching an investigation to settle the matter.

"If the Sasquatch exists, why is there no evidence?" This question is asked because laymen and credentialed scientists alike, for the past fifty years have offered nothing more than personal opinion, based on little field investigation if any. The person rightly asking this question sees that there is no structured system for evaluating evidence.

Many people have become frustrated with the subject and with those who participate in it because of the lack of structure in investigative work, and because they see no evidence being produced.

However, this author has been involved in the topic for forty five years, and has seen and collected much material supporting what I saw with my own eyes regarding these creatures.

The problem is this: what *is* evidence of Sasquatch, and how do we determine this evidence is valid?

Sometimes I enjoy watching true crime shows on television, they can be very entertaining. I noticed that it was common for people to routinely receive convictions with very little evidence to support the decision of jurors or judges.

I wondered just how the legal system might handle the subject of the Sasquatch? I began discussing this with a good friend who is a forty year veteran trial attorney and through our discussions we realized that the law provides a very structured way evidence in the subject of the Sasquatch would be determined and categorized without the "opinions" that have so far driven the topic.

My attorney friend Tony and I originally envisioned creating a fictional trial setting in which to offer evidence, bit I felt this would detract from my main purpose of writing this book, and that is simply to show what the law says is evidence, the types of evidence and how they might be presented.

Before I proceed, let us imagine that a legal proceeding has been filed with a court. This could be done for a variety of reasons, but let's say for a loose framework that a professional person's credibility has been challenged because word got out that they had encountered a Sasquatch, and the reason for the impending court proceeding is to vindicate the persons professional standing.

This indeed can be a very real situation as I have spoken many times to persons in lofty professional settings that rely very much on credibility and any hint of something like a Bigfoot encounter would destroy a career overnight, so this is plausible.

To help provide a simple framework for us to use I will not follow the path of a trial with all its nuances, however for the sake of the flavor of this setting as the author I will be the judge allowing evidence to be entered into our fictitious record. We will have two opposing councilmen mostly for the entering of evidence. You the reader are the jury. The evidence however is real, and that will be entered into record for your consideration.

Before we begin, the following information is the framework we will be using for the evidence that will be presented.

First we need to understand what constitutes evidence, and this is not opinion. All attorneys and trials are strictly governed by what is called the federal rules of evidence; each state in the United States has adopted these rules with some minor variations. The following material I will be quoting directly from the federal rules of evidence, and all materials contained within this book fall under these rules.

The following material is used in the United States and has been adopted by all fifty states with minor alterations in some. The Federal Rules of Evidence was adopted to make a standard for governing evidence. Other countries in the world often have similar rules and they are not too different than the following. This standard ensures that evidence is determined, and utilized in a uniform way and is strictly governed by law.

The Federal Rules of Evidence can easily be found and researched by anyone interested, and I did not wish to get the reader mired in too much of this, my intent was to provide enough to show that the material presented fits within the legal parameters of evidence and the types of said evidence.

First what is the definition of evidence?

Every type of proof legally presented at trial (allowed by the judge) which is intended to convince the judge and/or jury of alleged facts material to the case. It can include oral testimony of witnesses, including experts on technical matters, documents, public records, objects, photographs and depositions (testimony under oath taken before trial). It also includes so-called "circumstantial evidence" which is intended to create belief by showing surrounding circumstances which logically lead to a conclusion of fact. Comments and arguments by the attorneys, statements by the judge and answers to questions which the judge has ruled objectionable are not evidence. Charts, maps and models which are used to demonstrate or explain matters are not evidence themselves, but testimony based upon such items and marks on such material may be evidence. Evidence must survive objections of opposing attorneys that it is irrelevant, immaterial or violates rules against "hearsay" (statements by a party not in court), and/or other technicalities.

The main difference between the use of evidence in criminal and civil cases is the <u>burden of proof</u> . For a guilty verdict in a criminal trial, the prosecution must prove guilt "beyond a reasonable doubt." But for a civil defendant to be found liable, the plaintiff generally need only prove culpability "by a preponderance of the evidence" (a lower threshold).

What are the rules of evidence?

Definition of evidence:

In legal terms, evidence covers the burden of proof, admissibility, relevance, weight, and sufficiency of what should be admitted into the record of a legal proceeding. Evidence- crucial in both civil and criminal proceedings- may include blood or hair samples, video surveillance recordings, or witness testimony. The Federal Rules of Evidence govern the admissibility of evidence in federal trials, but state rules of evidence are largely modeled after the federal rules.

There are four general types of evidence:

1: Real evidence – Tangible things, such as a weapon.

2: Demonstrative – A model of what likely happened at a given time and place.

3: Documentary- A letter, blog post, or other document.

4: Testimonial- Witness testimony.

The following information is quoted directly from the federal rules of evidence:

EVIDENCE:

Any matter of fact that a party to a lawsuit offers to prove or disprove an issue in the case. A system of rules and standards that is used to determine which facts may be admitted, and to what extent a judge or jury may consider those facts, as proof of a particular issue in a lawsuit.

Until 1975, the law of evidence was largely a creature of the common law: Evidence rules in most jurisdictions were established by cases rather than organized, official codifications. Legal scholars long pushed for legislation to provide uniformity and predictability to the evidentiary issues that arise during litigation. Following a lengthy campaign begun by the American Law Institute, which drafted its Model Rules of Evidence in 1942, and the National Conference of Commissioners on Uniform State Rules, which drafted the Uniform Rules of Evidence in 1953, Congress in 1975 adopted the Federal Rules of Evidence. The Federal Rules of Evidence are the official rules in federal court proceedings. Both state and federal rules of evidence serve as a guide for judges and attorneys so that they can determine whether to admit evidence- that is, whether to allow evidence to be observed by the judge or jury making factual conclusions in a trial.

One important benchmark of admissibility is relevance. Federal Rule of Evidence 402 states, in part, "All relevant evidence is admissible, except as otherwise provided." The goal of this rule is to allow parties to present all of the evidence that bears on the issue to be decided, and to keep out all evidence that is immaterial or that lacks probative value. For example, the fact that a defendant attends church every week is immaterial, and thus irrelevant, to a charge of running a red light. Probative value is a tendency to make the existence of any material fact more or less probable. For instance, evidence that a murder defendant ate spaghetti on the day of the murder would normally be irrelevant because people who ate spaghetti are not more or less likely to commit murder, as compared with other people. However, if spaghetti sauce were found at the murder scene, the fact that the defendant ate spaghetti that day would have probative value and thus would be relevant evidence.

Let's take a look at the four types of evidence:

1: Real evidence – Tangible things, such as a weapon.

The term "real evidence" describes any **evidence** that is a tangible object, as opposed or oral **testimony** or **documentary evidence**, which records information that is offered as evidence. "Real evidence" is often used interchangeably with "physical evidence" to describe objects that are used to prove or disprove arguments in **trial** or at a hearing. Real evidence is used to prove a fact based on the characteristics of all or part of an object.

For instance, suppose that in a **products liability** case, the **plaintiff** was injured when the blade protector on the power saw she was using suddenly fell off, causing the saw to jump and severely injure the plaintiff's arm. At trial, the plaintiff introduces the defective saw, with its now-detached plastic blade protector, into evidence in order to show the **judge** and the **jury** the actual defective saw that injured her. In this situation, the saw and blade protector are examples of real or physical evidence.

Physical evidence is also common in criminal cases, and it frequently shows up on popular TV crime shows. The alleged murder weapon may be admitted into court as a piece of real evidence, or another object may be admitted. The infamous blood-soaked glove that didn't fit O.J. Simpson's hand in his 1996 murder trial is another example of real or physical evidence.

Real evidence should not be confused with "documentary evidence." Documentary evidence also involves physical objects, like written documents, cassette or CD recordings, and videotapes or DVD recordings. However, when evidence is "documentary," these physical objects are only the carriers of the evidence – they are not the evidence itself. The actual evidence is the information recorded on the paper, tape, or disc.

One way to think about the difference between real evidence and documentary evidence is to ask, "If I changed the actual physical object, would it change the information I'm trying to show the jury?" If the answer is "yes," the object is real evidence; if the answer is "no," the object is documentary evidence.

For instance, suppose that in a criminal shoplifting case, the prosecution brings out two pieces of evidence. Exhibit A is a DVD movie in its box. Exhibit B is a DVD recording showing someone who looks like the defendant taking Exhibit A off a store shelf and hiding it under his coat. In this situation, Exhibit A is real evidence, because it is the actual tangible thing the defendant is accused of stealing. Exhibit B, however, is documentary evidence, because the DVD is merely the carrier for the video of the defendant stealing something.

If you changed Exhibit A to a VHS tape, you would no longer be showing the jury the object the defendant stole, but something else. If you moved the video on Exhibit B to a VHS tape, however, you could still show the jury the recording of the defendant stealing a DVD. Therefore, Exhibit A is real evidence, while Exhibit B is documentary evidence.

The line between real and documentary evidence is clearer in some cases than in others. Written contracts can be particularly confusing, because a **breach of contract** case may deal with both the existence of the contract and the information contained in it. In these situations, the contract itself may be both real evidence (because it shows that the contract exists) and documentary evidence (because it records the terms of the contract on its pages).

Luckily, the difference between real evidence and documentary evidence is not a concern in most cases. It most often comes up when one of the parties challenges the admission of the evidence under the **best evidence rule.** The best evidence rule requires that an original or a highly accurate copy of a document or other object be brought into court.

In best evidence rule arguments, sometimes documentary evidence is not enough; real evidence is necessary. For instance, in the shoplifting case above, suppose that instead of admitting Exhibit A (the DVD the defendant is accused of stealing) into evidence, the prosecutor decides to take a photograph of the DVD and admit that into evidence. The photograph is documentary evidence showing that the supposedly-stolen DVD exists, but the defendant might **object** on the grounds of the best evidence rule, because the photograph is not as accurate and thorough a way to show the jury what was stolen as actually letting them see and handle the supposedly-stolen DVD would be.

Whether or not a best evidence rule objection can force a party to use real evidence instead of documentary evidence depends on the case. Sometimes, it is simply not realistic to use real evidence in court, even if it has not been destroyed through an accident or **spoliation.** For instance, suppose that in a **personal injury** case, the plaintiff was injured when she was hit by some cables hanging off the side of a speeding locomotive. In this situation, photographs of the locomotive and the cables may be admissible. Even though the photos are documentary evidence and thus may not be as helpful as the locomotive itself, it would be so difficult to bring the actual locomotive into the courtroom that the photographs are deemed "good enough."

2: Demonstrative – A model of what likely happened at a given time and place.

1. *Evidence other than testimony that is presented during the course of a civil or criminal trial. Demonstrative evidence includes actual evidence (e.g., a set of bloody gloves from a murder scene) and illustrative evidence (e.g., photographs and charts).*

2. Many trial attorneys view the presentation of evidence to the jury as analogous to the presentation of information by a teacher to students. As in the classroom, the involvement of more than one of a juror's senses in the courtroom increases the amount of information retained by that juror. For example, combining verbal testimony from witnesses with before and after X rays, or introducing a defective machine part that jurors can hold in their hands for inspection, makes for compelling courtroom activity. In a modern, "show-me" society, the ability of a trial lawyer to use demonstrative evidence effectively can make the difference between winning and losing a case.

3. One common and effective example of demonstrative evidence is the still photograph. Photographs of a plaintiff's bruises taken immediately after an accident can help a jury understand those injuries in a trial that occurs months or even years after the accident, when the injuries may have healed. Aerial photographs of the scene of a vehicular accident can show how a particular intersection is laid out, and can make more clear an ambiguous description of a blind intersection given by a witness.

4. X rays and medical models and illustrations can be very helpful to a jury in physical injury cases. These examples of demonstrative evidence help the jury "see inside" the victim to understand the nature and extent of the injuries. X rays can show not only fractures but also permanent metal pins and plates. Accurate models of a plaintiff's head and neck can show the interaction between the cervical area of the spine and the surrounding muscle and tissues in a soft-tissue injury case. Sometimes, partial or full skeletons are brought into courtrooms to demonstrate losses or restrictions of movement due to injuries. Modern computer-generated illustrations can show the exact injury to a specific plaintiff, as opposed to the generic injury represented in a stock medical illustration.

5. Graphs and charts are perhaps the most useful forms of demonstrative evidence. These tools can vividly illustrate a loss of earnings, a decrease in life expectancy, and past and future medical bills. Clear and concise charts can help a jury to arrange a complex set of events in a chronological fashion. These time lines can be crucial in organizing evidence, whether in a criminal trial or in a complex securities litigation. Often, maps and other geographic charts are used to show water flow, elevation, and other physical characteristics of real property (land).

6. Graphs and charts can be presented to a jury in a variety of ways. In addition to offering the standard large prepared poster board on an easel, some attorneys prefer to create charts as they speak to the jury, using large blank pieces of poster board and colored marker pens. Other attorneys like the dramatic effect of dimming the courtroom lights and using an overhead projector or computer screen to focus visual attention on their illuminated charts and graphs. Whatever the style of presentation, well-constructed charts and graphs that make good use of color and are clear and easy to understand are appreciated by jurors and can have a big effect during deliberations.

7. Articles and objects are also forms of demonstrative evidence. In addition to actual evidence that is introduced at trial (like the knife from a murder scene), other physical articles and objects can be used to help the jury understand the testimony. For example, in a product liability action based on a defective artificial hip, giving the jury models of ball-and-socket joints to manipulate and examine with their own hands can clarify testimony regarding the replacement joint that is still inside the plaintiff. Three-dimensional models and mock-ups of roadways, accident sites, or proposed buildings can simulate the outside world inside the courtroom to give proportion and scale to a witness's testimony.

8. With the permission of the judge, attorneys may be allowed to take the jurors to the scene of the crime or accident. Here, all a juror's senses are at work, and

testimony presented in court can be compared to and contrasted with the physical scene. A list prepared by both attorneys of items to "notice" may be read by the bailiff at the scene. Many juries appreciate not only the chance to get outside the courtroom but also the opportunity to see for themselves the place where it all happened.

9. With the advent of low-cost videocassette players and recorders, it has become more and more common to see videotape in the courtroom. A "day in the life of ..." video can graphically demonstrate the activities of a plaintiff living with debilitating injuries. For example, a plaintiff witness may say, "I can't pick up my children," whereas a video can actually show the plaintiff's young children milling about with the plaintiff able only to sit by and watch them. Videotapes can also show the traffic volume at a busy intersection or provide a driver's-eye view of a road sign obstructed by brush and leaves. If a jury is unable to leave the courtroom to visit the scene of a fire, a video camera can provide a tour through the burned-out remains of the family's residence. Some attorneys have actually begun hiring stunt persons to re-create vehicular accidents, driving comparable vehicles at the speeds they were going when the accidents occurred, and filming the results. Unlike a controlled dramatic re-creation, this kind of actual re-creation, with its inherent danger yet accurate representation of accident conditions, can be an effective tool at trial.

10. Though waning in popularity owing to the greater availability and lower cost of computers, slide projectors and human-created animation are still used by some attorneys. By taking two slide projectors, superimposing their projections, and connecting them with a sophisticated mechanical device, an attorney can make a before picture fade into an after picture with dramatic results. As with a presentation using an overhead projector, the dark courtroom and brightly-lit screen of a slide presentation focus the jury's visual attention. Animated cartoon shorts, hand inked by artists, are eye-catching and can portray exactly what the attorney wants to emphasize to the jury: for example, a cutaway "operating" engine might show how a defective part can cause the engine to break down.

11. Computers and computer-generated displays are at the cutting edge of demonstrative evidence. Computer-enhanced graphics can demonstrate anything from the speed of a vehicle to the loss of range of motion on an injured portion of the body. Computers also provide high storage capacity. One CD-ROM disc can store thousands of still photos, graphs, charts, digitized video clips, and even three-dimensional computer animations. An attorney who uses a computer to coordinate a presentation can combine many different forms of demonstrative evidence into a cohesive and dramatic whole. Still photos of an injury might be followed by a digitized video showing limited physical abilities after the injury. X-ray images can fade into graphs showing a loss of earning capacity. All these exhibits can be stored in a laptop computer and presented with minimal setup and distraction to the jurors. And the attorney making the presentation can instantly return to a particular demonstrative exhibit when making a point during closing arguments.

12. Another significant development in courtroom technology is the use of bar codes. This technology is helpful in organizing evidence in cases with numerous exhibits. Bar codes function in court much as they do in the department or grocery store. Exhibits, be they photographs or documents, are stored on CD-ROM according

13. to bar code. By entering or scanning the number, the item is immediately retrieved and can be displayed on the computer screen.

14. Many newer courtrooms are now equipped with individual computer terminals, so that jurors may view computer displays by attorneys on individual screens in the jury box. A future development may be the use of virtual reality—where individuals see and hear computer-generated images and sounds, and through body sensors "see" their hands and body within the simulation.

15. No matter the technology, demonstrative evidence must still conform to standard evidentiary rules. The trial court may disallow any item of demonstrative evidence that is inaccurate or incomplete. Courts can also strike evidence if it is unnecessarily cumulative: for example, 30 photographs of one bruise that can be seen clearly in one or two photographs constitute evidence that is unnecessarily cumulative.

16. An attorney must keep in mind that demonstrative evidence is not real evidence: it merely illustrates the points being argued to the jury and court. Computer-generated animation may only portray evidence that has been properly presented to the jury through testimony or as physical evidence. A chart or graph may only present numbers and amounts that have been properly calculated and proved. No matter how exciting the "show," the attorney must remember that items of demonstrative evidence are merely props, and that the witnesses and their testimony are still the primary method of presenting evidence to a jury.

17. 3: Documentary- A letter, blog post, or other document.

18.

19. Documentary evidence is a form of evidence that is presented and allowed as evidence in a trial or hearing. It is distinguished from oral testimony and physical evidence. Photographs, tape recordings, films, and printed emails are all forms of documentary evidence. However, a piece of evidence is not documentary evidence if it is presented for any purpose other than the examination of the contents of the document. It is to be noted that documentary evidence is subject to the best evidence rule, which requires that the original document be produced unless there is a good reason not to do so.

20.

4: Testimonial- Witness testimony.

21.

The most common form of evidence is the testimony of witnesses. A witness can be a person who actually viewed the crime or other event at issue, or a witness can be a person with other relevant information- someone who heard a dog bark near the time of a murder, or who saw an allegedly injured plaintiff lifting weights the day after his accident, or who shared an office with the defendant and can describe her character and personality. Any competent person may testify as a witness, provided the testimony meets other requirements, such as relevancy. When it comes to the legal field, the difference between testimony and testimonial is of great importance. As we all know, there are many terms within the field of Law that appear to have the same meaning, but yet have subtle distinctions. Once can say that the terms 'Testimony' and 'Testimonial' illustrate this point best. They present a conundrum in that many of us often understand the terms as meaning one and the same thing when, in fact, there is a slight difference between the two. This difference is so subtle that it almost blurs the distinction resulting in a trail of confusion. Most of us are somewhat acquainted with the term 'Testimony' which traditionally refers to the sworn declaration of a witness in court, or a declaration made by a person under oath or affirmation before a court of law. The definition of the term 'Testimonial' however, particularly in a legal context, is not that familiar to many of us.

As mentioned above, Testimony is conventionally defined as **a solemn declaration by a witness under oath or affirmation**. This declaration is generally made before a court of law. A Testimony can typically be given in written form or orally, although the latter is a more popular method of declaration. This declaration made by the witness involves the statement of facts pertaining to a certain incident, circumstance or occurrence. It is also recognized as a type of evidence, given to prove a certain fact or facts in a case. Keep in mind that when a person makes a declaration in such form under oath or affirmation, he/she is swearing or promising to declare the truth. Thus, a person found to be making a false declaration or stating false or incorrect facts will be charged with perjury.

2 INTRODUCTION OF EVIDENCE

I mentioned in the previous chapter that my intention was to avoid becoming distracted by the trial setting, so we will move directly to the evidence. I do think that introducing possible opening arguments by attorneys may be useful in demonstrating the opposing views currently held regarding the subject of the Sasquatch.

With each type of evidence presented, I will also add arguments by each side to help demonstrate what often happens in dialogues between those who are for and against the Sasquatch existing.

In addition to my wish of not being bogged down in a trial setting, the evidence I will present comes from numerous sources and would not likely come from a single encounter with Sasquatches.

A possible opening statement by an attorney for a plaintiff might be something like the following:

"We will demonstrate that there is overwhelming evidence to support the existence of large primate creatures in the wilds of North America, as yet unrecognized by science, known by many names but commonly called Bigfoot or Sasquatch."

The opposing counsel might make an opening statement something like the following:

"There has never been any proof of the existence of these imaginary creatures other than local legends and folklore, no physical or photographic evidence exists and there has been nothing more than the over active imaginations of people inventing stories of said creatures, honestly this proceeding is a waste of the courts time."

At this point the judge may direct the plaintiff to begin introducing evidence into the court record.

What I will do here is to begin introducing evidence, indicating the type of evidence as defined by the Federal Rules of Evidence.

PLAINTIFF: Your honor, at this time I would like to enter into the court record six written testimonies of eye witnesses, there are many more but if the court will allow this number should be sufficient at this time, there will be additional witness statements as we move forward. (Note: in an actual court case thousands of witness testimonies could possibly be entered into the record if a judge allowed such, for the constraints of a book however five is the number I am using for this demonstration.)

JUDGE: proceed counselor.

PLAINTIFF: I would like to enter the following witness testimony as witness statements 1A, 1B, 1C, 1D,1E and 1F for the record. (Remember, witness testimony according to the Federal Rules of Evidence may be in either written or oral form.)

(For privacy protection I will not be using names or altering names, in a real court proceeding names and addresses would be entered into a court record.)

Witness statement -1A:

"I'm originally from Southern Illinois and became interested in Sasquatch after the whole Big Muddy Monster thing in Illinois in the early 1970s. I was about 6 when those events occurred and for a while it was big news. I remember my dad watching shows about Bigfoot (and my mother scoffing) during that time. I started reading everything I could find and that continued through my middle school years and our move to Florida when I was 11. I don't recall ever having an experience in Illinois, other than a vague impression of being watched from the woods as my brother and I played at a playground in a camping area.

Once we got to Florida, things changed. I had absolutely no clue that these creatures were here. None. Not until much later. My mother's parents had moved down a year prior to us moving and had purchased land adjacent to property owned by my grandmother's youngest brother and his family. My parents also purchased land adjacent to both properties. My uncle and my grandparent's properties had been cleared and totaled together roughly 3 or so acres. My folks bought a 4 acre plot that consisted of land that had been mined for phosphate so many years prior that the mining had been done with horse-drawn equipment and the land had been allowed to return to its wild state. There was ridge that ran about 3 or so miles from some orange groves to the west to the end of my folks' property line and behind the ridge was swamp. There was a dirt road leading in to the property which is still there and is my folks' driveway. My siblings and I, before my parents had the house built, used to roam the drier areas of this property and the property to the west of it. I recall one day being on the dirt road and hearing something just beating the hell out of a tree trunk with a branch. We got spooked having no clue what could be doing that, and we took off back to our grandparents' house and spent the rest of the afternoon indoors. I was roughly 12 or 13 at the time, my brother was 10 or 11 and my sister would have been 7 or 8. One of my brother's friends was also with us that time.

A few years later, when I was 15 or so, I found a track on the property west of my folks' place. Didn't see anything else at that time but this was after the house was built and I had heard plenty of odd noises over the couple of years I had lived out there by that time. A friend of mine and I also got chased out of the woods on that property by something big about a year or so after I found the track.

Fast forward to when I'm in my 30s, married with a small daughter, and living elsewhere in the area. My grandmother was still living at the time and had been given a computer by one of our cousins. Having no use for it, she gave it to me. I was to pick it up one evening and arrived a bit early. My grandmother and my parents were out to dinner so while I waited for them to come home, I let my daughter, who was about 2-2 1/2, play in the sandbox by my parent's front deck while I sat in the large A-frame swing a few feet away. It was early summer, so it didn't get dark until after 8pm. It was just starting to get towards dusk and you could hear insects and birds. I was just sitting there enjoying the evening and listening to my daughter chattering to her toys when the hair on the back of my neck stood up and the insects went silent. I got a really strong sense of being watched coming from the far west side of the property. We were on the east end, almost to the property line. What really struck me as weird was that my folks' dogs, two 70lb boxers, were silent as well. I started to get really nervous, mostly because my daughter was there. I didn't at that time have a key to my folks' house or I'd have been inside and getting one of my dad's rifles, which I do know well how to use. Instead, since I did have a key to my grandmother's house and since my car was parked there anyway, I told my daughter that the mosquitos were coming out and we needed to go in. I didn't want her scared, and I didn't want whatever was watching us to think I was as scared as I was because I didn't want to provoke a predatory response. We calmly put the lid on the sandbox and walked back down to my grandmother's house, with me keeping myself between my daughter and the trees. Once we were in the house, I turned the TV on for my daughter and was getting her a snack when the most god-awful scream I have ever heard in my life came from outside. It shook the glass in the windows, it was that loud. I told my daughter it was an owl, but that was no owl. About 20 minutes later, I heard the automatic door open in the garage and my dad pulled my grandmother's car in. I didn't really want to go outside but I didn't want to deal with my mother's skepticism and sarcasm either so I went and everything was normal again. I loaded the computer and left pretty quickly.

About 6 months after that I was ghost hunting with my best friend about 20 or so miles south (this is in central Florida, south of the Green Swamp) in a cemetery adjacent to an old church. The cemetery was bordered on 3 sides by woods and there was a creek running along the rest side that I'm pretty sure runs into the Alafia River at some point. We were sitting in the car and I was watching the cemetery while my bestie was watching the tree line. I saw movement in the center of the cemetery but before I could mention it, my bestie said that a tree was moving on her side. I looked over, but it had stopped so I looked back towards the cemetery. I had been there many times, both at night and during the day, and knee the layout well. In the center, there was an evergreen bush that stood about 7 feet tall. When I looked back, there was a figure standing next to the bush, and it was about a foot taller than the bush. It was dark, so I could only see the silhouette of the figure: head directly on the shoulders, massive shoulders, long arms and covered with hair. I said something like: I'm seeing something I didn't notice before. My bestie turns to look (she was the driver) and says: Holy shit! I said: Time to leave. She started the car and we peeled out. The whole way back, we went back and forth about did we really see what we thought we saw? I went back during the day about a week later and took pictures, which I still have now 13 years later, of my daughter standing where this thing stood. She was exactly 3 feet tall at the time and would have stood mid-thigh level on this thing.

I have had no other experiences since then. My parents still live on the same property and my sister now lives on the property that my grandparents owned. There are fewer people out there now than there were, the water management agency used eminent domain to purchase all but 2 or 3 of the houses on the one street south of my folks' property because they were raising the level of the lake across the highway. There's a dump east of this area too, about a mile or two east, and a wildlife preserve. There is a series of lakes and creeks that connects this area to the Green Swamp to the north and to the Peace River to the south. The most recent sighting of a skunk ape that I know of was in 2013 and less than 2 miles as the crow flies south of there."

Witness statement -1B:

"I am 44 years old and I am a security officer for the Muckleshoot Indian Tribe. I have been a commercial fisherman for most of my life; I just recently started working a regular job. My first sighting was just a short encounter when I was probably 17 years old; myself and a few friends were sipping on a case of Rainier beer. We had just got the beer and I think we were on our first beer each. Our main spot for hanging out and drinking beer was a new building on our reservation just behind my house about 200 yards. There was a big front door area with a big awning over it; we used to hang out under. Just as we got relaxed and started joking and laughing, all of a sudden the dogs at the house nearest to us started freaking out and barking and growling. No one else was paying much attention to it, but it caught my attention and I moved out from under the awning and started looking toward the house where the dogs were barking. At first I didn't see much and suddenly I saw a slight movement out of the corner of my eye, and I saw a huge black figure peeking out from behind this green bushy tree that was kind of out in the open. At first I thought it was just my eyes playing tricks on me in the dark then it pulled itself back behind the tree!!!! I said out loud "HOLY SHIT!" and my friends didn't pay much attention to me and I told them I had just saw something peeking at me and they just laughed at me and kept talking. Just then it moved back out again and really quickly went back behind the tree. It was then I realized how big this thing actually was, it must have been between 10 and 12 feet tall because this tree, although it was a young tree, was about 15 to 17 feet tall, and this thing went most of the way to the top of the tree. I told my buddies "hey man let's move out of here and go under the new big light pole they just put in down the street". They laughed and said no let's just stay here. I couldn't handle staying there after what I just saw so I told them "no man I'm serious let's go under the light". They still disagreed with me so I had to tell them that since I was the one who bought the beer that

I was taking it with me to the big new light pole to sit and drink and if they wanted some of my beer they had to go with me. It was then that they realized how serious I really was, and they got real scared looks on their faces and said "oh shit, you are serious". I said I told you I'm not kidding around and I don't want to be here right now. We quickly packed up our beer and smokes and moved to the new light. We called our neighborhood god Woody to come and sit with nus because he was an awesome early warning system telling us when something wasn't right at night time.

The second sighting was a brief roadside sighting, me and my cousin were coming from a housing project which had a long dark road to get to the highway, and just as we were pulling out of the light it looked like someone tall was standing on the side of the road facing from our right to our left looking down at the ground, my cousin flipped on the bright lights and it looked up at us real quick. We got a real good look at this thing and it was a very scary moment because he looked right at us. We went right by him and we both looked at each other and said at the same time "DID YOU SEE THAT?" I don't know about him because he was driving but I got a real good look at this thing and it looked pretty scary!!! It was real stocky looking and had hair all over its body. It wasn't like most descriptions I hear about that say it didn't have hair on its face, it had hair on its face, its whole face was covered and I couldn't see any skin at all. The hair on the end of its arms by its hands was longer than the rest of the hair on its arms. Its eyes didn't shine in the light, I don't know if it was just the angle it was facing but I did not see any eye shine. The freaky thing was it didn't seem real big in comparison to a human; it seemed normal size which made us think maybe someone was playing a prank on us. We went back the next day to check out the spot where we saw this thing and to our surprise the trail on the side of the road where it was standing sloped down lower than the road about 3 to 4 feet below the road level, so this thing had to about 9 or 10 feet tall. This is the scary sighting that made me question whether I ever wanted to go into the woods again for about a year!!!!

I went hunting with my brother when I was about 24 or 25 years old and we brought his son, my nephew with us. We came up this road that was kind of steep, and when we got out of the thick timber there was a truck parked on the side of the road. After we went past this truck, the road kind of wrapped around this mountain curving to our left and above the road it was thick old growth timber and below the road was a very large clear cut that went all the way to the bottom of this valley where there must have been a creek because there were trees all along the bottom of the valley, then more clear cut on the other side of the valley. We went up and around this mountain and my brother said he would jump off right here and I'll go up over the top of the mountain and you drive back down the road and park on the corner and come up over the top of the mountain toward me and we will meet somewhere at the top. He said leave my nephew in the truck and lock the doors, my nephew was only 3 years old, but he knew how to wait in the truck because he always hunted with us. I was only going to   be away from the truck for 5 minutes tops. I locked my nephew in the truck and headed up towards the top of the mountain we were on. I got about 200 feet up in the thick woods and I walked up on a bow hunter in camouflage, I spotted him right off and I walked up to him quietly and asked him if he seen anything? He said he saw a couple does and that was all, he was a little perturbed that I was molesting his hunt, but I didn't do it on purpose. He got up and headed down the mountain and instead of going the rest of the way up the mountain I headed down also because he was going to have to go past pour truck where my nephew was. I got down to the road and started heading back to the truck, I could see it just down the road, so I stopped to check out the clearing just below the road. As I was scanning the clearing I thought I saw a big burnt stump just on this side of the trees at the bottom of the valley. I kept scanning and didn't pay it much attention. After scanning the whole clearing, out of curiosity I looked back at the burnt stump and it moved, at first I thought it was a bear standing on its hind legs but it never went back on all fours so I thought "Ahhh I'm just seeing things", but I couldn't help but pick up my 3 X 9 scope on my 300 Savage rifle, that's when I got a good look at what I was seeing!!!! I almost lost my breath and I started shaking, I was looking at a giant!!! It was black, not dark brown, it was black. It had hair from head to toe and I could see its eyes, they were jet black with no whites. Its hair was very long all over its whole body, like real long, probably about 10 or 12 inches long like a guy in a guilly suit but there is no man that big in this world. I know I was about 200 to 250 yards away but I could tell this thing was massive. My first instinct was to run as fast as I could down to the truck. I stepped back so it couldn't see me and thought to myself calm down, don't panic, and take a couple deep breaths and just calm down. That's what I did, I took about 4 deep breaths and calmed down, I was still shaking but I calmed down a lot. I then stepped back up to the clearing and pulled up my scope, it was still standing there, I was it looking around. Unlike most descriptions I have heard it was turning its head and looking around, it wasn't turning its whole upper body it was turning its head like a person. I started freaking out again and stepped back out of sight, I wanted to run, and I wanted to just take off as fast as I could to the truck but I talked myself out of it once again. I slowly started walking toward the truck making sure I was out of sight of this creature. I stopped and walked up to the edge and looked through the scope again. I could see everything about this creature, its hands, feet, arms, legs, and face. It was VERY VERY scary to look at its face!!! I realized that I had the cross hairs right between its eyes! But the thought didn't even cross my mind to pull the trigger, when I realized I was aiming at it I pulled the scope down and was looking at it with the naked eye then I realized there were 2 hunters just on the other side of the trees from it wearing blaze orange vests. I know they were farther away than this creature but they looked tiny compared to this thing, maybe half its size. I whispered to myself to get out of there you guys he's right there, then I looked through the scope again and the creature acted like he heard or sensed these guys were close by. He reached out with a hand just like a man's hand and grabbed a green leafed branch in front of him and let out a very high pitched scream like a woman getting killed, it was long and drawn out but towards the end of the scream it dropped into a low almost growl sound that scared the shit out of me, the hair on the back of my neck stood up and I once again felt like running!!!!!! I could see the 2 guys look at each other and to my relief started high tailing it away from the creature. Then I thought enough was enough and I walked briskly to the truck, my nephew unlocked the door and I jumped in and sat looking forward thinking about what just happened.

My brother came back pretty quickly and we left the area, I did not tell him what happened, I kept it to myself thinking he would call me crazy. I told a couple of my close friends later and word got to my brother. He pulled me off to the side at a family gathering and asked me if I saw something in the mountains. When I told him yes he got pissed, he told me "goddammit!!! When you see something in the woods you tell me right away!" I got real emotional and teared up and said I'm sorry bro, I just didn't think you or anyone would believe me. He said I'm your brother, you can tell me anything especially things like that, and I almost started crying and I'm not one to cry over just anything but what I was keeping inside me about this incident was eating me alive, and it was a relief to let it out to someone close to me like my older brother. "

Witness statement -1C:

"My dad has told me this story since I was a child (I am 54). He would drive by the area on our way to my Grandma's and slow down there and I remember seeing the foundation to the cabin. If it was at night he would slow down as he was telling the story and my brothers and I would encourage him to speed up and get out of there. The woods were thick, close and creepy. I have asked my dad to elaborate on the story recently. The date is iffy, as it was so long ago.

The area is on old Highway 30, that runs by Beaver Falls, in between Rainier and Clatskanie Oregon. Back then it was the main highway. My dad said he believes it had to be before November and thinks it was in the year 1949.

He was driving home late one night and it had been raining (which is common any time of year in that area). He was driving a '34 Ford. As he came around a corner, just after Beaver Falls his headlights illuminated a creature standing off the side of the road a ways (ferns were covering the lower half of its body) with "something" in the crook of his arm on the side of it's body. My dad saw what he believed was long gray hair hanging down from what the creature was carrying.

The back story on this is that there was a woman that lived in a cabin off the side of the road. She raised goats and the "kids" called her the "Goat Lady". My dad immediately felt it was her the creature was holding in the crook of its arm. That lady turned up missing and was never seen again.

Mr. Hucklebridge stated that it could have been taking her, after death, to where the creatures bury their relatives. I have had other people mention this scenario. I don't know. I have no clue if this could have been the situation. My dad feels it was a creature, either having killed her or knocked her out and was not doing a friendly gesture.

To further add to the story: Within a short time of the Goat Lady disappearing there was man "over the ridge from this sighting" who was found with his head chewed off. I understand (but am not sure) that the head and body were found in different locations...like one in the yard and one in the house. the man had a dog that would not let anyone near either the body or head. I don't know if the dog had to be euthanized to get to the man. I think some action had to be taken with the dog to be able to access the man. My dad was clear on the fact that the authorities checked and it was not the dog who had killed the man, and I believe they checked and felt it wasn't a bear either.

I asked my dad what was his first thought when he saw the creature and he said "Ford, don't fail me now!". He had fears of engine failure, flat tire, or anything else that would hamper his escape.

My dad said that he "knew" what it was, even though this was before the hoopla at Bluff Creek with the road builders and the Patterson-Gimlin film . There had been other reported sightings around the area.

He told me of a story of some high school kids swimming on Beaver Creek. One girl didn't want to swim and was sitting at a picnic table and her friends were all swimming (he even elaborated on some of their names). She looked up and a few feet away from her was a creature holding back some bushes looking at her. She let out a scream of all screams. Her friends came running up from the creek. After she screamed the creature let go of the bushes and disappeared into the dense woods. When her friends got to her she was so traumatized she couldn't tell them what happened. She was crying and terribly upset. They took her into Clatskanie and after they got to "Brock's" (Dad called it-a little soda shop that served burgers and stuff) she finally got calmed down enough to tell them what had happened.

My dad's mind is very sharp. The difficulty in remembering the dates has to do with so much time having passed. He is very literate and intelligent. My dad is a down to earth person. He hunted for many years around Saddle Mountain and the Mist area. If you know the area, it is thick rain forest. He knows what a bear looks like and knows what he saw was a Bigfoot as he calls it now."

Witness statement -1D:

"I guess, for some back story, as someone had noticed in the Intro thread by my screen name, I served just under five years in the Army Infantry. I go by Charlie Hotel on here because my real name (first name) starts with a C and my real last name starts with an H. And the phonetic alphabet for C and H is Charlie Hotel. Anyway, I joined right out of high school before I had even turned 18, and wanted to get out and see the world and get out of Indiana. I did my basic training at Fort Benning (like all Infantrymen) and was stationed at Fort Drum, in New York. In 2004, my unit deployed to Iraq and we spent a year operating in and outside of Baghdad. I was wounded in April of 2005, and we returned in June of that year. By that point, I had been promoted to Specialist with a waiver, and was in a Team Leader position, due to being one of the more "squared away" guys as they say. After the deployment, our unit saw a lot of turnover (guys leaving for other units, people reenlisting to go other places) which is normal for that sort of thing. Our unit had been given the East Coast QRF (Quick Reaction Force) after the 82nd Airborne had been called to help after Katrina hit... which meant that we weren't going to be deployed again right away, and that we would be doing a lot of training on post.

In the middle of September 2005, I got called in to my 1st Sergeant's office during a workday out of the blue. Usually, that only happens when you're in trouble. So, naturally, I was nervous. He told me that I was being assigned an additional duty assignment detail from S-1 and gave me some orders with the number to contact the 1LT in charge of the detail. He didn't really know much more about it, other than that they needed someone from the company with a Security Clearance, and since I had attended Javelin Trainers course, and wasn't a screw up, they picked me. The orders didn't really say much (I'll attach the copy I have of them at the end of this) so after I got out of the First Sergeant's office, I was just relieved to not be in trouble. I pretty much just figured I'd be pulling fireguard duty for a bunch of government contractors while they researched birds or turtles or something (a lot of that stuff had been going on at Drum anyway because of the expansion of the base). I didn't think much of it, but figured it would at least be something different to do.

I called the 1LT from the paper and talked to him about the assignment, he told me that I would be attached under his command starting the 14th and ending once the detail was completed. He was from one of the other Infantry Battalion's HHC units and asked if I could break away from my duties and come meet him in order to pick up a packing list and fill out some other paperwork. I asked my Platoon Sergeant, and he said it was fine, and since I would be assigned to the LT that following Monday, I may as well go ahead. So I went and met up with him, and got all my paperwork filled out, and got the packing list, and found out when the next time I needed to meet with him was, which turned out to be the following morning at the Brigade HQ. Beyond that stuff, he didn't really say much of anything.

So, the next morning I meet up at the Brigade HQ, and met the rest of the guys who got picked from the different units to be a part of the detail. It was all Infantry guys, and one Medic. The LT had us all load up in a LMTV (a truck) and we head out to one of the Ranges. Which turns out to be one of the furthest Ranges on the entire installation. It's like a thirty to forty minute drive out there from main post and gets to be pretty much out in the middle of nowhere. They use those ranges for a lot of different types of training, and most of it is combat related stuff. Most of the Ranges have buildings that are used for briefings, preparations, and for when it's cold out. There were a bunch of civilian POVs and trucks outside of the building, when we got inside, they had a bunch of chairs and tables set up. A lot of people were milling about and talking amongst themselves when we came inside, and we were shuffled in seats at the back of the rows. The LT went up to the front, and spoke with a couple of people, which I assumed at the time were in charge (which turned out to be true).

I had learned (up to that point in my Army career) that it was best just to keep your mouth shut, ears open, and do what you are told and you'll go a long way. And I figured that whatever we were doing, it would be a good chance to maybe get some special recognition, as it was apparent that whoever all these people were, they were important. I was planning on going to the promotion board soon and becoming a Sergeant, so whatever I could do to stand out, I was going to do it. That included, sitting around and listening to a bunch of scientists lecture on boring subjects or guard a bunch of tents or roads all day and night for a couple of weeks while they research stuff.

But, once the first person started to talk, I knew right away that we were listening to something completely unexpected and not normal. The first person to talk was an Agent from the 10th Mountain Criminal Investigation Command, or CID. He went over the seriousness of Security Clearances, and the sensitive nature of them and what it means to breach them. In hindsight, I may or may not be doing now, and has played a major role in what has been keeping me from telling this story for so many years. The next person to speak was a scientist or something like that from either the U.S. Fish and Wildlife Service, or Bureau of Land Management (I don't remember which) talking about the nature of what they do, and what the impact of their research means to the environment means. I don't exactly remember much, as it doesn't really matter too much to the story.

Finally, another person got up to speak; this person was a Special Agent with the U.S. Fish and Wildlife Service. They had a PowerPoint presentation (the others did as well) ready to go. They told us that in August, some Soldiers conducting rifle qualifications at a Range had witnessed what they first thought was a bear downrange and issued a cease fire (which was the standard operating procedure). They stated (all later in written form by the Company Commander) that they witnessed the animal "stand up" and proceed to "walk like a human at a steady rate" from one tree line to the other. They had made jokes with each other that they had just seen a "Big Foot" and that they should have shot it. The CO contacted Range Control and told them that they had witnessed what was at first believed to be a bear, but was unusual in size, gait, and appearance. The CO was asked by the Range Control Officer to make a written statement, which was later passed on to 10th Mountain Headquarters.

Apparently, whenever something like this is sighted, Range Control is supposed to notify the Post Commander's Office and let them know (not sure if that is an Army or Military wide thing, since this is my only experience, but if it's a Directive, then it is possible). The Agent then told us that they cancelled all the training scheduled for the ranges in and around this area (from the one we were at to about three back and two north if that makes sense, so about six total). He then went on to explain that they would be investigating the sighting and determining the validity of it. They never outright said what it was we were looking for, at first, but seemed to be clear on the fact that it wasn't just a "bear" that they were out looking for. And it seemed like a lot of effort to me just for a bear sighting. We were all (meaning the regular Soldiers) thinking the same thing: Big Foot.

The 1LT got up next, and just went over our mission next, stating what our duties would be, which I found to be odd as soon as he explained that we would actually be conducting PSD style security for the Government teams. I found it kind of strange that they would need us following them around fully armed in the woods while they searched for a bear or whatever it was, and even weirder that they wanted us doing it using actual tactical movements and they had planned on doing most of this late at night and in the early morning hours using our NODS (night vision goggles). The whole thing was just odd to me once the initial briefings were over (which took about six to eight hours including a lunch break). The Operation was planned for a later date, and we were to be prepared and ready to go by that time. The Platoon Sergeant (PSG) of the group was a cool guy, and seemed to just take the whole thing in stride and kind of just take it as a joke in a way. He was making Big Foot jokes (not around the LT or any of the Government people) like the rest of us were.

We had a few more briefings like that the following weeks, and a couple more training days just to get used to working with each other as a Platoon. They seemed to want to get us used to the idea that we could very well be interacting with some kind of unknown creature and yet, never outright said it in any of those briefings. And all of my buddies in my normal unit kept asking me about the detail, but I just had to tell them that it was just some boring science thing. It was kind of an odd situation, and I just wanted to get it over with. It was planned for early October, which was nice at least, since Drum usually gets super miserable and cold by the end of the month.

Anyway, the night of the operation finally comes, and we all head over to the staging area to link up and get ready to board the trucks to head out. The PSG kind of relied on me to be the guy who goes back and forth between him and the LT because I wasn't a moron and that just meant I had even more tasks to do to get ready. It was getting chilly at night, and we had a lot of packing and prepping to do in the parking lot of HQ. We loaded up, and drove out to that same Range building parking lot. Once there, we linked back up with the Agents from the Government, and the research teams. They went over the plans as far as where we would be looking, and what the plans were in terms of what to do. I wasn't exactly a part of these talks, since I was only an E4. So I don't know what was said in any of these talks, but I'll get more into this later. We ended up moving out not long after, once everyone was ready to go. The platoon had set up with a split team movement, meaning that we had a parameter surrounding the government team so that we could provide security on all sides of them while we went through the woods. Our LT guided the movements, with the Agents and leader of the Land Management team navigating.

I was in the back of the movement, with the Platoon Sergeant during the movements, just sort of scanning my area. I had my night vision up, since I didn't feel like I really needed it, and was just scanning back and forth. I always liked that sort of thing, it was one of the reasons I joined the Infantry, the chance to walk around in the woods and "play" Army. Even after a yearlong of fighting in Iraq and I still loved that stuff. I was enjoying myself, even when we'd stop for twenty or thirty minutes, and the Government people would do whatever it was they were doing... picking up samples, tracking, etc.

The first night went on like this until morning, around 0845 or so. We made it back to the Range Control building, tired and worn out and didn't seem to find anything too interesting. Everyone was just ready to crash and try again the next night. Since we were just there to provide security, we didn't have much to do other than clean our weapons and BS with each other during the day, while the Government people actually worked on the stuff they picked up overnight. The same thing happened the next night, as we had left at the same time, and found nothing of note, in a different path. Though, we had thought we had heard something, but it might have just been some other kind of animal.

By night three, I think our (PSG?) had figured we were just part of a big rib and wondered why we were taking this whole thing so serious. It started to rain early in the evening and was cold and pretty miserable. None of us wanted to even be out there, and nobody really thought we were actually looking for anything, because nobody believed that those guys had seen anything but a bear anyway. After all, they were just dumb Soldiers anyway. But, at around 0245 or so, we learned that we weren't just wasting our time after all. And that the Government people knew that the whole time. That's where this story becomes even harder to tell. We had come across an area of really thick bramble (I think that's what it's called, the prickly stuff) brush that had been matted down in some areas and pulled up around in others. It looked like something had made some sort of shelter out of it, and used it to keep things out of the area in a way. The research people took some photos of it, and looked around for some samples and we were there for maybe twenty minutes. Then we started to head back out... again, I was in the rear of the formation.

About three or four minutes after we started back off walking, the sound of gun fire erupted in the woods. It was a sound I hadn't been startled by since Iraq, and wasn't expecting to hear at all on this detail, even though they told us it might have been part of our assignment. Our training kicked in, and we all got down on a knee and quickly scanned our area, we heard yelling, and cease fire. Then I heard someone yelling for our Medic to come forward. Our Platoon Sergeant went up with him. I stayed in the back and continued to pull security. There were maybe six to ten shots in rapid succession total, if that. Our nerves and adrenaline were on edge, and I just remember looking back and forth to the other couple guys in the back of the group and sort of just shrugging and wondering just what the heck had happened up there.

After a long, unknown, our PSG finally comes back and says to us something along the lines of "You're not going to f***-ing believe it. They just shot and killed something big up there, something not human." I still wasn't sure what he was talking about, and asked him pretty much that. And he had this baffled look on his face, and just said something like "I don't know, just go look." So, I got up, and went up towards the front of the formation to where most of the Government people and the PL (Platoon Leader; Lieutenant) were at. They had their flood light out and the Medic had her Aid Bag out and opens on the ground. I saw (right away) something huge and dark on the ground in the middle of them. Steam was coming off of it, lots of steam. That's the one thing I'll probably never forget from that night.

My eyes were probably the size of dinner plates, and I remember saying "What is that?!" Somebody from the Government team said "It's an illusory hominid. They're more common than you realize, but not nearly as many as there used to be." Or something like that. I just remember that term "elusory hominid, as it would come up many times after that. That is apparently the term used for the creature by that specific team, though could be that agency, again I'm only speaking on what I know from this operation. I got closer, and looked down. The animal (or creature, or whatever you'd like to call it) was lying in a slumped over position, in a familiar position to someone who had just been shot. It was a common pose that I was used to seeing. It happens when someone is lunging or running and is shot. They tend to "crumple" over like that. It was clearly a male, as it had male genitals visible from behind its legs, and it had that long, course hair that I guess a lot of people who see these kinds of creatures would agree they tend to have. It was night, so at the time, the hair appeared to be rather dark, but seeing the animal later in the morning, it was more of a brown color.

It had noticeable twigs, leaves, and other things caught up in the hair as if it had been running through the trees, which may have been from when it was lunging at the front of the team and not from its normal routine... hard to say, as I wasn't an expert. I couldn't see its face, since it was face down at the time, but I could see a lot of dark blood pooling in the dirt from that area, and from around its chest. Its hands and arms were up underneath its chest, as though maybe it grabbed its chest when first shot instead of trying to brace the fall. I remember the bottom of the feet were very white compared the rest of the body, and stood out, and one of the feet were up in the air because of the position of the body and the way it fell.

I couldn't take my eyes off the body, just like I seemed to always have a problem with in Iraq. Something about the reality of death always affected me that way, and I always had an odd feeling being confronted with it. Added with the fact that I was being presented with the hard truth of something that "wasn't supposed to be real" all of sudden, and it was a very surreal and strange moment. I also remember hearing a few of the Government people arguing and talking about whether or not they should continue looking for more, or if they should just wrap it up and take this one back and consider it taken care of for now. I asked one of the Infantry guys up from who shot him, and one of the Team Leaders said that they think they all probably got a couple shots off. It surprised the crap out of them and came out of nowhere, and said they didn't even see it or hear it until it was just about on top of them.

I ended up going back to the back of the formation while the Government people took pictures, samples, and did more of whatever else they do, and we were there another hour or so. Finally, we got ready to move out again. They had gotten a body bag out, and volunteered some guys to carry the animal back to the Range building. I remember watching as they tried to fit the animal inside of the bag, it was a normal size body bag, and this thing was probably over 7 feet tall and probably a few hundred pounds, and dead weight. They wrestled with it and finally got in it, and had to drag it back through the deep woods and mud. We traded out a few times, but since I was carrying an M249 (machine gun) I never had to actually carry it, thankfully. By the time we made it back, the guys who did, looked pretty much smoked and covered in mud. It was getting light out, and the rain had stopped by this point at least. I had noticed that one of the Government trucks that had been there before had been prepped and ready to go; it was a large silver semi-truck with white cab. They had the guys carrying the animal stop and open the bag back up, that's when we all got another look at it. They had them pull the animal back out and the Government people took some more pictures, this time of the face, the hands and feet, and the bullet wounds. They added some tags to the lips and nose. It looked a lot like those old cave man people but also kind of like a monkey or ape, but just huge. Again, it's probably cliché to say it, but it really does look like what a lot of people who say they see them say they look like.

Our PL kind of rushed us away from it though, and didn't seem to want us standing around and looking at it, and didn't want us to even really talk about it. We had to go inside of the building and start our usual weapons cleaning and after-action stuff. None of us were as tired, because of the curiosity of the situation. We all were on edge and excited because of what had happened and wondered what was next. We had no idea what we had just found and wondered if we were going to be famous now for having discovered a new creature, being the first to discover Sasquatch. Our PL told us just to shut up about it, and told us to remember our mission and that we're not supposed to talk about it at all until we know more for sure. By the time we had everything all cleaned and done, and got back outside, the silver semi-truck was already gone, and some of the government people were gone. The body was gone too.

The PL talked with the Fish and Wildlife Agent and CID Agent and some of the other people, and we were told just to go ahead with the rest of the OPORD plan and wrap things up. They would take care of everything else, and he again stressed to keep things on the hush and hush. So we packed everything up, loaded up the trucks, and headed back to the Brigaded HQs. As I mentioned before, the PSG kind of had me doing a lot of the back and forth with the PL, so I had a copy of the OPORD and knew was all the steps were and knew what was involved as far as downturn. We turned our weapons back in, turned the trucks back in to the motor-pools, and were released for the remainder of the next week while they worked on the After Action Report and the debriefing.

This happened the following week, at the same Range building. It'd be the last time we all (meaning the Platoon detail and the Government people) would be working together. They stressed how good of a job we did, how professional everyone was, how exciting it was to have been successful in the operation, and again how we all needed to abide by the security clearance keep quite on the matter. It was vital on this point because of reasons that we weren't to be included on, but that we needed to understand were important to the security of the United States and the population. At the time, I just figured that as the usual case of "You don't need to know because you're just dumb Infantrymen." which was probably true. Take it for whatever you will, I don't know. We also went over the final AAR, which was now being called OPERATION CLOUDED MOHAWK (I guess because of the Natives in that area). An AAR is an After Action Report and just goes over the basics of "what the plan was; what you were trying to do; what you did; what the outcome was; and what you could have done better." We all got a handshake and some other perks I won't mention, and went back to main post after that final meeting.

The LT had me make some copies for him at the Brigade HQ because he would be sending off reports of the AAR to whomever, that's where I come into play in all of this, as I mentioned earlier. I was sort of the middle man because I wasn't dumb. I spent that entire week after that night we killed that animal thinking about it and wondering what it was, how smart it was, how it lived, why it was there, and why we did what we did. And I didn't like the way it was treated after we encountered it. The whole thing just seemed weird and I didn't like it, so I felt like maybe I should make copies for myself, so that I'll at least be able to remember the details of it. So, since I was sitting in the empty S-shop of the Brigade building making copies for the LT, I made copies of the AAR and all the other paperwork for myself and left them in the printer. I came back out, and handed him his copies. After I said my final goodbyes to the guy, I went back into the office, picked up the stack of papers, and put them in a black manila folder and got out of there.

I've had that folder ever since buried away with all of my other Army paperwork. I have tried to just sit on it and forget about it, but like I said, it hasn't really been easy and it's something that just always seems to stand out and bother me. And lately, the Government has been giving me good reason on a personal level to want to not exactly be quiet anymore about it at all. I can't say for sure whether or not I'll ever release the entire AAR (which has the complete report, in detail of the event, include many things I haven't mentioned) but who knows, maybe I will. I don't want to get in trouble, and maybe I will anyway, but sometimes you reach a point where the truth matters more.

I eventually left Fort Drum and became an Instructor at Fort Benning at the Javelin School, served a couple more years before having to get out because of complications from my injury in Iraq. I served honorably and don't want people to think that any of this is me bashing the Army; this isn't what this is about at all. I loved my time in the Army; I just also love the truth, and served with a code of conduct and values that included Integrity and honesty. I realize now that many people are seeking the truth in this subject and many people want validity when it comes to these "elusory hominids" and I am now willing to risk bringing that truth to the forefront. I'm including my discharge papers, my state ID, and the appointment orders for now. I (As you'll see, the First and Last name's match up, the birthdates match up, the States and address of record match up, and the time frames match up to prove that I am who I say I am, and my service is the correct time frame. Without giving out too much information, so I hope to stay somewhat in secret to protect myself as much as I can give the information I've told in this thread. I only blacked out what I felt I needed to in order to protect myself.) Maybe I'll add more, who knows. I'm surprised I've even said this much honestly. Forgive me if I've left things out, there is just only so much I can or am willing to say, maybe will change. I'll be willing to answer questions, though I can't say how much of an answer I will be able to give on all questions."

Witness statement -1E

"Kevin G. told us that he had been to an area called Wyeth, Oregon, not far from what is called the Bridge of the Gods, which spans the Columbia River. He went there searching for a place to hunt game. It was a former logging landing near a heavily forested area. While there, he noticed steam coming from the ground and assumed that what he saw were volcanic steam vents.

He mentioned the steam vents to a friend of his, Hugh Brown, also of Stevenson, and suggested that he go there and see them for himself. Following up on the information, Hugh and a friend of his, Jeff S., went there the following day.

When the two men arrived at the location Kevin had given them, they found where steam was rising from the ground. They weren't there long when they heard the most unusual cry from an animal that either of them had ever heard. The sound seemed to be coming from down the slope of the ridge that they were on. The creature continued to scream, and each time it made those eerie sounds it seemed to be getting closer to where they were standing.

Suddenly, a large creature burst from the thick foliage about 100 feet below where they were stood. It then quickly darted back into the cover of the brush, and they didn't see it again. At first they thought it was a bear, but they couldn't be sure. The screams were also getting louder and closer, and Jeff S. became frightened. He fled the landing for the safety of the car.

Hugh stood where he was, trying to figure out what kind of animal was below making the strange noise. Shortly after seeing the animal they thought was a bear, a deer ran out from the brush not more than 5-feet away from where Hugh was standing. The deer looked very frightened and nervous. After the creature screamed again, very close this time, the deer darted off, away from the direction of the sound.

Only moments after the deer ran away, Hugh saw a huge, hairy, manlike creature come out from the thick underbrush just below where he was standing—it ran toward him as if intending to attack. He stood there in shock and complete amazement, not believing what he was seeing.

The creature approached within 15 feet down slope of where Hugh stood. It came to a sudden stop as Hugh just stood there motionless. The two just stared at each other for about 30 seconds. Just as suddenly as the creature had emerged from the forest, it turned to its right and casually walked back into the forest, and out of sight.

By then, Hugh had regained his composure and fled to the car. Once inside, he and Jeff S. quickly left the area, not to return until he took Carlo and me there to see the place for ourselves.

Both Hugh and Jeff S. seemed genuinely frightened when re-telling their account of what happened, and I have no doubt that they encountered something very strange. To help us understand, both men made drawings of what they had seen. These drawings are presented below. Hugh Brown drew the top figure and Jeff S. drew the figure on the bottom of what he saw burst from the brush."

Drawings made by Hugh Brown and his friend Jeff S. of the creature they encountered

Hugh stated details such as facial hair, eyes, teeth, etc., and his recollection was very good. He said the teeth were similar to human teeth. The creature's face was covered with hair, but not long like on the rest of its body, and that the hair was of varying lengths at different places over its body. He said the creature's eyes were large and deep set, and it looked as though it had a brow ridge above its eyes similar to something you might see in a book about Neanderthal humans.

Hugh wished he could have told more, but examining the creature in detail was not a priority for him at that moment. He was afraid that this strange creature might attack him, and he was relieved when it seemed to look bored and simply walked away.

Witness statement -1F

(The following is an actual sworn statement)

Bigfoot Encounter Alberta Canada – Affidavit of Mr. William Roe

Affidavit of Mr. William Roe, on August 26th, 1957.

Mr. William Roe approached the writer requesting the swearing out of An Affidavit in regard to a strange animal he had seen in British Columbia.

The affidavit was drawn up by a member of our legal department and sworn to in the usual manner by the writer.

I cannot state as to the credibility of the story.

We trust the foregoing information will be of assistance.

Yours truly,
(signed) W. H. Clark
Asst. Claims Agent

Affidavit.

I, W. Roe, of the City of Edmonton, in the province of Alberta make oath and say,
(1) That the exhibit A attached to this, my affidavit, is absolutely true and correct in all details. Sworn before me in the City of Edmonton, Province of Alberta, this 26th day of August, A.D. 1957,
(signed) Wm. Roe and then
signed by Clark under a
numbering D.D. 2822

EXHIBIT A

Ever since I was a small boy back in the forests of Michigan, I have studied the lives and habits of wild animals. Later when I supported my family in northern Alberta by hunting and trapping, I spent many hours just observing the wild things.

They fascinated me. The most incredible experience I ever had with a wild creature occurred near a little place called Tete Jaune Cache, B.C., about 80 miles west of Jasper, Alberta.

female bigfoot.

I had been working on the highway near this place, Tete Jaune Cache, for about 2 years. In October 1955, I decided to climb five miles up Mica Mountain to an old deserted mine, just for something to do. I came in sight of the mine about 3 o'clock in the afternoon after an easy climb.

I had just come out of a patch of low brush into a clearing, when I saw what I thought was a grizzly bear in the brush on the other side. I had shot a grizzly near that spot the year before. This one was only about 75 yards away, but I didn't want to shoot it, for I had no way of getting it out.

So I sat down on a small rock and watched, with my rifle in my hand.

I could just see part of the animal's head and the top of one shoulder. A moment later it raised up and stepped out into the opening. Then I saw it wasn't a bear.

This to the best of my recollection is what the creature looked like and how it acted as it came across the clearing directly towards me. My first impression was of a huge man about 6 feet tall, almost 3 feet wide, and probably weighing near 300 pounds. It was covered from head to foot with dark brown, silver-tipped hair. But as it came closer I saw by its breasts that it was female.

And yet, its torso was not curved like a female's. Its broad frame was straight from shoulder to hip. Its arms were much thicker than a man's arms and longer, reaching almost to its knees.

Its feet were broader proportionately than a man's, about 5 inches wide in the front and tapering to much thinner heels. When it walked it placed the heel of its foot down first, and I could see the grey-brown skin or hide on the soles of its feet.

It came to the edge of the bush I was hiding in, within 20 feet of me, and squatted down on its haunches. Reaching out its hands it pulled the branches of bushes towards it and stripped the leaves with its teeth. Its lips curled flexibly around the leaves as it ate.

I was close enough to see that its teeth were white and even. The head was higher at the back than at the front. The nose was broad and flat. The lips and chin protruded farther than its nose. But the hair that covered it, leaving bare only the parts of its face around the mouth, nose and ears, made it resemble an animal as much as a human.

None of this hair, even on the back of its head, was longer than an inch, and that on its face much shorter.

Its ears were shaped like a human's ears. But its eyes were small and black like a bear's. And its neck also was unhuman, thicker and shorter than any man's I have ever seen.

As I watched this creature I wondered if some movie company was making a film in this place and that what I saw was an actor made up to look partly human, partly animal. But as I observed it more I decided it would be impossible to fake such a specimen.

Anyway, I learned later there was no such company near that area. Nor, in fact, did anyone live up Mica Mountain, according to the people who lived in Tete Jaune Cache.

Finally, the wild thing must have got my scent, for it looked directly at me through an opening in the brush. A look of amazement crossed its face. It looked so comical at that moment I had to grin. Still in a crouched position, it backed up three or four short steps, then straightened up to its

full height and started to walk rapidly back the way it had come. For a moment it watched me over its shoulder as it went, not exactly afraid, but as though it wanted no contact with anything strange.

The thought came to me that if I shot it I would possibly have a specimen of great interest to scientists the world over. I had heard stories about the Sasquatch, the giant hairy "Indians" that live in the legend of the Indians of British Columbia and also, many claim are still, in fact, alive today. Maybe this was a Sasquatch, I told myself.
I levelled my rifle.

The creature was still walking rapidly away, again turning its head to look in my direction. I lowered the rifle. Although I have called the creature "it," I felt now that it was a human being, and I knew I would never forgive myself if I killed it.

Just as it came to the other patch of brush it threw its head back and made a peculiar noise that seemed to be half laugh and half language, and which I could only describe as a kind of a whinny. Then it walked from the small brush into a stand of lodge-pole pines.

I stepped out into the opening and looked across a small ridge just beyond the pine to see if I could see it again. It came out on the ridge a couple of hundred yards away from me, tipped its head back again, and again emitted the only sound I had heard it make, but what this half laugh, half language was meant to convey I do not know. It disappeared then, and I never saw it again.

I wanted to find out if it lived on vegetation entirely or ate meat as well, so I went down and looked for signs. I found it * in five different places, and although I examined it thoroughly, could find no hair or shells or bugs or insects. So I believe it was strictly a vegetarian.

I found one place where it had slept for a couple of nights under a tree. Now, the nights were cool up the mountain, at this time of year especially, and yet it had not used a fire. I found no signs that it possessed even the simplest of tools. Nor did I find any signs that it had a single companion while in this place.

Whether this creature was a Sasquatch I do not know. It will always remain a mystery to me unless another one is found.
I hearby declare the above statement to be in every part true, to the best of my powers of observation and recollection.

Signed,

William Roe"

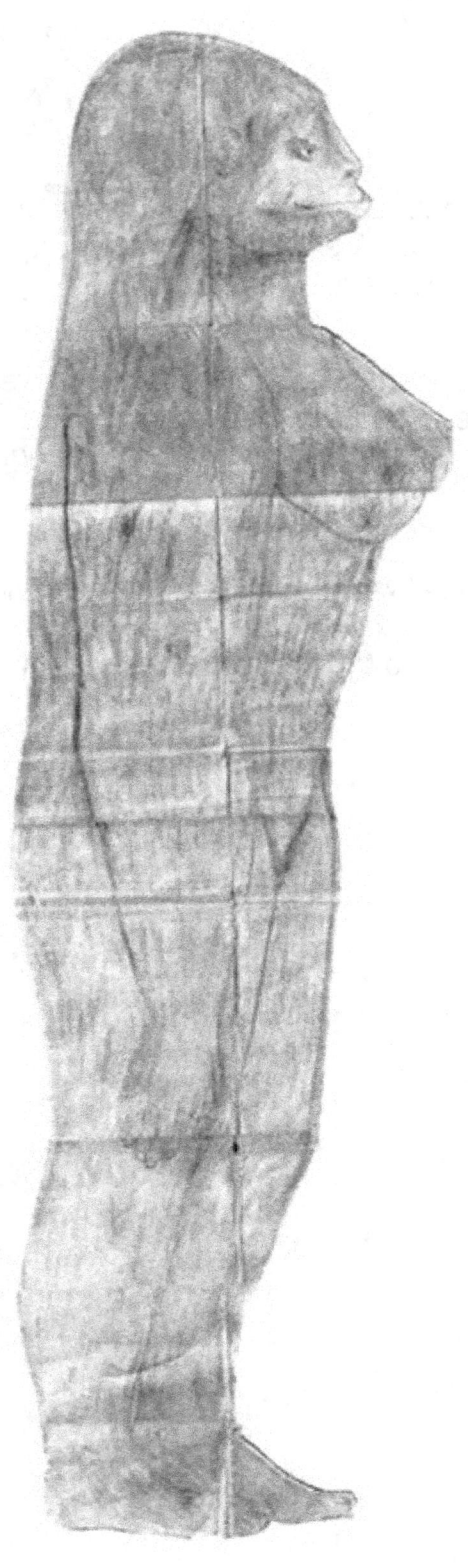

Drawing made under William Roe's direction.

PLAINTIFF: Your honor, at this time I would like to enter into evidence scientific proof that giant apelike animals have previously lived that will establish their existence and that more species of such creatures may continue to exist that have yet to be recognized and classified by science.

JUDGE: any objections by opposing council?

DEFENSE: None at this time your honor.

JUDGE: So noted, proceed council.

PLAINTIFF: I would like to introduce into evidence at this time items as 2A, 2B, 2C 2D and 2E.

JUDGE: the items will be so entered into the record.

Item -2A

"The first *Gigantopithecus* remains described by an anthropologist were found in 1935 by Ralph von Koenigswald in an apothecary shop. Fossilized teeth and bones are often ground into powder and used in some branches of traditional Chinese medicine. Von Koenigswald named the theorized species *Gigantopithecus*.

Since then, relatively few fossils of *Gigantopithecus* have been recovered. Aside from the molars recovered in Chinese traditional medicine shops, Liucheng Cave in Liuzhou, China, has produced numerous *Gigantopithecus blacki* teeth, as well as several jawbones. Other sites yielding significant finds were in Vietnam and India. These finds suggest that the range of *Gigantopithecus* was in Southeast Asia. There are presently three extinct named species of *Gigantopithecus*: *G. blacki*, *G. bilaspurensis*, and *G. giganteus*.

In 1955, 47 *G. blacki* teeth were found among a shipment of "dragon bones" (also called "oracle bones") in China. Tracing these teeth to their source resulted in the recovery of more teeth and a rather complete large mandible. By 1958, three mandibles and more than 1,300 teeth had been recovered. *Gigantopithecus* remains have come from sites in Hubei, Guangxi, and Sichuan, from warehouses for Chinese medicinal products, as well as from cave deposits. Not all Chinese remains have been dated to the same time period, and the fossils in Hubei appear to be of a later date than elsewhere in China. The Hubei teeth are also larger.

Chinese physical anthropologist and paleoprimotologist Dong Tichen suggested that Gigantopithecus bears a series of quite distinctly differentiated characteristics by its own. Thus it stands for a completely independent branch on the primate genealogical tree. Tichen considered Gigantopithecinae as a new subfamily, with Gigantopithecus as its type genus, which logically belonging to Pongidae, not to Hominidae.

Gigantopithecus blacki (named in honor of the friend and colleague of von Koenigswald, Davidson Black) is known only through fossil teeth and mandibles found in cave sites in South China and Vietnam. These are appreciably larger than those of living gorillas, but the exact size and structure of the rest of the body can only be estimated in the absence of additional findings. Dating methods have shown that *G. blacki* existed for at least a million years, going extinct about 100,000 years ago after having been contemporary with anatomically modern humans (*Homo sapiens*) for tens of thousands of years, and co-existing with *H. erectus*, who preceded the appearance of *H. sapiens*. In 2014, for the first time, fossil teeth and mandible of *Gigantopithecus blacki* were found in Indonesia. Some of the caves in which teeth have been found were not caves yet at the time the apes lived, but just fissures. It has been suggested that *Gigantopithecus* bones were brought there by porcupines, who chew on bones as a source of calcium. This may help explain the lack of *Gigantopithecus* bones today.

Gigantopithecus's method of locomotion is uncertain, as no pelvic or leg bones have been found. The dominant view is that it walked on all fours like modern gorillas and chimpanzees; however, a minority opinion favors bipedal locomotion. This was most notably championed by the late Grover Krantz, but this assumption is based only on the very few jawbone remains found, all of which are U-shaped and widen towards the rear. This allows room for the windpipe to be within the jaw, allowing the skull to sit squarely on a fully erect spine as in modern humans, rather than roughly in front of it, as in the other great apes.

The majority view is that the weight of such a large, heavy animal would put enormous stress on the creature's legs, ankles, and feet if it walked bipedally; while if it walked on all four limbs, like gorillas, its weight would be better distributed over each limb.

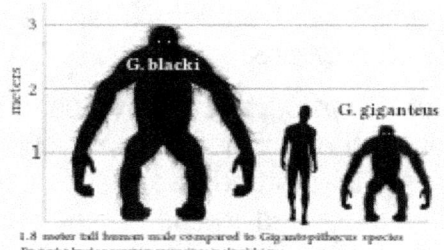

A comparison graph of a 1.8-meter-tall human male (almost 5' 11") in comparison to *G. blacki* (left) and *G. giganteus* (right): This graph is based on orangutan proportions while standing upright.

Based on the fossil evidence, adult male *Gigantopithecus blacki* are believed to have stood about 3 m (9.8 ft.) tall and weighed as much as 540–600 kg (1,190–1,320 lb.), making the species three to four times as heavy as modern gorillas and seven to eight times as heavy as the orangutan, its closest living relative. Large males may have had an arm span of over 3.6 m (11.8 ft.). The species was highly sexually dimorphic, with adult females roughly half the weight of males. Because of wide interspecies differences in the relationship between tooth and body size, some argue that it is more likely that adult male *Gigantopithecus blacki* were much smaller, at roughly 1.8–2 m (5.9–6.6 ft.) in height and 180–300 kg (400–660 lb.) in weight."

Item -2B Gigantopithecus teeth

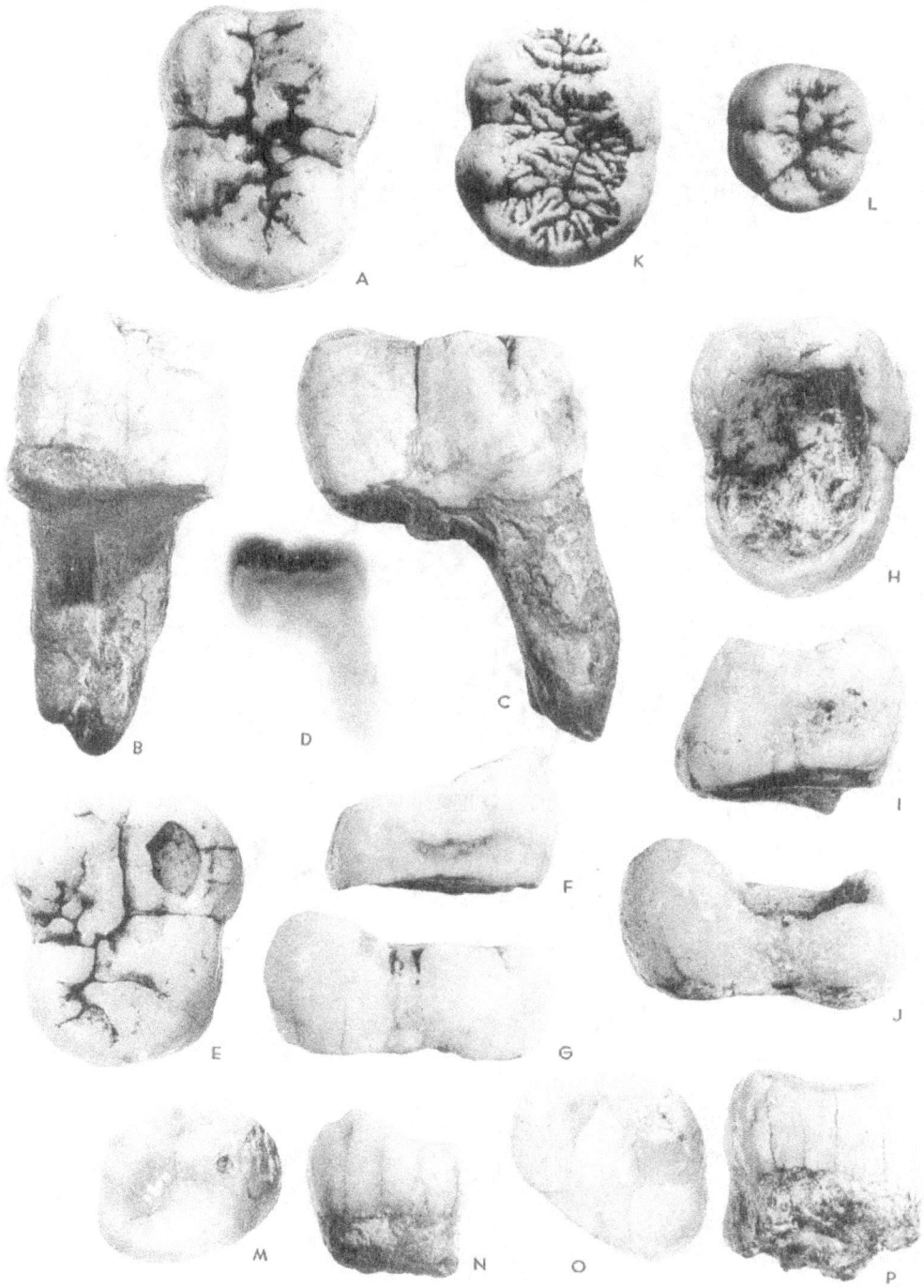

Item -2C Gigantopithecus teeth

Item -2D Gigantopithecus skull reconstruction

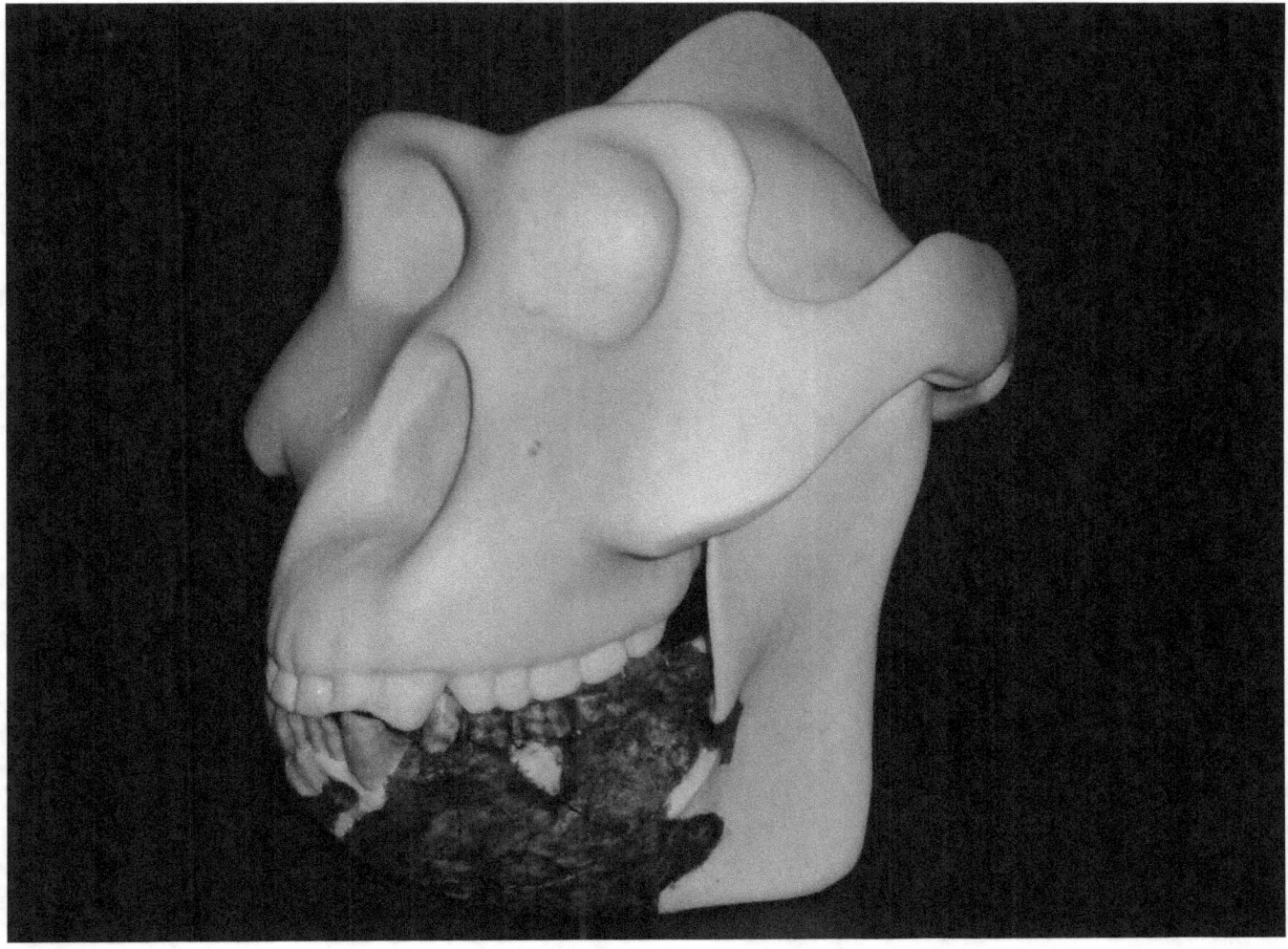

Item -2E Gigantopithecus jaw (actual fossil)

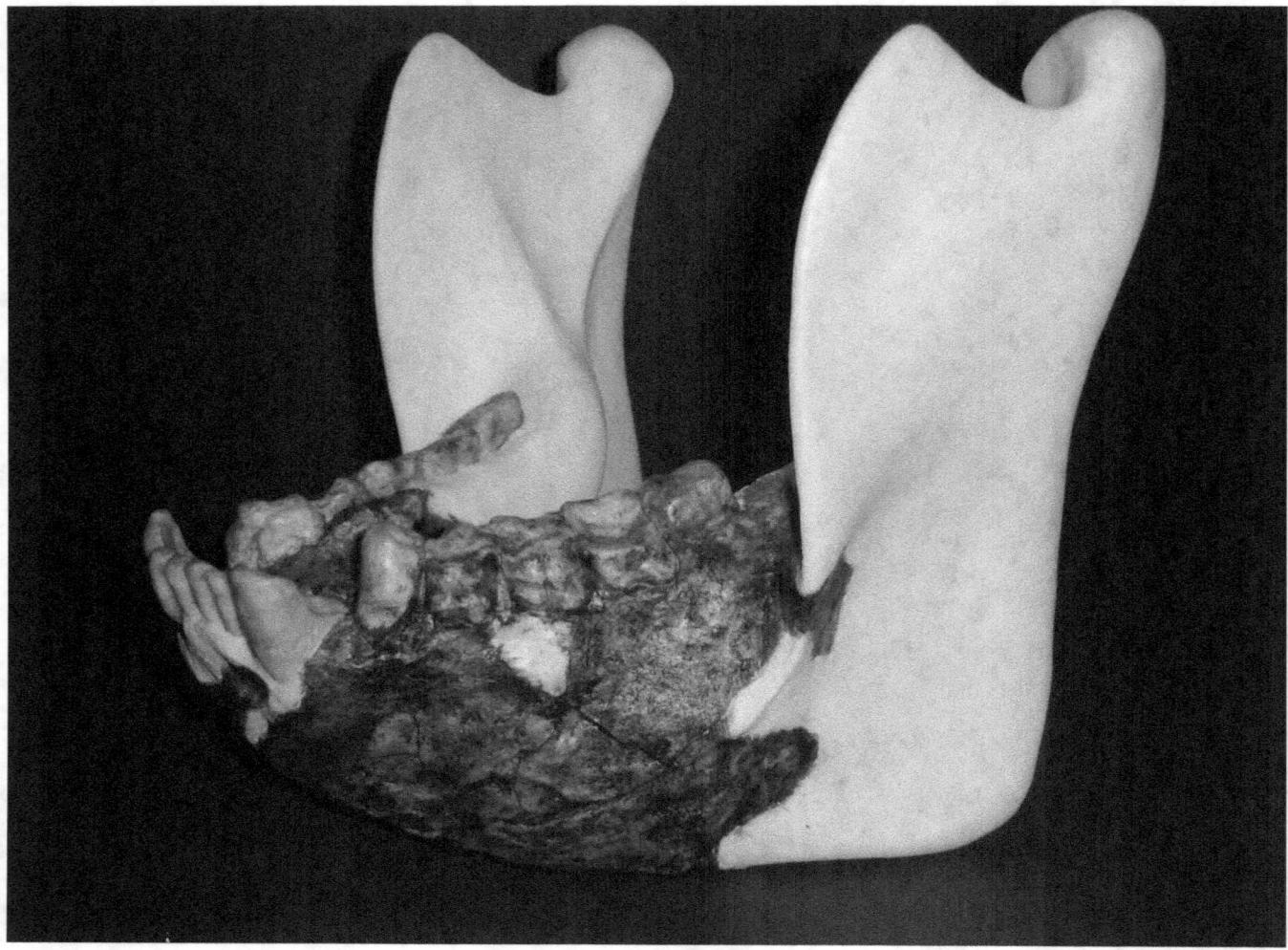

DEFENSE: Your honor, I will concede the fact that science has proof there are extinct species of primates that are similar to what the plaintiff is trying to say is inhabiting the forests of North America today. However there has never been one captured, and no remains of one found nor even any photographic or other proof of any such creatures existing beyond the fossil evidence scientists currently recognize.

JUDGE: Council for the plaintiff, do you have any evidence to support the purported creatures ever being captured, photographed or remains found?

PLAINTIFF: yes your honor, and if I may proceed I will introduce first some historical documentation showing at least one specimen was captured by reputable witnesses. I will then introduce evidence of testimony, photographic and trace evidence of said creatures.

JUDGE: Alright council proceed.

PLAINTIFF: I would now like to enter into evidence items 3A, 3B and 3C.

Item -3A

What is it?

——

A Strange Creature Captured Above Yale

——

A British Columbia Gorilla

(Correspondence of the Colonist)

Yale, B.C., July 3rd, 1882.

In the immediate vicinity of No. 4 tunnel situated some twenty miles above this village, are bluffs of rock which have hitherto been unsurmountable, but on Monday morning last were successfully scaled by Mr. Onderdonk's employees on the regular train from Lytton. Assisted by Mr. Costerton, the British Columbia Express Company's messenger, and a number of gentlemen from Lytton and points east of that place, who, after considerable trouble and perilous climbing, succeeded in capturing a creature which may truly be called half man and half beast.

"Jacko," as the creature has been called by his capturers, is something of the gorilla type standing about four feet seven inches in height and weighing 127 pounds. He has long, black, strong hair and resembles a human being with one exception, his entire body, excepting his hands, (or paws) and feet are covered with glossy hair about one inch long. His fore arm is much longer than a man's fore arm, and he possesses extra-ordinary strength, as he will take hold of a stick and break it by wrenching or twisting it, which no man living could break in the same way.

Since his capture he is very reticent, only occasionally uttering a noise which is half bark and half growl. He is, however, becoming daily more attached to his keeper, Mr. George Tilbury, of this place, who proposes shortly starting for London, England to exhibit him. His favorite food so far is berries, and he drinks fresh milk with evident relish. By advice of Dr. Hannington raw meats have been withheld from Jacko, as to make him savage.

The mode of capture was as follows: Ned Austin, the engineer, on coming in sight of the bluff at the eastern end of No. 4 tunnel saw what he supposed to be a man lying asleep in close proximity to the track, and as quick as thought blew the signal to apply the brakes.

The brakes were instantly applied, and in a few seconds the train was brought to a standstill. At this moment the supposed man sprang up, and uttering a sharp quick bark began to climb the steep bluff. Conductor R.J. Craig and express messenger Costerton, followed by the baggage men and brakemen, jumped from the train and knowing they were some twenty minutes ahead of time immediately gave chase.

After five minutes of perilous climbing the then supposed demented Indian was corralled on a projecting shelf of rock where he could neither ascend or descend. The query now was how to capture him alive, which was quickly decided by Mr. Craig, who crawled on his hands and knees until he was about forty feet above the creature.

Taking a small piece of loose rock he let it fall and it had the desired effect of rendering poor Jacko incapable of resistance for a time at least. The bell rope was then brought up and Jacko was now lowered to terra firma. After firmly binding him and placing him in the baggage car "off brakes" was sounded and the train started for Yale.

At the station a large crowd who had heard of the capture by telephone from Spuzzum Flat were assembled, each one anxious to have the first look at the monstrosity, but they were disappointed, as Jacko had been taken off at the machine shops and placed in charge of his present keeper.

The question naturally arises, how came the creature where it was first seen by Mr. Austin? From bruises about its head and body, and apparent soreness since its capture, it is supposed that Jacko ventured too near the edge of the bluff, slipped, fell and lay where found until the sound of the rushing train aroused him. Mr. Thos, White and Mr. Gouin, C.E., as well as Mr. Major, who kept a small store about a half a mile west of the tunnel during the past two years, have mentioned having seen a curious creature at different points between camps 13 and 17, but no attention was paid to their remarks as people came to the conclusion that they had either seen a bear or stray Indian dog. Who can unravel the mystery that now surrounds Jacko? Does he belong to a species hitherto unknown in this part of the continent, or is he really what the trainmen first thought he was, a crazy Indian?

I was very intrigued when I first read this story, and wondered what ever became of the creature called Jacko. The only answer I could get from anyone who had researched this matter was that no one ever really knew. The closest anyone knew was that the creature died during the trip to England, and the body was dropped overboard.

Item -3B

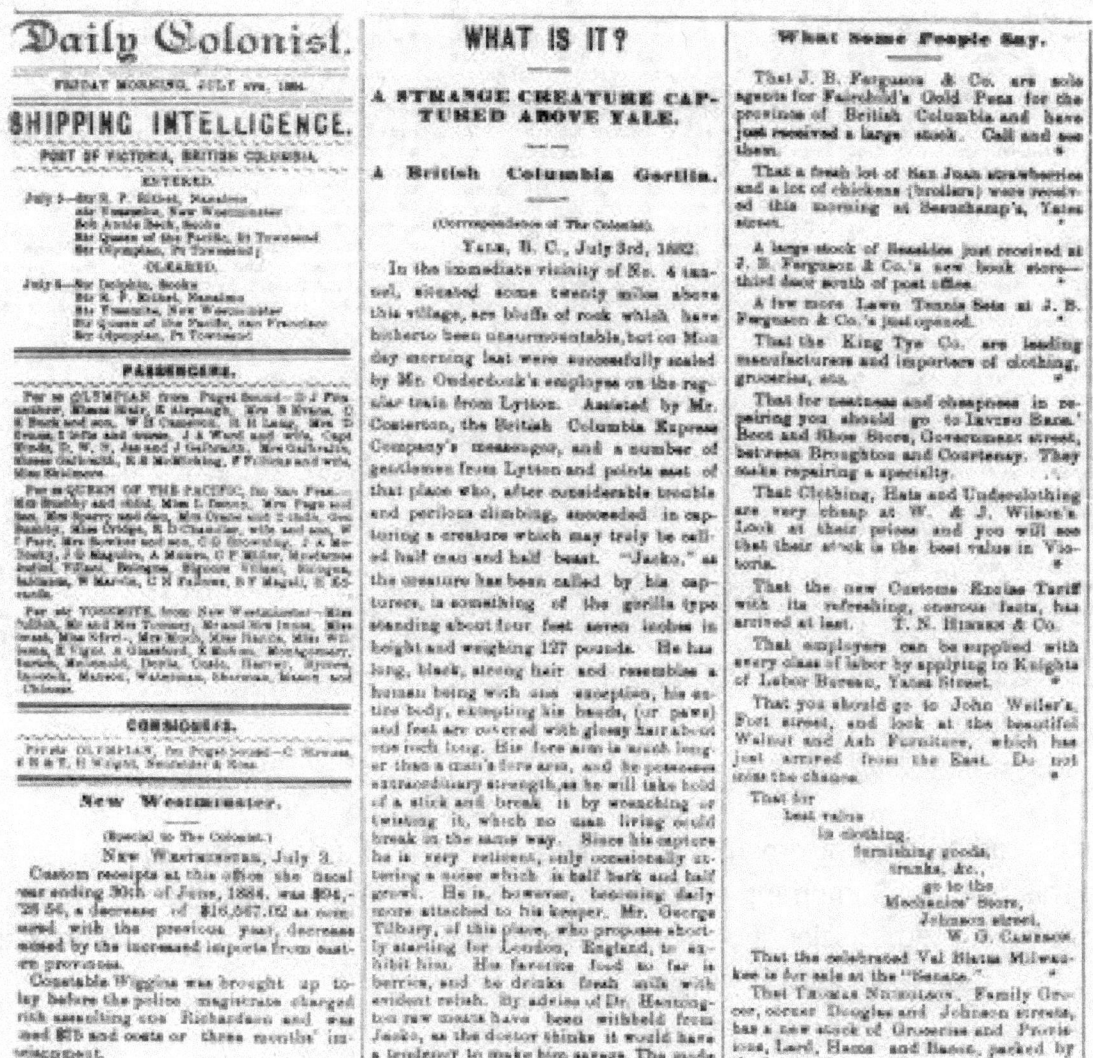

Item -3C

THE CLEVELAND LEADER, MONDAY MORNING, AUGUST 11, 1884.
A WESTERN WHAT IS IT?
A Mysterious Creature in British Columbia.

The village of Yale, B. C., is situated at the head of navigation on Fraser River, ninety miles above New Westminster, which was the capital of British Columbia until it was changed to Victoria. About twenty miles from Yale, on the line of the railroad, is a locality roughly known as "Tunnel No. 4," where the extraordinary occurrence about to be related took place during the early part of the present month.

Notwithstanding the improbability of any amount of prospecting resulting in turning up even the bones of the "missing link," much less in finding an actual living specimen of this much debated being, the actual facts which are related concerning the remarkable appearance near "Tunnel No. 4" would tend to bear out this theory of the subject. At different times during the past two years there has been seen in the hilly country about the settlements a being whose personal appearance is variously described.

One day about a year ago a party of young people from Yale went on the road as far as Tunnel No. 4, and there, disembarking from the cars, proceeded to spread themselves over the country in the form of a picnic party. The tempting meal had been spread upon the ground, and young men and girls were seated in a circle preparing to enjoy the viands, when there was heard a loud crashing noise above their heads, and in an instant, without further warning than was given by a most fiendish yell—something between the shriek of a hyena and the Indian war whoop—there dropped into the midst of the spread a horrible creature as large as a man, covered with hair from head to foot, with long arms which he brandished about in formidable style, as he vainly tried to extricate himself from the canned fruits, cold meats, jam pots, and oleomargarine into which he had unexpectedly tumbled. This was a "surprise party" for which no intentional preparation had been made, and in a moment there was a stampede.

Tumbling headlong down the hill on whose crest the elaborate meal had been laid, the frightened picknickers so hastened their departure as to be utterly unable to give any coherent description of what had frightened them to the railroad men whose assistance they implored. A party fully armed was at once made up, and the scene of the sudden onslaught was carefully approached. The unwelcome visitor had fled, but before leaving he had plainly helped himself to everything that took his fancy, and that seemed to have been guided by nothing but the opportunity. If he were a human creature and had eaten what was certainly gone, selected from every imaginable article of food, his remains would undoubtedly be found in a few hours. No idiot Indian or other kind of man could possibly have eaten such a mixture and live.

But if such was the case, the most careful search failed to result in finding the body, and after a protracted search, which lasted, after a desultory fashion, for several weeks, the idea of his having died of indigestion or gout was reluctantly abandoned. One fact which was demonstrated by the circumstances of this visitation caused the believers in the Indian theory to be very deeply shaken in their convictions. This was that he had fallen from an overhanging limb of a tree, carrying a large piece with him, and the size of the limb was a good indication that the creature must be as heavy as an ordinary sized man, and hardly an Indian, as they do not usually climb trees. A few months later another view of this strange being was had by some workmen on the railroad, but, though they gave chase, they were not able to come up with him. He was not seen again until about three weeks ago, when he was not only seen, but caught. The spot where he was discovered was a series of bluffs, deemed inaccessible. A train was running from Lytton to Yale, when the engineer saw what he supposed to be a man lying close to the track. He whistled down brakes, but just as the

train stopped the object sprang to its feet, and in an instant the object was climbing the side of the precipitous declivity with the greatest ease. The conductor, brakemen, express messenger, and a number of passengers at once gave chase, and after some perilous climbing succeeded in corralling the creature on an overhanging shelf of rock from which he could neither ascend nor descend. The ingenious, though rather cruel, method was now adopted for securing him, of dropping a piece of stone from above, which, falling on his head, stunned him, and he fell insensible.

The bell rope was now procured, and, after some expert climbing, he was reached, tied, and lowered gradually down to the foot of the cliff. He was placed in the baggage car and successfully transported to Yale, when it was found that he had recovered from his insensibility, and was tractable and docile. One of the men in the railroad machine shop assumed the care of him, named him Jacko, and very soon made his friendly acquaintance. And even then, and up to the present time, it has not been satisfactorily ascertained to what race the new discovery belongs. He is of the gorilla type, but not definitely enough to be declared a gorilla, which is, moreover, a creature unknown to the latitude of British Columbia—while there has been no menagerie there to introduce even a monkey. He is about 4 feet 7 inches in height, and weighs 127 pounds. His entire body, except his hands and feet, is covered with black, glossy hair about one inch in length, but his forearm is much longer than that of a man, and so strong that he will break a stick—by wrenching or twisting it—so large that no man could possibly accomplish this feat. He makes a noise, half bark and half growl, but is generally quiet. His favorite food is berries, and he drinks fresh milk with evident relish. His captor intends taking him to London for exhibition. Then his exact position in natural history will probably be discovered.

PLAINTIFF: It was customary at that time period to have disposed of a dean animal, and human remains in this fashion. Something of this nature would have been little more than a curiosity, and unless presented to scientific circles of the time would have been of little interest to those who were the creatures captors.

PLAINTIFF: I would now like to introduce evidence of a now famous case of one said creature being filmed in California on the 20th of October 1967. This has remained controversial since that day, however it has been mostly the subject of opinions and conjecture as to its authenticity. However by the rules of evidence it has a strong position in support of it being authentic. I would now like to enter into evidence: first the testimony of one of the two witnesses present that day, second photographic evidence (two of the frames as it is not possible to place the film in book form and is not necessary for this demonstration of the evidence) and third, trace evidence in the form of footprints left by the object in the photographic evidence.

JUDGE: Proceed councilor.

PLAINTIFF: First I would like to enter the witness testimony as item 4A into the record.

JUDGE: so entered.

Item- 4A

On October 20, 1967 at a place known as Bluff Creek California two men captured on film a creature that has been the source of much controversy since.

There have been many theories and claims regarding this film, some supportive and some claiming hoax. The following interview by John Green of Bob Gimlin on videotape at Gimlin's home in Yakima Washington in 1992 recounts events in Gimlin's own words.

"Green: This is John Green talking to Bob Gimlin in his home in Yakima Washington. This is with regard to the movie that Bob and his friend Roger Patterson made 25 years ago in

Northern California (Bluff Creek area). But we'll start a little further back than that. You've known Roger for a long time haven't you?

Gimlin: Yes. I knew Roger in the early 1960's. I met Roger about 1958 – 59.

Green: So that was before he got interested in Bigfoot?

Gimlin: Yes. I can't recall just exactly when he did start talking to me about Bigfoot, but it was probably in the early 1960's.

Green: Did you go out with him at all, looking into this?

Gimlin: Yes. Roger and I had gone out many times in different areas and over in the Mt. St. Helen's area and actually up in this area here because there was a fellow who said he sighted one right up here at Cowiche Canyon which is about 20 miles from here. I went up there with Roger on that investigation. Of course we covered as many of them as we could when they'd call or somebody would give us a report on something that's happening in the area. Roger and I rode (horseback) in the mountains quite a bit because I was training the horses at the time. Of course O rode a lot in the mountains and Roger would go along with me and he'd play tapes and talk to me about the creature. I was a skeptic in those days. I trusted Roger's thoughts and his knowledge, but I wasn't really convinced that they existed.

Green: How did you come to take this particular trip to California?

Gimlin: Well Roger and I had been over in the Mt. St. Helen's riding the roads and just more or less going by the lava rock caves and things when we came back from there... well, let's go back a little here... it started raining real heavy over there and this was in the last part of August and the first part of September. When we got back to the Yakima area, somebody in California had phoned Roger's wife and left a message that there had been tracks sighted on new roads they'd been pushing back into the Bluff Creek area that they were building logging roads into. So that is the reason we went into that area.

Green: Did Roger usually carry a movie camera with him?

Gimlin: Yes. Most of the time he had a camera that I can recall. I wasn't much on cameras but Roger did have a camera and prior to that he had been working with a guy up in this area here and that's when he bought the camera. I knew he had that camera; he usually kept it in his saddlebags on his horse.

Green: When you went to California, did you have some definite time you were going to spend there?

Gimlin: Yes, well we didn't know exactly because I was working construction at that time and I was in – between bobs, so I said yes, I can take off and go down there. I cannot recall the exact amount of time I was going to stay down there with him but we stayed longer than I'd planned on staying. In fact we stayed a week longer than I planned.

Green: How long were you there?

Gimlin: I think we were down there (California) a total of three weeks.

Green: and what were you traveling with?

Gimlin: I had a one-ton truck with a horse van on it to haul the animals and all of our equipment. Of course we took all our supplies to stay as long as we needed to stay, the hay, the grain, our own food...because once we got in there, we never went into town.

Green: How many horses did you have?

Gimlin: We had three horses, two saddle horses and a packhorse. I had a saddle horse and Roger had a saddle horse and of course we had a small packhorse along.

Green: What was Al de Atley's role in this?

Gimlin: Well, Al de Atley was Roger Patterson's brother in law and he backed Roger financially with whatever expenses it took to go to these places. He was supposed to help me on some of the expenses which I never did receive.

Green: So you provided the truck and the...

Gimlin: Yeah, and the fuel, my own horse and my own food. The agreement when we left on any of those investigations was that whatever Roger spent that we would split the expenses with me but Al de Atley was backing Roger, because Roger didn't have a job at the particular time.

Green: So in fact he only financed Roger; he didn't finance your share at all?

Gimlin: No, he didn't finance my part of the trip at all. I had my own horse, my own equipment and my own food. I didn't expect somebody else to support me on that. It would have been nice if I could have gotten part of the fuel and expenses on the truck.

Green: So you went to an area where you heard tracks had been seen fairly recently?

Gimlin: Yes. Just prior to the time we had gotten there, they had sighted tracks on that Tuesday after being off over the Labor Day weekend. It had also started raining all up and down the West coast. By the time we got down there, these tracks supposedly were three different sizes and were just globs in the mud as far as I was concerned. We couldn't get any plaster cast definition of them at all.

Green: I never realized that you went down there for that specific set of tracks.

Gimlin: Yes, that's the reason we went into that area. I wasn't real anxious to go down there because I needed to go back to work, but Roger kept saying these guys were pretty good down in that area, I can't remember the fellow's name that called up here.

Green: Probably Al Hodgson.

Gimlin: Yes! It was Al Hodgson, but there was somebody else who had talked to Roger too, a guy that worked for the forest service.

Green: Syl McCoy maybe?

Gimlin: Yes, I think that was his name, yeah, McCoy…. Something like that. 'Course it took me a while around here to get things ready, so my wife could do my chores because I had animals at that time, to be able to feed them and take care of them, to be gone that long, why I had to make provisions for her to take care of the animals.

Green: That is interesting because I was there and saw those tracks you're referring to and when I was there Al Hodgson told me he was expecting Roger, well maybe he'd called him already by then.

Gimlin: May have.

Green: I took that to mean that Roger already had a trip there planned before that.

Gimlin: Uh huh, well I don't recall whether he had a trip planned prior to the call or not, in fact I don't think he did. Like I said, we'd been in the Mt. St. Helen's area and when I came back here I was going to go back to work in two weeks. Then I talked to him (Roger) again. We said we were kind of in between jobs so we can take a couple weeks off and that's mainly the reason I went on down and Roger went with me because it was my equipment.

Green: So what did you do when you got there?

Gimlin: Well first we set up camp of course, Then the way we do is just e the roads, when these guys were working on the roads with bulldozers and everything, as quick as they'd quit working, we would ride up in that area and search for tracks or whatever we'd run into then we would take the one ton pick up when the equipments off the road, so we could drive the roads. We would drive the roads at night real slow looking for tracks crossing the road. Of course in the day time we couldn't drive the roads 'cause they were working on the roads up in there. They had started logging in some areas and the logging trucks had started coming down from there. We covered as many miles as we could with the amount of time that we had. We could only go out so far then we had to go back to camp. I mean, we did ride back to camp and use the truck to drive the roads at night time.

Green: What happened on this particular day?

Gimlin: The day we got the film footage, I left early in the morning and Roger slept in, I just rode out and around, I always got up early and so I rode on out. My horse loosened a shoe and I came back in to tack the shoe on tighter. About 10:00, mid morning or so, I sat around there for a little while, because Roger was gone when I got back. Supposedly he had gone down the creek there, ah Bluff Creek there and after awhile he came back and asked what area I had covered that morning? I told him and he says why don't we ride up into this area we had ridden into before, a desolate type area down a couple of canyons, there's a creek running through it. So we went ahead and fixed lunch and he said let's get our gear together so when we ride out we can stay if we have to and stay a little bit later into the night if we need to. We packed up the packhorse and it was about midday, perhaps a little bit after noontime when we went around this bend in the creek bed. There was a fallen tree and as we came around it there was this creature standing by the creek. That's when everything started happening. The horses started jumping around, raising the devil and spooked from this creature. Roger, well his horse was rearing up and jumping around, he slid off him, got his camera out of the saddle bags and started trying to get pictures of this creature as it was walking away.

The film footage that you see (The Patterson film) is what was acquired from that particular sighting in the few seconds that we had to take pictures with, and then Roger ran out of film in the camera. The reason for him running out of film was, as we were riding up there, we just took our time and fooled around. It was in the fall of the year, the maple trees were turning red and it was kind of pretty and Roger was taking pictures of me riding up the canyons, pictures of the trees and photographing the surrounding areas. So when this all happened, he didn't have much film left in the camera unfortunately. Of course, some of it was kind of blurry because he was running across the creek to get a better view, a closer view of the creature in a better way and get more pictures of it. When he did run out of film, why naturally it was one of those old cameras, that he had to get under a poncho to change film.

We went to catch his horse and the packhorse because I kept my horse under control. I had my horse with me all the time. So we caught his horse, got the new film out of the saddlebags, he got under this old poncho and changed the film around. Then we tried to track the creature on up from where we had last seen it. We didn't have much luck doing it. Then we decided it was getting late in the afternoon. In that area, that time of year, the sun goes down about 3:30 or 4:00 o'clock. We wanted to get back and take plaster casts of the tracks and then go on into town to see if we had anything on film. We weren't sure from Roger stumbling and falling on the sand bar and getting up and running, we didn't even have an idea that we had anything on film at that time, in fact it was doubtful that we did have anything.

Green: So you cast the tracks the same day?

Gimlin: Yes we did. In fact right that afternoon. By the time we got the tracks cast and the different deals that we did to cast the tracks done, it was getting late. It was almost dark by the time we got back down to the truck and got the horses fed and tied up. By the time we got into town at Al Hodgson's store, it was good and dark. I imagine it was about 8:30 or 9:00 o'clock. Then we went on over to... oh whatever town that was to mail the film up to Al de Atley, Roger's brother in law, so he could take it and get it developed to see if there was really anything on the film.

Okay, I'll go back a little bit to the casting of the tracks. I rode the big horse. The horse that I was riding was around 1200 – 1300 pounds. I rode him along side the tracks with this new film in the camera, Roger took pictures of how deep the horse's prints were in the soil compared to the creature's tracks. Then I got up on a stump, which was approximately three to four feet, you know? We didn't measure it, probably should have. Anyway I jumped off with a high heel boot as close to the track as we could. Then we took pictures of that to illustrate the depth that my footprint went into the same dirt with a high heel cowboy boot and at that time I weighed 165 pounds. These were all things that we did prior to leaving the scene. It was a good thing we did, because that night when we came back, 'course we were pretty excited about just seeing it and we sat there and talked about it until about 12:30 or one o'clock in the morning.

Around 5:30 a.m. or so it started raining and it was just a pouring down rain. I told Roger we better get up there and do something about the tracks or they'd wash out, and he said no, it would stop raining after awhile. I went ahead and got up, put the saddle on my horse and decided I would ride up there while it was raining really hard and Roger says "ah it'll quit, don't ride up there" I said "no, I'm going to go ahead and ride on up there." I had gotten a couple of cardboard boxes from Mr. Hodgson's to cover these tracks the night before. So when I went outside to get a couple of these boxes that were folded up out there, they were just soggy old pieces of cardboard. I disregarded taking those back up there, so I rode back up to the scene, pulled some bark off some trees and covered up the tracks as best I could and went back to camp.

By then we decided it wasn't going to quit raining. The little creek that was six or seven feet across was now ten or twelve feet across and four feet deep! We were on the side of the creek, which had to be crossed with the truck to get out to the main road. I said, "Well I'm going to go ahead and cross the creek with the truck and get started out. "And of course Roger thought it would stop raining and he suggested I leave him there and come back and pick him up.

In the meantime, why ah... they had called the track dog people in Canada and they were supposed to come down. I think they had also phoned you. Mr. Green and Rene' Dahinden. I'm not sure when all that happened but I do remember the people in Canada had been called with the track dogs to come on down to see if we could track it up through the mountains from where we last saw it.

Green: I think it was the B.C. Museum that was called, cause that was the people who phoned me.

Gimlin: Was that it? Oh, I couldn't recall just exactly how that went.

Green: A man from the museum had come down with me at the beginning of September, come down after I was there and told them the tracks were there.

Gimlin: Oh was that it? Okay well, I didn't remember just exactly how those sequences happened.

Green: Yes, well it was from him I learned of the movie, the call must have gone to the museum.

Gimlin: Must have, yeah, well Roger didn't do that; I think it was Al Hodgson. I think Roger had talked to him about the calling, well they had talked about it, but I was not present at the time they did.

Green: About how far was it from your camp to where this a...

Gimlin: Oh a calculated guess, I think it was about four miles.

Green: That movie you took, comparing the depths of the tracks, that would be the one that you showed at the university of British Columbia?

Gimlin: Yes. That is the one shown in British Columbia.

Green: Are you aware that movie has been missing almost ever since?

Gimlin: Yes I am aware of that. I asked before Roger passed away and his reply was that Al de Atley had that somewhere. He didn't tell me exactly where. He (Roger) said that Al has the film in his possession somewhere. Of course I asked Al de Atley about it and he denied having it and denied it ever existed. That seems strange to me because I knew it existed and Roger knew it existed!

Green: And so did all the people at the University of British Columbia!

Gimlin: Exactly. See... so why the film disappeared, I'll never know and probably never find out.

Green: Sounds almost as if Al lost it.

Gimlin: Or sold it. Who knows what happened to it?

Green: Well you'd think if had been sold it would have shown up sometime.

Gimlin: Well you know Al and Roger toured with that film afterwards and it's hard telling what went on in those days and of course Roger made some deal with American National which I never did know.

Green: But you know Rene' Dahinden and I were the first people to make a deal for the use of the film itself. Al brought to Seattle the film of the creature and a great deal of footage of that Roger had taken of the waterfalls and trees and various things like that. The footprint film was supposed to be there but it wasn't.

Gimlin: Was it supposed to be on the same role of film?

Green: Oh no!

Gimlin: It was just a different role of film then?

Green: Well, I don't remember now if he brought a lot of little boxes or whether this film had already been spliced.

Gimlin: Yeah, see.

Green: But anyway, we showed it expecting to find the footprint film but it wasn't there.

Gimlin: Yes, but as I didn't know much about movie cameras or splicing film or any of that sort of thing, anybody could have shown me the film and I wouldn't have been to detect a splice except I knew what was taken, we all saw it, you know? Course the film footage of the creature wasn't that good but the other film footage was plain. It was taken during sun light hours and I thought it was good film. I don't know what you guys thought about it, but I thought it was a pretty good film.

Green: Oh yes, as I remember I only saw it once but it was perfectly clear I thought.

Gimlin: Well I saw it at the same time you guys did. I don't really recall everything that happened way back then you know. Course there was a lot of speculation at that time and Roger and Al had big dollar signs in their eyes you know. They were just going to go here and go there, and well we did travel a lot with that film. There was a lot of money spent. Course, Argosy bought one article at that particular time. I think it was the fall of 1967, Argosy bought the article. After that Al and Roger traveled with the film and promoted it somewhat.

That was about the time I went back to work because I didn't have any income. They just kind of cut me completely out of the thing. It me forever to kind of even, well even after Roger died, I had to go to court to get any rights at all out of it which, you know was kind of an odd thing. But between Mrs. Patterson's attorney and her it was a deal where they did not recognize that I had any interest at all in the film. At one time I was supposed to be one-third partner on everything that happened. If there was money coming in, but then that all changed. The film itself, now maybe Al lost it. I really don't know what happened to that film footage where Roger and I took film of the tracks, my boot tracks and the horse's and so forth.

Green: Remember how deep the horse tracks were compared to that of the Sasquatch tracks?

Gimlin: The horse tracks were not as deep as the Sasquatch tracks of course. I just walked the horse through. I walked him as slow as I could but you figure he is distributing his weight on four feet. The tracks were better than half as deep but they weren't as deep as the tracks of the creature.

Green: But the area of the four hoof prints wouldn't be any greater than two of those footprints, would it?

Gimlin: No, no, the hoof print area if your familiar with sizes of horses hoof prints, well the horse wore a size one shoe, which is not quite 6 inches in diameter, probably more like 5 inches in diameter with a number one shoe on the front feet. The shoes were a little bit smaller on the back feet. They were size ones trimmed down is what they were. Of course I rode the horse too, so there was my extra weight plus the horse's weight plus the saddle and tack and everything I had on him. There was probably a total weight of about 1400 pounds.

Green: How about when you jumped off the stump?

Gimlin: Now when I jumped off the stump with a high heel boot in the dirt, the footprint went almost as deep as the creature's footprint. We didn't actually measure, we didn't have a ruler, we just took pictures of it. Viewing it (the film) you could actually tell better for depth. By looking at it and making a judgment on the sight of it, it wasn't as deep as the creature's footprint. They weren't exactly side-by-side either, they were probably two or three feet between my track and the creature's track but there was some distance between them. The soil was practically the same. That soil had all been washed in there from the flood a year prior. There could have been some variation in the soil. We really didn't get into it that deep, it was a thing where we were pretty excited about it all and there was a time element there to get all these things done before dark.

Green: You know when you walked around the tracks, when you took that movie; your boot tracks were there too, weren't they?

Gimlin: Yes, right! We walked around it quite a bit trying to stay out of the tracks as much as possible.

Green: But still you would have been close then?

Gimlin: Oh yeah, just walking, we were close but the boot prints lacked a whole lot going as deep, considerable amount going as deep as the creature's tracks were.

Green: Going back now to what happened, when you first saw the creature, how did it come into view?

Gimlin: You mean when we first saw it John?

Green: Did you come around a corner or did you see it from a distance or?

Gimlin: No, it wasn't exactly a corner. We came around a bend. We were riding the creek beds, is what we were doing and so when we came around the bend in the creek; this thing was standing alongside the creek. Stand upright. We were about 60 to 80 feet away from it when we first saw it. Then at different times we were different distances from it. At one time I was probably as close as 60 feet to it when I rode across the creek and got off my horse. When Roger ran across the creek, the thing immediately started walking away. Then whenever it was that the horses started spooking and throwing fits, the commotion started and the creature just started walking away.

Green: So it was standing when you first saw it?

Gimlin: It was standing still, right at the edge of the creek when we first saw it, yes.

Green: Right at the edge?

Gimlin: Right by the edge of the creek, yes.

Green: But fully upright?

Gimlin: Fully upright, standing upright, yes.

Green: What exactly did the horses do?

Gimlin: Well Roger was in the front and his horse tried to spin around and come back. I was riding behind him on the big horse leading the packhorse along. My horse was kind of spooky but not near as bad as Roger's horse. Roger's horse was a spooky little horse. He was a young horse of course. The horse I was riding was an older cow horse, been roped on and used for a lot of things. Roger's horse threw all kinds of fits and when Roger got off the horse, he ran off and the packhorse jerked free from me and ran off back down the way we came.

Green: Did Roger's horse buck?

Gimlin: No, it never did buck, just reared and jumped all around. His horse was in front of me and of course I wasn't looking straight at him all the time. This all happened in a couple of heartbeats you know. It happened fast!

Green: But then Roger's horse didn't go down?

Gimlin: No, it didn't fall down, just reared up is all.

Green: Because this has been said since, you know that Roger's horse fell down?

Gimlin: No, no his horse never did fall down. No.

Green: Okay, that's interesting. So did he get the camera while he was still on the horse?

Gimlin: Yes, while he was stepping down off the horse, Umm, a lot of people have asked me about that and they probably don't realize the agility that Roger had. He was a tremendous athlete. Roger had tremendous agility! He had been a rodeo rider, he did gymnastics and this wasn't a full size horse Roger was riding either. It was a pony, a small horse.

Green: Yeah, I've seen those little horses; he used to haul them in a Volkswagen bus.

Gimlin: Yeah, we used to haul two of them in a VW bus. Roger rode these horses because they were easy to get on and off of because Roger wasn't a very big man. So actually when he was getting off his horse, he always kept that saddlebag ready. The saddlebag had two flaps on it to keep it buckled down. He kept one buckled and one of them unbuckled so he could get his camera in the event he needed it in a hurry and this was the case at that particular time.

Green: So he practiced getting the camera out of the saddlebags in a hurry?

Gimlin: Oh yeah, lots of times. Yes, he did, that was his theory that if he ever had to get it, ah kept the one buckle on there so it would not bounce out while he was riding and the other one loose so he could get it out in a hurry.

Green: Did Roger have a gun at all?

Gimlin: Yeah, Roger had a 303 British rifle in his saddle scabbard and I had a thirty ought six rifle in my saddle scabbard.

Green: Did you have any expectation that you might see one?

Gimlin: No. I surely didn't. I don't think Roger did either! We always carried rifles with us when we went into the mountains, at least I always did and I'm sure Roger did too.

Green: Had you discussed whether you would shoot at one of these creatures if you saw one?

Gimlin: Yes, many times. We had talked about it but decided unless it was necessary, we would never shoot. In other words, unless it was violent or attempted to attack us or something in that sense of the word, you know?

Green: So when Roger was off of his horse and ran after the creature with the camera, what did you do?

Gimlin: Roger said, "Cover me" as he pulled the camera out. If they don't understand what that means, well he didn't have any protection, just the camera in his hand and in case something were to happen.

What I did was ride across the creek, pull my rifle out of the scabbard, stepped down off the horse and just stood there with my rifle. I never raised the rifle like I would shoot or anything like that, just held it in my hand and with the other hand held my horse to keep him from getting away from me.

Green: So there was never a gun pointed at the creature?

Gimlin: No never. I didn't point the rifle at the creature.

Green: Did you ever feel the creature was acting at all threatening?

Gimlin: No, it kept walking away all the time. It turned and looked around, once at Roger and once at me. The first time it turned and looked was the time I rode across the creek. I was off to it's right, behind it and that is when it made one turn with its head. Then Roger relocated himself on a log, steadying the camera at one time, then when he ran to another position to get a better view and a better picture the creature turned it's head a second time and I assume it was looking at Roger. When you view the film, I never could really decide whether it turned to look at me or Roger because all these things happened tremendously fast and I was trying to hold onto my horse and a rifle at the same time and also keep an eye on the creature and Roger.

Green: Do you have much of a mental image now of what you saw as opposed to what you saw on the movie since that time?

Gimlin: I don't think that it's changed that much. Yes I still have a mental image of what really happened that day. There may be a few things I've over looked or forgotten over the years but basically the time of the day and how the thing moved and what we did is pretty much still in my mind. Pretty exact in my mind because even though we were excited, you never seem to forget those things.

Green: When you first saw it, how big did you think it was Bob?

Gimlin: I thought it was about six and a half feet tall and I would have guessed its weight at 250 to 300 pounds. It did have tremendous muscle bulk. This was an estimated guess at the time of course. I'm not used to seeing things like that. I was just guessing weight compared to the amount of muscle quarter horses have, it was as big as a quarter horse naturally and the height because we were up on our horses at the time we first saw the creature. Therefore it probably didn't look as tall as it really was. Now the horse I was riding was a 16-hand horse. One hand is 4 inches on a horse. My horse was 16 hands tall plus my saddle. That would make him approximately sixteen and a half hands high. Now of course, with me sitting up there, you can figure me eye level was about 9 feet high. So anything actually less than nine feet you would be looking down at it.

Green: Was it obvious whether it was a male or female?

Gimlin: Well, it appeared to be a female, but you know I had never seen one. I had never even seen a track until that day so I couldn't even make a statement whether it was male or female. But the film indicates that it had mammary glands, so we assumed it was a female.

Now they had told us that the tracks they found in the road were three different sizes. We talked about that at length and discussed it and assumed there was a male, a female and a younger one with those three different sized tracks. So our first assumption was it was a female.

Green: What color did it appear to be to you?

Gimlin: It was a dark brown, brownish color.

Green: Then it wasn't as dark as it looks in the film?

Gimlin: No, it wasn't as dark as it looks in the film. It was a long ways from being tan, but it wasn't a very dark brown like it shows in the film. It was a lighter color brown. Of course it was lighter in different areas of it's body too, I suppose where the hair was shorter it was lighter or vice versa, it might have been darker where the hair was shorter.

Green: Can you remember details on its face?

Gimlin: Yes I can. The face would have a flat type nose, the lips, I can't really remember what the lips looked like except it did have lips and we could see its teeth. The eyes were large eyes but not big round eyes like a horse or a cow but there were large eyes. The hair on its face was short. There wasn't a whole lot of hair around its cheeks and down along side the face, the best I can remember is the face didn't have a whole lot of hair on it.

Green: What would the skin color be then?

Gimlin: It seemed like it was a brownish color skin.

Green: Was it doing anything with its hands?

Gimlin: You mean a...

Green: Well in the film they were just swinging.

Gimlin: Well John, that is all I ever saw. It never raised its arms or anything to that effect. It just walked with an easy type motion away from us and swung its arms like a human being. The best I can remember is the hands were about the same color as the face.

Green: The bottoms of its feet looked quite light colored but that could be the sand.

Gimlin: I think that is the case. The sand wasn't a white sand, it was kind of a funny type soil there where the creature walked and it was lighter colored dirt. I think you can remember the color of the soil John.

Green: Oh yeah.

Gimlin: It was pretty light colored soil in there and might have been why the soles of the feet looked light in the film footage.

Green: In the movie, it hasn't quite disappeared when the picture stops because it looks as if it's about to disappear behind a big pile of, well it looked like a stump or pile of wood of some kind.

Gimlin: Yeah, it hadn't disappeared when the film footage, ah, when Roger ran out of film because it traveled on, oh probably not half again the distance of where he, but another thirty or forty yards. There was some trees down in that area. I suppose from the flood and so forth. There were many fallen trees and different things in that area. Then when the creature did disappear up a little draw, why I wanted to follow it. Of course Roger didn't want to follow it because he was on foot and he didn't want to be left there. We thought there was the possibility there were the two others around, we didn't know at the time whether that was one of the ones that had made the tracks up above the scene or not.

Roger was a little bit upset about that so he wanted to catch his horse and get some more film in the camera. It took quite a while to catch the horse and to catch the catch horse as well and tie them up. Then we rode on in pursuit of the creature. Now see, the way it went to see if we could see more tracks or, I don't know. I thought maybe we could see this creature again. I don't really know why I was thinking that. We never did see it again, but we saw scuffs in the gravel and in the creek bed there that indicated where it had possibly ran when it went out of sight. We measured 68 to 72 inches in the stride which was not even close to accurate because it was, as I have said, just scuffs in the gravel. Then we tracked on up the creek bed quite a ways. We saw one wet half of a footprint on a rock as it went up into the mountains and that was as far as we went with it.

Green: So there wasn't sand to show footprints beyond where you saw it?

Gimlin: No, it was gravel mostly, but there was sand and dirt where it went across the creek, but it never left a footprint in the sand or in the dirt or soil. It did leave a wet mark on the rock in the creek where it went across and went on into the hills from there.

Green: Were you ever closer to it than Roger was while he took the pictures?

Gimlin: Yeah, I was. When I rode across the creek and got off my horse I was closer than Roger was with the camera at that time. I rode fairly close to the creature.

Green: And I suppose Roger wouldn't have had much of a look at it because he was looking through the lens of the camera all the time.

Gimlin: Well yes, I feel that I had a better look at it. We talked about it like I said when we got back to the camp that night we stayed up and talked about that for hours. You know, talked about what each one of had seen. There was things that I had seen about the creature that Roger didn't. Of course, he couldn't see it too well, because he was looking through the camera.

Green: When you got off the horse, what size did it appear to be then?

Gimlin: Well, to be plum honest with you, I didn't even think about sizes at the time it was going away. It was large, but I never gave any thought to how high it was or how heavy it was because it was moving away from me. That was about all that was in my mind at that time. That this creature was of no threat to us and oh yeah, I was trying to keep my horse under control cause you know I never had any idea what might happen and I sure didn't want to be on foot! So I knew I could get back on my horse and maybe if I had to, well if I had to, if I had to shoot it and it didn't go down, I could get on my horse and I could get out of there, and Roger would have to fend for himself. I'm not a coward, but I'll be darned if I was going to stick around if this creature got violent, you know? So I was concentrating on keeping my rifle in my hand and my horse under control.

Green: There is of course, this widespread opinion that this was some kind of masquerade, having the film; of course there is a certain amount of blurring and a certain amount of under exposure of the creature itself. You can't see the face, for instance. You had a much better look at it than that, what was your impression?

Gimlin: My impression is that there is a creature and I don't feel it was a man in a suit. If it had been a man in a suit, I don't know how they would have gotten him back into that particular area. I have heard this story and thought about it many times. God! At one point with the film circulating all around and people criticizing, I was almost to the point of not being even sure myself. But I thought about it all these years and I'm quite sure it wasn't a man in a suit. I saw the face. I saw the expression on its face. With all the muscles in the arms and legs, I don't know how it could be a man in a suit! Plus I never had anything to do with a man in a suit and if Roger did, how would he know I wouldn't shoot it? In my opinion, that creature was not a man in a suit.

Green: Could you see the muscles move when it walked?

Gimlin: Yes, I could see the muscles clearly and that was one of the deciding factors in my opinion that was no man in a suit. The thighs, the buttocks, the arms and shoulders, you could see it move clearly underneath the hair.

Green: You have estimated this thing to weigh a great deal less than the horse and yet the footprints were deeper, what explanation could you think of?

Gimlin: Well you asked my estimation when I first saw it.

Green: No, no but.

Gimlin: Oh you mean afterwards? Well god John there was no way of really knowing. We knew it had to be heavier than it appeared to be when we first saw it. Of course, we thought the horse's weight was distributed on four feet and I'm not good with the mathematics of such things but ah, if you figure 1400 pound horse distributed on four feet would be about 350 to 400 pounds, so we figured it must have weighed much more than we originally figured. Course Roger did some research by going over to the zoo in Seattle, watched the gorillas there and asked how much they weighed and so forth. They had one over there named Bobo and I don't remember his weight exactly but I do remember he weighed more than it looked like he weighed.

Green: Yes, I did the same thing with those same gorillas.

Gimlin: Uh huh.

Green: And there was a female gorilla there that was quite small but was tremendously heavy.

Gimlin: Yeah John, that is what Roger was telling me. I wasn't all that interested at the time, whatever it was you know? In the end it probably weighed approximately 500 pounds to make such tracks that deep in the dirt. Of course, when it walked, it kicked up a certain amount of dirt from the pressure of the toes pushing away.

Green: Well it would have to distribute the weight on different parts of the foot when it walks otherwise there is no way it could have made a deeper print than the horse.

Gimlin: Yes, right.

Green: If its feet were put down flat each foot would have an area as big as three of the horse's feet.

Gimlin: Yes.

Green: You would have to roll that imprint in some way or another.

Gimlin: Yeah, right.

Green: So when you saw it, up until that moment you had never seen a track?

Gimlin: Never, never seen a track at all, that's right.

Green: And you weren't at all convinced that there were any such animals to be seen?

Gimlin: That is true. I was not convinced that they really existed. You know, I figured Roger must have had a reason. He showed me plaster casts and I heard different stories from people who had seen them, so I thought well maybe there is something to this but I just didn't believe in them basically, didn't believe it was possible they could exist. Even after we got the film many people said "ah they don't exist" and still people tell me it's a bunch of malarkey you know? There will always be a certain amount of people you just can't convince less they see one.

Green: Well when you did see it, there wasn't any doubt you were looking at an animal was there?

Gimlin: There is no doubt in my mind at all.

Green: Okay, that ought to do it Bob, thanks a lot!

Gimlin: Your quite welcome John."

PLAINTIFF: I would now like to introduce into the record two of the still photographs from the film. The film is 23.85 feet long (preceded by 76.15 feet of "horseback" footage), has 954 frames, and runs for 59.5 seconds at 16 frames per second. I would like to enter the following evidence as items 5A and 5B.

Item -5A

Item -5B

PLAINTIFF: I would at this time like to introduce photographs of a number of the footprints that were cast in plaster at the film site as items 6A, 6B, 6C, 6D, 6E, 6F and 6G.

Item 6A

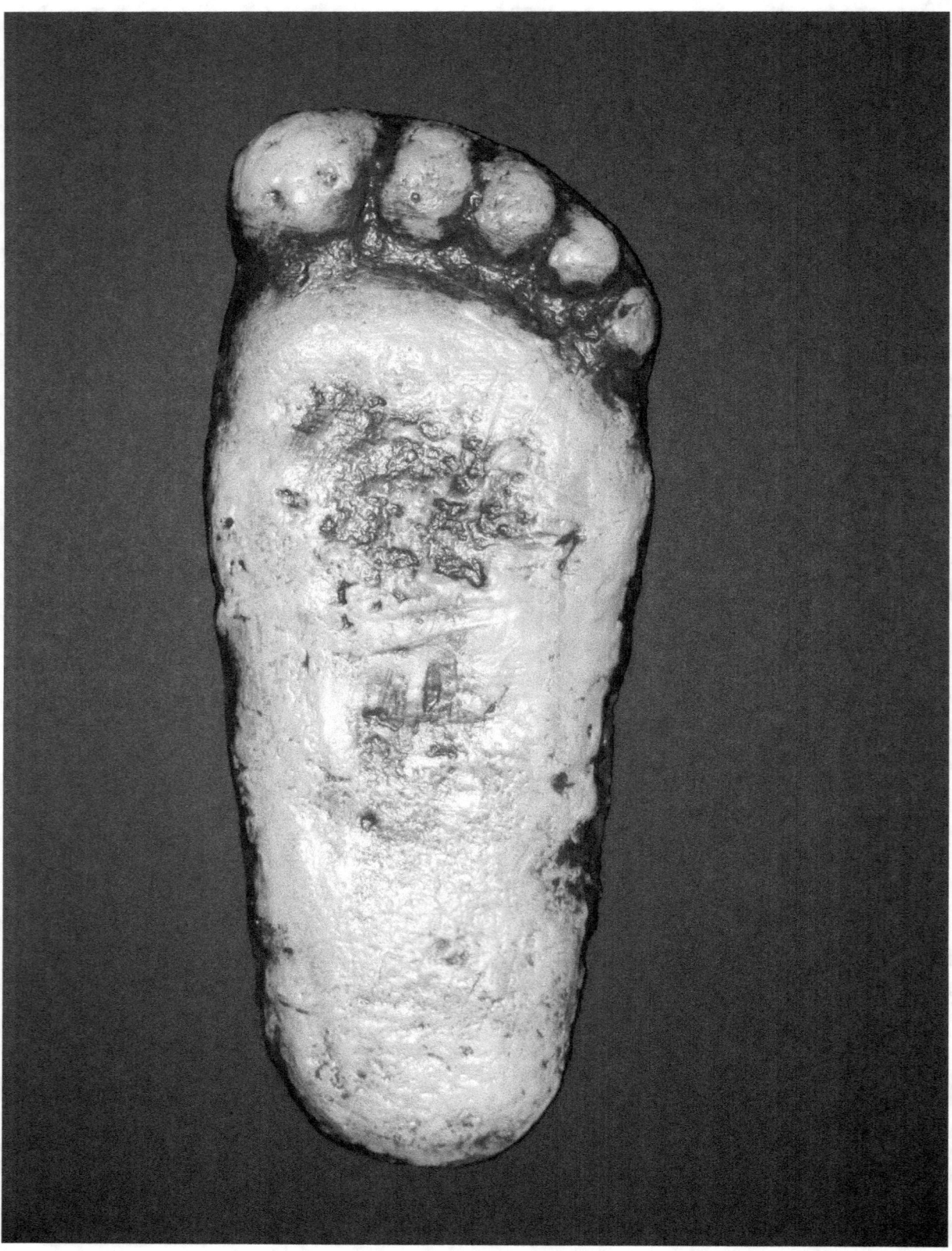

Item 6B

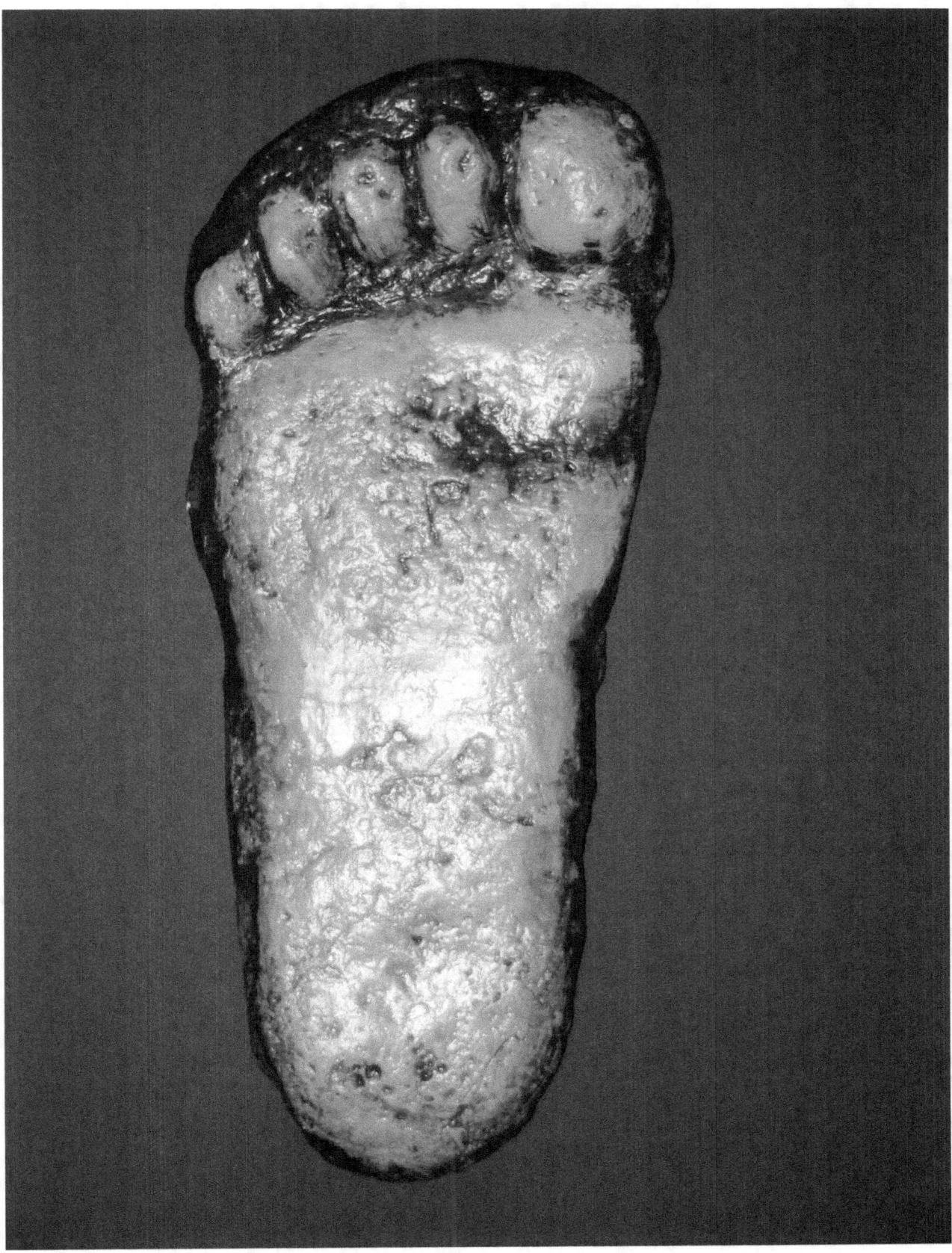

Item 6C

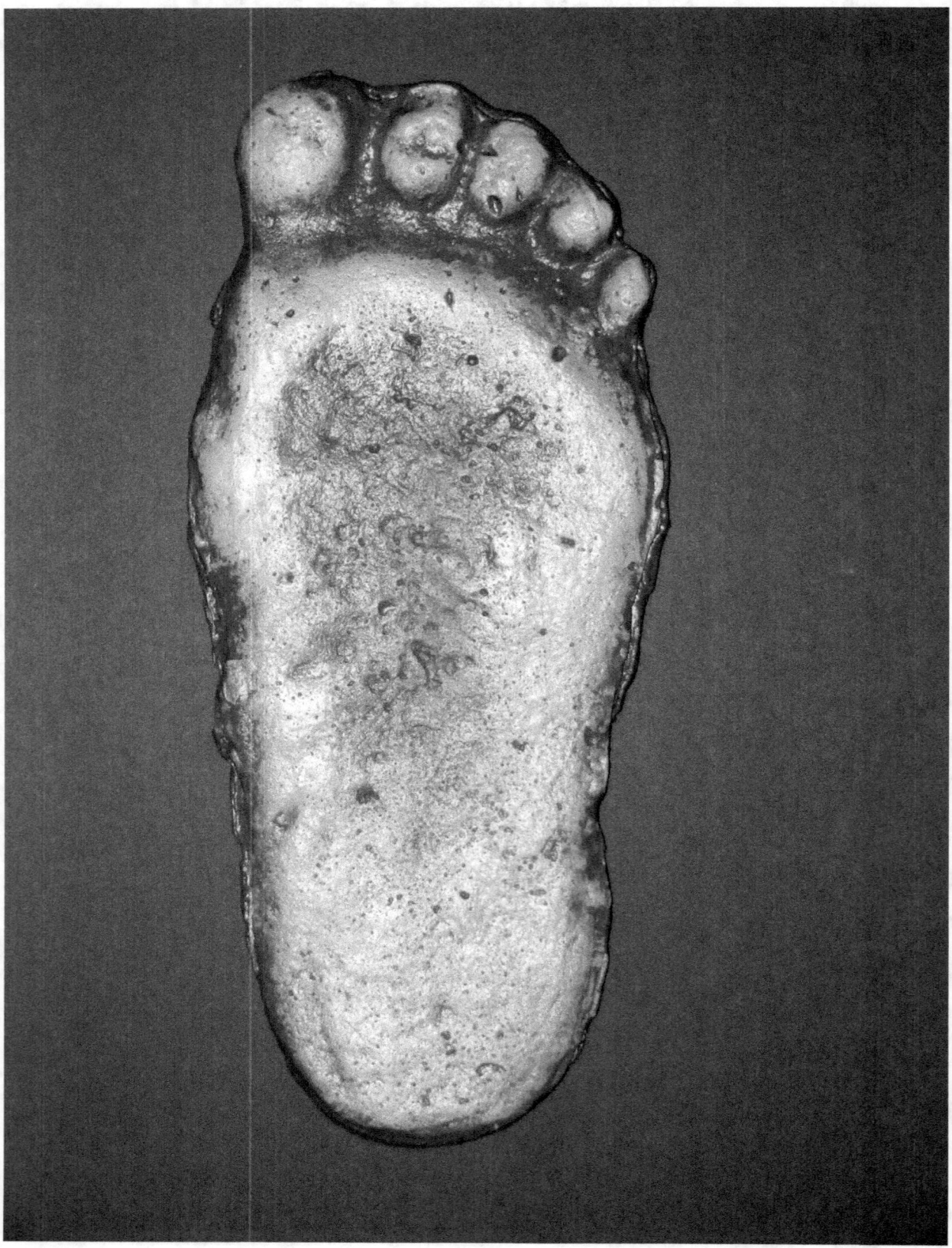

Item 6D

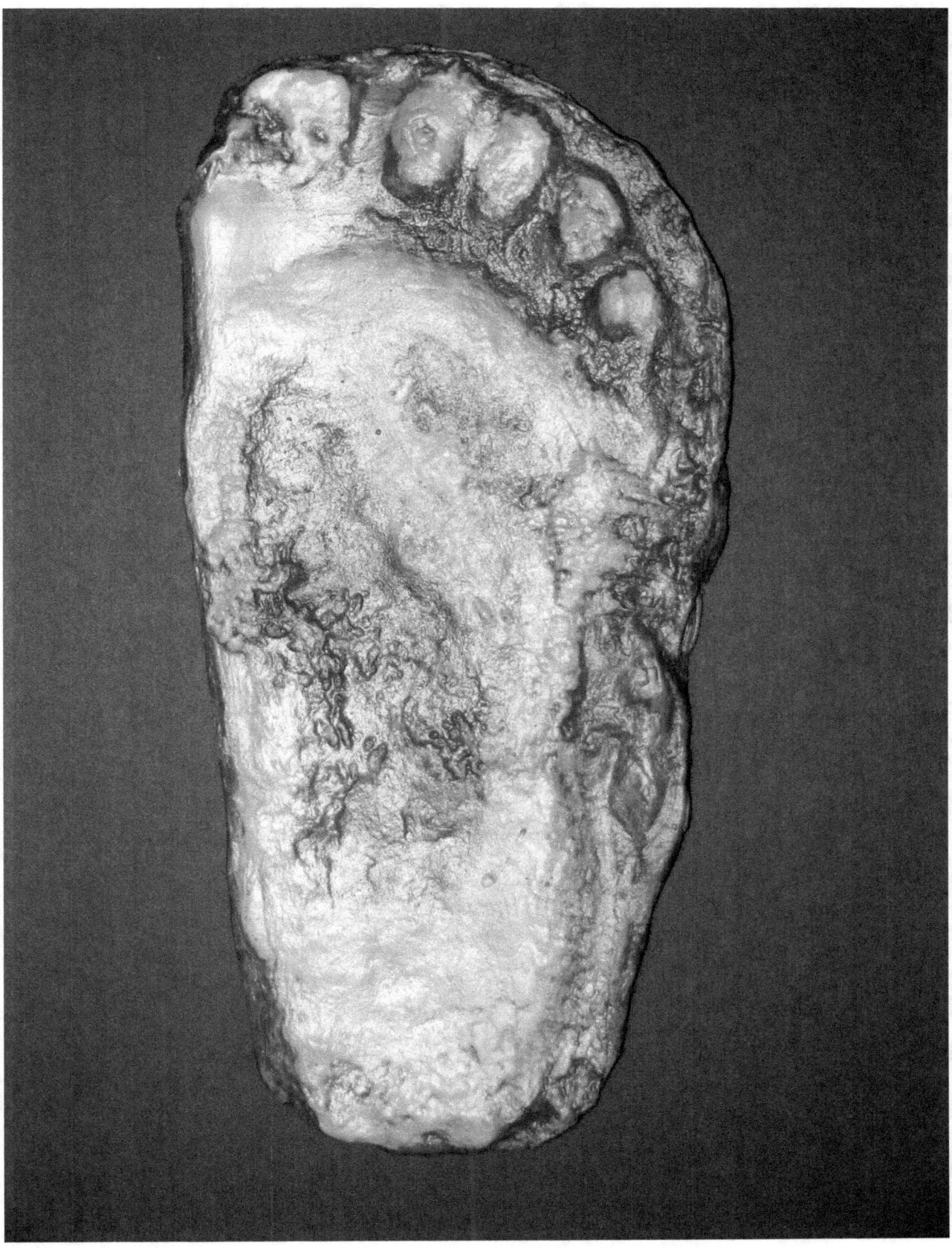

Item 6E

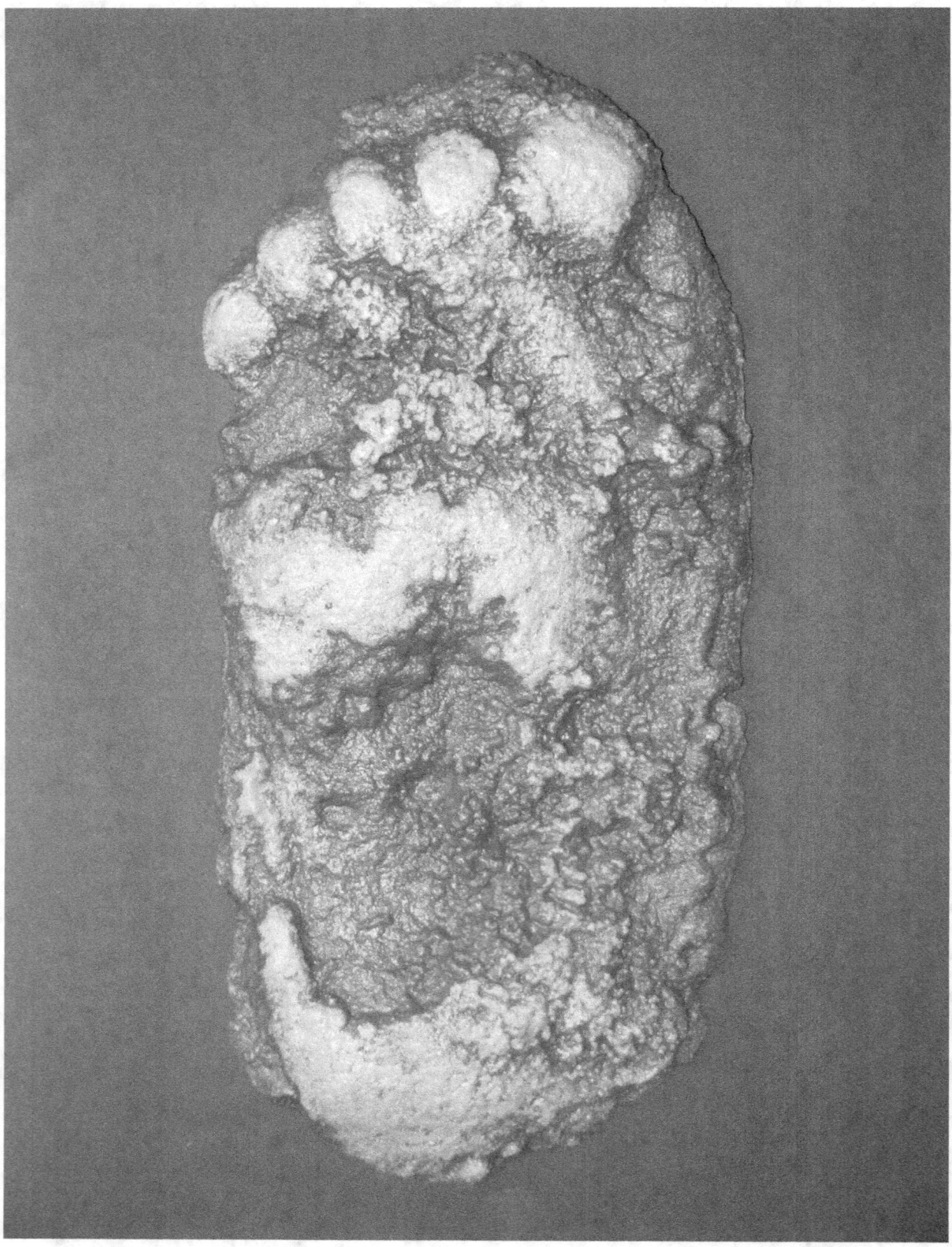

Item 6F

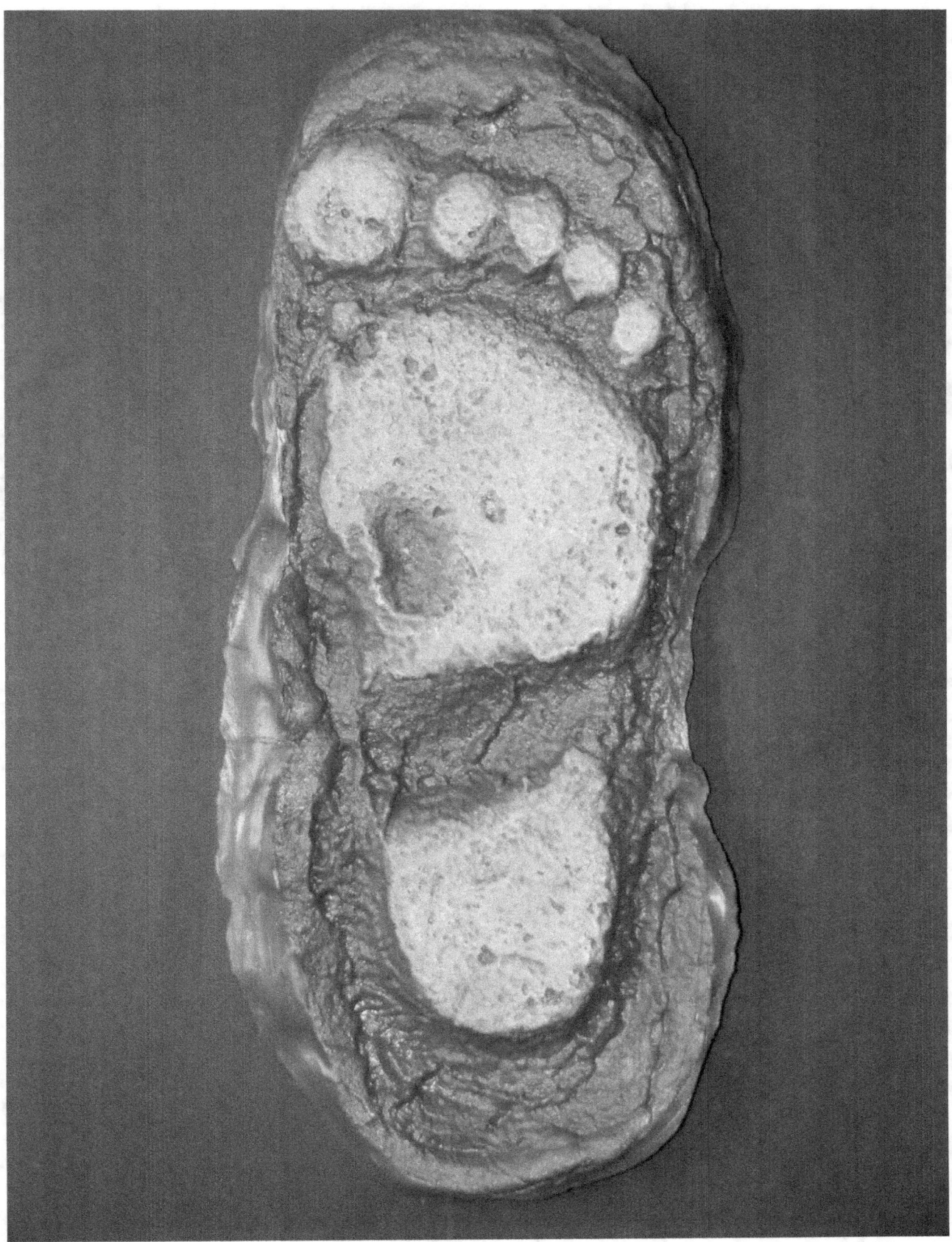

Item 6G (this a photograph of item 6F)

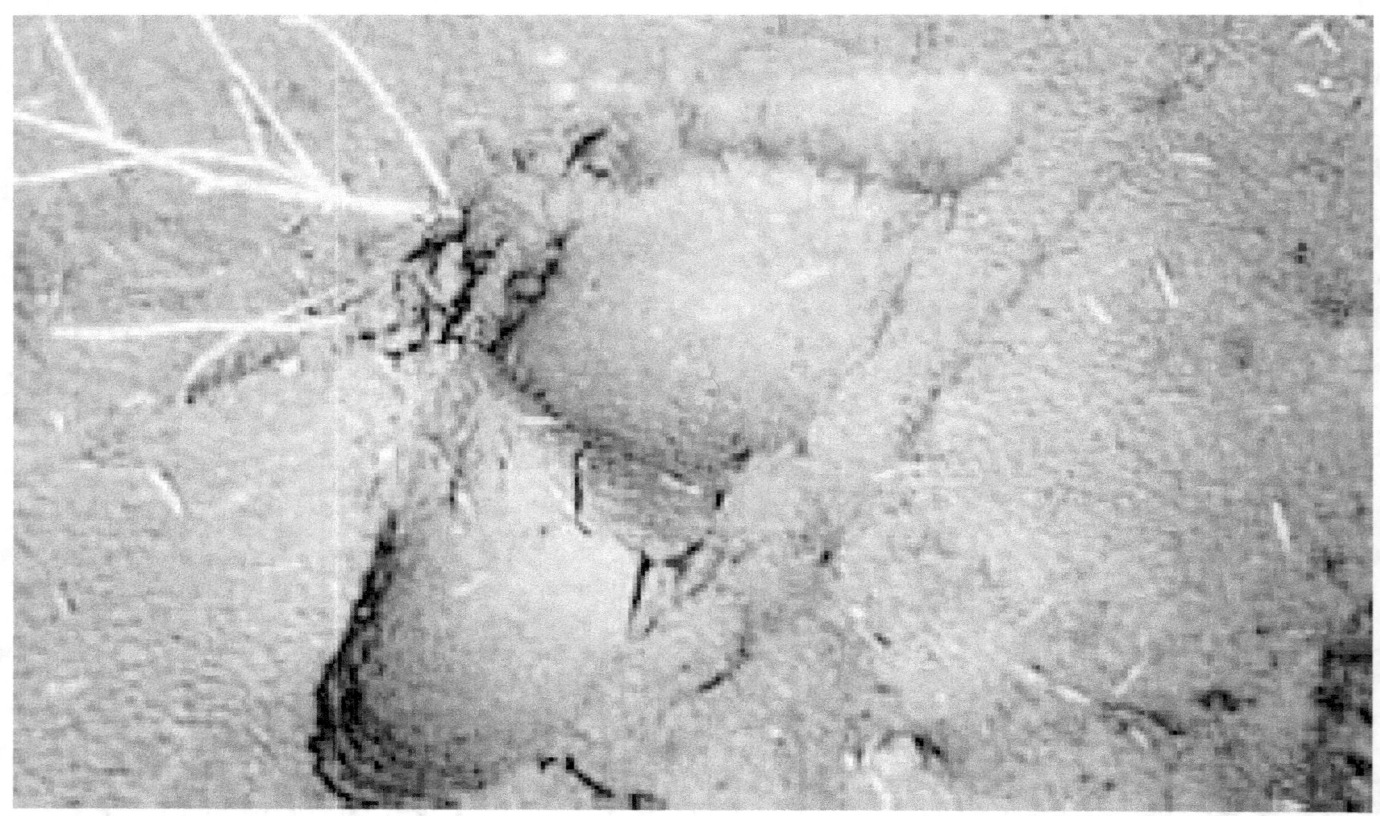

DEFENSE: Your honor, This film has never been proven real. A man named Bob Heironimus, claims to have worn the gorilla suit seen in the film. He also claims that Bob Gimlin offered to pay him $1,000.00 dollars in exchange for a day's work.

PLAINTIFF: Your honor this film has been the intense object of scrutiny for more than fifty years to date. Mr. Heironimus has never produced **1:** said suit. **2:** any financial documentation proving any suit was ever created. **3:** proven any connection to either Mr. Patterson or Mr. Gimlin. **4:** No witnesses place him in the vicinity of the Bluff Creek film site when Patterson and Gimlin were present. There were road construction employees living on the work sites at that time who recounted seeing Patterson and Gimlin but only those two men. **5:** immediately after filming the object seen in the film, Patterson and Gimlin took the film to Al Hodgson in the town of Willow Creek to have it sent to be developed, Hodgson never saw any additional people aside from Patterson and Gimlin. **6:** Forest service personnel went to the film site the following day, there was never any evidence noted of anyone present other than Patterson and Gimlin. **7:** approximately ten days after the film was obtained, Bob Titmus went to the film site where he made careful study of the site and tracked the creature. **8:** Titmus cast a number of the footprints as also Patterson and Gimlin had. Titmus noted that there were no signs of anyone other than Patterson and Gimlin at the film site and surrounding area. 8:

Heironimus has no explanation of how he created the footprint impressions and was unable to match even closely the depth of the impressions. **9:** Mrs. Patterson has stated numerous times that Roger and Bob Gimlin were construction workers, which was intermediate employment at best during the time period the film was obtained, Roger seldom had much money often relying on relatives and friends generosity in the form of twenty or thirty dollars to help pay for gas and food to explore regions for signs of Bigfoot let alone having large sums of money to have a suit made or to pay anyone to wear such a suit. **10:** The film was taken to the top Hollywood special effects people at the time, the statement regarding the object in the film was "we wish we could do something that good, but we cannot'. Now it should be noted that in 1967 the suits in the Planet of the Apes films were regarded as state of the art, The "Apes" in the film wore clothing, ever wonder why? The reason was in 1967 suits could be manufactured however they could not be closed seamlessly in the back which is where the actor would enter the suit, and large visible anchors were used that were necessary to hold the suit together, these had to be covered with something to hide the fasteners so the apes wore clothing to cover them. It can rightly be asked how two periodically employed construction workers hastily had a suit made being far better than any Hollywood experts were able to produce make something that is obviously seamless in the film? Today digital special effects is how Hollywood overcomes obstacles of this kind, but we must remember this was in 1967.**11:** Prosthetics expert and suit creator Bill Munns has extensively examined the Patterson/Gimlin film and has stated that when making any suit for Hollywood much can be done but that the suit limb joints must match up the actor inside, it's impossible to move the suit in a convincing way if at all. **12:** Many investigators such as world famous investigator and author Rene Dahinden, who himself spent twenty years attempting to prove the film was faked was ultimately unable to do so and finally determined it was genuine.

Your honor the claims of this film and attendant evidence having been faked does not hold up.

JUDGE: I tend to agree with you councilor.

DEFENSE: Your honor, if this film is authentic, then why is there no other photographic evidence aside from this film?

PLAINTIFF: I will agree that much in the public social media sites and elsewhere are the products of fabrication. However there are photographs that are likely authentic. I will enter two such items into the record, the first item has no witness testimony. The photograph was taken in 2009 in the state of Michigan, the photograph was given to a family friend, the direct witnesses wish no discussion regarding the photograph, they deny what is in the photograph and even one child of the witnesses claims the object in the photograph is a bear. It us unknown why the witnesses wish nothing to do with the photograph or object in the photograph and we can only conjecture as to why. The photograph unlike so many claimed to be of a "Bigfoot" creature that typically are blurred and difficult to determine is a mid-day shot and quite clear. The object in the photograph appears to be running away from the photographer. Three of its four appendages are off the ground, something no bear is capable of, and one can see clearly the bottom of the objects right foot facing the camera and details are clear. I wish to enter into evidence items 7A, 7B, 7C, 7D, and7E.

Item 7A (original photograph)

Item 7B (what you are seeing in photograph) sketch by Justin Mark

Item 7C

Item 7D (three of the four appendages off the ground as it moves)

Item 7E (bottom of right foot, similar to Patterson film)

PLAINTIFF: I now wish to enter another photograph into evidence. This photograph was taken by a Native American gentleman in Alaska. He states that there were three such creatures in his hunting area and while hunting one night took the following photograph. I will enter this photograph as Item 8A.

Item 8A

PLAINTIFF: There have been other such creatures photographed in the past in other regions of the world. One such item was called "De Loys ape" I wish to enter this into the record as supporting evidence that animals may exist that we have yet to know or recognize scientifically.

JUDGE: I will allow this councilor, please proceed.

PLAINTIFF: I would like to enter into the record items 9A, 9B and 9C.

Item 9A

François de Loys, a <u>Swiss</u> oil <u>geologist</u>, led an expedition from 1917 to 1920 to search for <u>petroleum</u> in an area along the border between <u>Colombia</u> and <u>Venezuela</u>, primarily near <u>Lake Maracaibo</u>. The expedition was unsuccessful, and furthermore suffered greatly due to <u>disease</u> and skirmishes with <u>natives</u>; of the 20 members of de Loys' group, only four survived.

According to de Loys' later report, in 1920, while camped near the <u>Tarra River</u>, two large creatures approached the group. Initially, de Loys thought they were <u>bears</u>, but then noted that they were <u>monkey</u>-like, holding onto shrubs and branches. The creatures – one male, one female – seemed angry, said de Loys, howling and gesturing, then defecating into their hands and flinging <u>feces</u> at the expedition. Fearing for their safety, the expedition shot and killed the male; the female then fled. De Loys and his companions recognized that they had encountered something unusual. The animal resembled a spider monkey, but was much larger: 1.57 m tall (compared to the largest spider monkeys, which are just over a meter tall). De Loys counted 32 teeth (most <u>New World</u> monkeys have 36 teeth), and noted that the creature had no tail.

They posed the creature by seating it on a crate and propping a stick under its chin. After taking a single photograph, de Loys reported, they skinned the creature, intending to keep its hide and skull. Both items were later abandoned by the troubled expedition.

According to other reports, more photographs were taken but were lost either in a flood or during the capsizing of the scientists' boat.

Item 9B De Loys ape

Item 9C

1040   THE ILLUSTRATED LONDON NEWS   JUNE 15, 1929

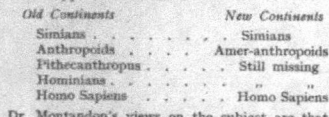

A GAP FILLED IN THE PEDIGREE OF MAN?

A SENSATIONAL DISCOVERY IN SOUTH AMERICA: A NEW AND STRANGELY HUMAN SPECIES OF THE ANTHROPOID APES (HITHERTO UNKNOWN IN THE WESTERN HEMISPHERE).

By FRANCIS de LOYS, B.Sc., D.Sc. F.G.S.

ANTHROPOID apes have been known since the days of earliest discovery in Asia and Africa, where they are represented by the *genera* orang, gibbon, chimpanzee, and gorilla. Their existence and their great similarity, anatomically and physiologically, to man, had always been one of the main factors in support of the Evolution Theory. The lack of them in the ancient and recent fauna of the American continents, and the fact that the races populating these continents are probably of allogenous stock, lent a substantial argument in refutation of the same theory.

Indeed, had it not been for the fact that the continuity of succession essential for the acceptance of evolution was broken over such a major area of our globe, the tenets of the evolutionist's creed would have had to be accepted indubitably. The fact remained that, however plausible the deductions of the evolutionist, and however well founded they were on facts observed in the old continents, man, the last link in the sequence, was found on the American continents — where processes required for his appearance through evolution had stopped short at the lower stages of the simian group.

In the stage of knowledge then prevailing, the sequence of evolution was set forth as follows—

Old Continents.	New Continents.
Simians	Simians
Anthropoids	Nil
Pithecanthropus	"
(*Neanderthal Species*)	
Hominians	"
Homo Sapiens	Homo Sapiens

The gap, then, between the simians and man was absolute.

A discovery which was made some time ago by myself and was recently communicated by Mr. Bouvier to the Académie des Sciences de Paris (*séance* of March 11—" Un Singe Anthropoïde actuel en Amérique," by Dr. G. Montandon), makes possible the partial filling of this gap, and brings considerable support to the Ologenic Theory recently set forth by Dr. Montandon, of the French Anthropologic Institute (" L'Ologénèse Humaine"; Paris, Alcan, Editeur). I was exploring at the time the untrodden forests in the neighbourhood of the Tarra River, itself an affluent of the Rio Catatumbo, in the Motilones districts of Venezuela and Colombia, and I came across two animals the nature of which was new not only to myself, but also to the native woodsmen of my party.

At a bend of a western—minor—affluent of the Tarra River, these two animals broke out upon the exploring party, then at rest, and, owing to the violence of their attitude, had to be received at the point of the rifle. One of the two was shot dead at very close range; the other one, unfortunately wounded, managed to escape, and disappeared in the jungle, the great thickness of which prevented its recovery. The animal shot dead was examined, sat into position on a packing-case, measured, and

immediately photographed from a distance of ten feet. Its skin was afterwards removed, and its skull and jaws were cleaned and preserved. The hardships met with by the party on their long journey across the forest, however, prevented the final preservation of either the skin or the bones.

At first examination, it was found that the specimen was that of an ape of uncommon size, whose features were entirely different from those of the species already known as inhabiting the country. From the sole of the feet to the apex of the skull it measured 157 centimetres in height, whereas the weight (guessed, it is true, without scales) was probably well over eight stone. The body was entirely covered with a thick coat of coarse, long, greyish-brown hair, and entirely devoid of any trace of a tail. The ape was an adult female. The jaw, carefully examined, revealed the presence of thirty-two teeth only, without, on the back portion of the mandible, any protuberances hinting at the possibility of a greater number of embryonic molar-teeth.

These remarkable features—size, absence of tail, number of teeth, and ground habits, together with the strongly humanoid aspect of the face and the ruggedness of the build, reveal the fact that there does, indeed, exist an ape different in most respects from the monkeys of the New World with which it could be compared. The brachyteles and the ateles, in fact, are characterised by having thirty-six teeth, long, prehensile caudal appendages, and long slender limbs adapted to their arboreal habits.

A comparison with the anthropoids of the Old World, on the contrary, is easier, the body resembling, on a much larger scale, that of the gibbon, whilst the limbs, with their reduced thumb, resemble most those of the orang. The discovery of this new species of giant ape with an anthropoid, though platyrhinian, aspect, does not entail the rejection of the prevailing division of simians into catarhinian and platyrhinian sub-orders. It has been found advisable, on the contrary, to introduce a new family amongst the platyrhinians, that of the Amer-anthropoid, consisting, for the time being, of this one genus only, the Amer-anthropoïdes Loysi (Montandon).

The correlation with the sequence of Old World types thus becomes—

Old Continents	New Continents
Simians	Simians
Anthropoids	Amer-anthropoids
Pithecanthropus	Still missing
Hominiana	"
Homo Sapiens	Homo Sapiens

Dr. Montandon's views on the subject are that we are dealing, in this instance, with a case of parallelism. This discovery shows that America has developed its anthropoids, just as Asia and Africa developed theirs, thus contradicting the accepted theory whereby Central Asia was the cradle of humanity, owing to the peripheral distribution of anthropoid apes — chimpanzee and gorilla on the Guinea Coast, gibbon and orang in the East Indies and Malaya.

My discovery of an anthropoid ape that is properly American thus brings considerable support to the Ologenic theory, whereby anthropoids as well as hominians, and, indeed, man himself, originated independently on the whole of the earth.

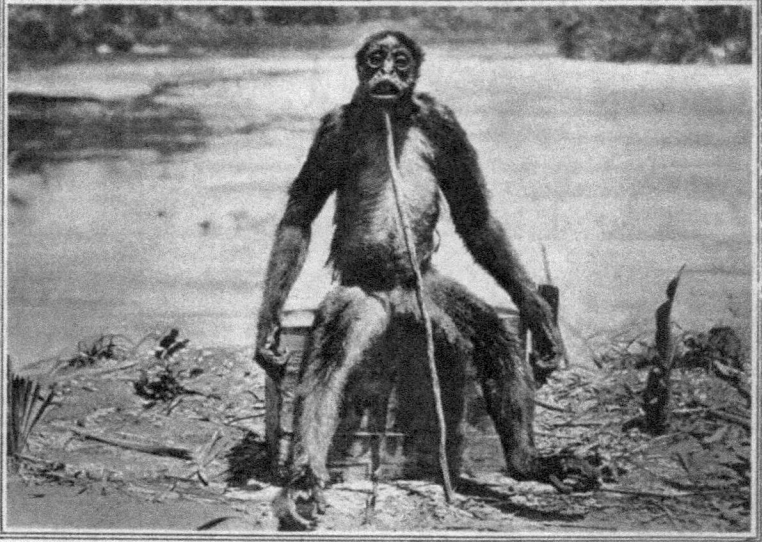

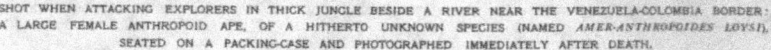

SHOT WHEN ATTACKING EXPLORERS IN THICK JUNGLE BESIDE A RIVER NEAR THE VENEZUELA-COLOMBIA BORDER: A LARGE FEMALE ANTHROPOID APE, OF A HITHERTO UNKNOWN SPECIES (NAMED *AMER-ANTHROPOIDES LOYSI*), SEATED ON A PACKING-CASE AND PHOTOGRAPHED IMMEDIATELY AFTER DEATH.

AN ANCESTRESS OF MAN ON THE AMERICAN CONTINENT, HITHERTO BELIEVED TO BE DEVOID OF ANTHROPOID APES? THE HEAD OF THE CREATURE KILLED WHEN IT AND A COMPANION ATTACKED AN EXPLORING PARTY—A *POST-MORTEM* PHOTOGRAPH SHOWING THE STRANGELY HUMAN FIGURE, EYES AND EXPRESSION.

PLAINTIFF: Your honor, I have several additional types of evidence to introduce into the record. If it pleases the court I would like to proceed.

JUDGE: Proceed councilor.

PLAINTIFF: Thank you your honor, I will begin with some behavioral evidence. For something to be judged real as in this instance unknown primates we must look at behavioral as well as physical evidence that would in many cases be similar to other primate species. There are two kinds I would now like to introduce into evidence, I will begin with possible tool usage. I have had discussions with a physical anthropologist regarding this, and he explained that all primate species utilize objects in their environment in various forms of tool usage. He said if the Sasquatch did in fact exist that they too would exhibit some form of tool use. I will present witness testimony, then photographic evidence and finally a possible explanation based on my discussions with the anthropologist I mentioned previously.

I would like to introduce the witness testimony as item 10A.

Item 10A

"I was supposed to be watching a catskinner as he was fire trailing, but it was awful cold, and I walked a mile or so down the trail, because he had no need of anyone at that time, and I thought I'd warm up and see the country. Up where he was, it was a cold east wind blowing; a little further down it was a west wind coming in. It was late fall, the last weekend in deer season I think, in 1967.

"It was a mountain trail - they have several of them up there - footpaths, and for horses. The elevation was about between four and five thousand feet. I came out lower down, into the fog, before I saw anything, and the fog was freezing on the trees because it was so cold, but if the wind would blow, the fog would break, and fall off. That made it kind of noisy, it sounded like walking.

"I came around a bend - well, first I noticed some rocks that were turned over. All the other rocks were wet, because of the fog, but these rocks were dry. Then I looked up, about forty or fifty feet, up on a ridge of rock, and I saw these animals there - looked like human or just about. Large male; the female wasn't so large; and a small baby - well, not really small. It was moving with them. It was standing up, mostly. The two older ones were squatting down and sort of bending, as they picked up rocks and smelled them. They were kind of careful. They moved on for a few minutes, and then finally the male found possibly what he was looking for and dug real fast down into the rocks, which were large boulders - not the round-type of rocks, but the flat, sharp kind.

"I could not explain why these rocks were there; there hadn't been a slide or anything. They were on top of the ridge, so they wouldn't have come down from anywhere. They are loose, quite a few holes underneath them, and they are as if they had been broken up - definitely not the round river-type rock. But they (the animals) would pick them up, and, after they smelled them, they would lay them down, on top of each other. They didn't just lay them back where they had picked them up, they stacked them up, in piles. And when the male found what he was looking for, he really made the rocks fly. The big rocks weighed 50, 60, or even possible 100 pounds; he just jerked them out with his hand. He didn't seem to take any precautions for his safety. Later on I looked, and there was some rock there that could have fallen on him, but he wasn't concerned.

"He brought out what appeared to be a grass nest. Possibly some stored hay that small rodents had stored there. He dug through that, and brought out the rodents. It seems they ate them. The rodents appeared to be in hibernation, or asleep, or something. There were about 6 or 8 rodents. The small animal, I noticed, only got one, but the others got 2 or 3 apiece.

"But about that time they became aware of my presence. And well, just became alert. I was alongside of this trail that follows the ridge. I didn't remember getting there, but I was squatting down beside a small tree when I became aware of where I was. As soon as they realized I was there, they suddenly began to move. Real quiet, behind some low-hanging limbs on a tree there. I didn't see them again after that.

"I tried to follow their tracks in the direction I thought they would have to go, but I couldn't find any, although there was frost there. But the next day I found 2 tracks, I heel print, and the front part of the foot, the toes, but they were in a different direction - the direction from which I had come - and I never did get to connect them up with exactly which direction they had gone or know anything about them.

"The footprints, I would say, but there wasn't enough of the track to tell. They were possibly 5 inches wide, I don't know, at the widest point. I don't think they could have been 6. I didn't know if it was one of the animals I had seen that had made the footprints.

"I saw the toe print as it came out of the old landing. I saw the heel print as it went in. The heel print gave me the impression that the heel protruded. The tracks were in dirt. It was just as if you had a level piece and scooped it out for about 2 feet deep, and it would cave in some. It (the animal) had stepped down into that and left a heel print, and as it stepped out on the other side you could see the toe print.

"When I left the catskidder, he was on Low Creek, but I had walked to Jim's Meadows, possible a mile or more. I saw the footprints between where the catskidder was, and where I had seen the other animals.

"After the animals disappeared I watched and looked for a few minutes and then decided I didn't want to go in that direction. So I just headed back. I didn't tell the catskidder about seeing them. I didn't tell anybody about it... until _____ asked me to ask among my crews - maybe some of them had seen them. That was the only time I had even mentioned it to any of the fellows out there, because I didn't want anyone to think I was a nut or something or other.

"The only time I saw their faces was when they became alert. They gave me an impression of having a face a little like a cat, without the ears. I couldn't remember seeing the ears. It seemed like the nose was much flatter - it didn't stick out like a human's. The upper lip was very short, and seemed very thin. I couldn't remember that it had a chin, like a human has. So somehow or other, I felt that it was a face more like a cat than a human.

"The male was darker than the female, a dirty brown, where the female was a buckskin or fawn-colored animal. The male had much longer hair on shoulder, head, and neck, and hung in strings, like you see it on an Angora goat. He was much heavier in the shoulders than the female. From just above the hips, the male got larger; he had a very wide "small" of the back. From there on up, he just got bigger and bigger. They had very rounded or stooped shoulders. The head was set lower on the shoulders than on a human. They don't seem to have the neck "stand up" as we do.

"Most of the time they were not standing, but were squatting down and leaning forward to pick up the rocks. I didn't see them stand actually erect until they became alert that I was there. I didn't see them walk, as such. The only movement I saw was when they made a quick, short dash to get behind the limbs of the trees. I saw them move alright, but in a humped-up, stooped-over position, just moving across the rocks. But they were upright when they made that quick dash at the end. It seemed to me that the mother picked the baby up on her lap and ran holding the baby in front of her, possibly right below the breast, and her breasts hung real low, much lower than on a human.

"I couldn't say how thick through the body these animals were, but they were very heavy-set - particularly thick and heavy at the small of the back, and on up through the ribs. I think the male was over 6 feet tall, but I'm an awful poor judge of height and weight or anything. I didn't think the female was a tall as the male, in fact I think she came possibly up to his shoulder, but I saw them standing up so little, I didn't know, but they were much larger than a human, much bulkier. The baby didn't come up to the mother's hips actually, I don't think, but I don't remember for sure. The first time I saw them standing up was as the male stepped out of the hole he dug with the grass but it was only a very short while until they took off. I didn't see them after that.

(Q. How did they eat?) "They ate by just taking it in their hand and eating it as one of us would if we were eating a banana. They ate it skin, feathers, and all-just bit it in two, and as they would bite part of it well then just cram the other right on in. The little one though, he had a little more difficulty, because he didn't have quite enough room for all of it, where the older ones did. It wasn't like a human would band the food to the baby, he had to get his--he was scratching through the grass that they bad and got it himself, and the female did the same thing. They gave you the impression in that way of not taking care of the baby, like people would. I've been wondering now if that group lived together as a family, and I hope to go back and look into it deeper.

(Q. Did you form any impression of the proportions of, say, the legs in relation to the rest of the height? Would they be like a long-legged man, or short-legged?) "I don't know; I couldn't say for sure; but the arms were such that when they squat down they have to bend forward to pick up anything-their arms are not long enough to reach. This one that was digging just seemed to go right on down. I didn't remember seeing him get up, but as he was down here, he was just digging and kept going on down, and ... well, at that time I couldn't see exactly where he was, because I was down, and they were up a little bit on the side of this rock, which kind of levels off some, and he went down, and so I couldn't see exactly what he was doing in there, but I did see when he came out. At that time I was a little bit nervous.... I'm not sure, now, about half of it-seemed like it was a bad dream for a while. I just couldn't believe it was really happening. It just couldn't be, but it is.

(Q. Did you notice the hands at all?) "I noticed that it had hands; I did not notice if it had thumbs. I couldn't tell from the way it worked-it didn't seem to use the thumb. And I didn't see any ears. I didn't see any knees projecting when it squatted. They were in an awkward position because of the rocks, and they couldn't just squat down like we would on a floor. They would be on different levels; and off too far to be comfortable. That's as close as I could explain it.

"When they went from place to place they would shift in position, according to the terrain. The male, well, actually both of them, seemed to be moving in a certain direction, possibly from tracing the small rodents. I thought possibly it was the scent left by the rodents coming up through the rocks, because it was not a runway that they could have been picking, because they were just picking the rocks up anyplace, and as they picked it up, they'd turn it over and smell it, and then lay it on the stack. They left it very definitely in a pile. They would leave anywhere from three to fifteen or twenty in one pile, as they would reach back, and then, oh, six to eight feet farther, they would leave another pile-start laying them in another.".

With Rene and my daughter Kathryn and son Jim, I went with this man last July to the spot where he had seen the three creatures. We found the piles of rocks to which he referred, not only at the spot be showed us, but on almost every other area of broken rock we found in two hours of scrambling around on the mountain. They were obviously piles manufactured by something or someone, the rock could not have rested that way naturally, and there were dozens of them.

The hole he saw the male Sasquatch dig was about five feet deep and almost as steep sided as a well. No bear or anything else without hands could have lifted out the rocks. A man could undoubtedly figure out a way to do it if he had any reason to take the trouble, but in this case the story had only come out as the result of an enquiry from someone else who had seen footprints in the snow in January of this year, and there was no reason to expect that anyone would be coming to look over the site.

(as the author the following photographs are those I personally took, they are from eight different sites in the states of Washington and Oregon. Many know of the first site where logger Glen Thomas witnessed the creatures stacking rocks and digging the hole, however Rene Dahinden discovered many others and I also have discovered some. To date I know of nine told of a number of others from witnesses.)

PLAINTIFF: The following photographs I will enter into evidence supporting the witness testimony in Item 10 will be numbered 11A through 11U.

Item 11A

Rock stack from the Glen Thomas site.

Item 11B

Three rock stacks silhouetted against the sky.

Item 11C

Rock stack.

Item 11D

This is more of a pile than distinct stack.

Item 11E

Rock pile.

Item 11F

Note the stack to the left leaned until it came to rest against a boulder, or was it intentionally constructed this way?

Item 11G

This is the author standing inside the hole logger Glen Thomas witnessed the Sasquatch dig.

Item 11H

Another perspective of the hole dug by the Sasquatch.

Item 11I

The author standing in the hole dug by the Sasquatch at ground eye level.

Item 11J

View of the hole dug by the Sasquatch with nothing for perspective.

Item 11K

The author sitting next to a stack at another site.

Item 11L

Rock stacks are typically 3 or 4 rocks in each stack, this was the average but there were exceptions.

Item 11M

This is a pile at another site.

Item 11N

More piles, there were nine such piles at this site.

Item 110

Sometimes there were stacks with only two rocks but this did not occur often.

Item 11P

Three stacks at the original site.

Item 11Q

Accounting for slippage, it can be seen the creatures possess a high degree of intelligence.

Item 11R

Originally I thought these stacks and piles might be used as markings, but as can be seen here they are not generally seen unless one is relatively close to them.

Item 11S

Another pile of rocks, I have yet to determine why sometimes rocks are stacked and other times piled.

Item 11T

The author taking a break near one stack.

Item 11U

The author sitting at the original site note the stacks in the background. I eventually found a total of 57 stacks and piles at seven different sites from the locations Rene Dahinden directed me too. I found a number of sites on my own after this and continue to learn of more to this day.

PLAINTIFF: Your honor, I mentioned my consultation with a forensic anthropologist regarding tool use, and he believes the rock stacking behavior presented may in fact be a form of this.

First we need to ask what does science consider tool use and how is it defined?

Tools are used by animals for purposes including acquiring food and water, grooming, defense, recreation or construction. Originally thought to be a skill only possessed by humans, some tool use requires a sophisticated level of cognition. There is considerable discussion about the definition of what constitutes a tool and therefore which behaviours can be considered as true examples of tool use. A wide range of animals are considered to use tools including mammals, birds, fish, cephalopods and insects.

Primates are well known for using tools for hunting or gathering food and water, cover for rain, and self-defence. Chimpanzees have been the object of study, most famously by Jane Goodall, since these animals are more-often kept in captivity than other primates and are closely related to humans. Tool-use in other primates are lesser-known as many of them are mainly observed in the wild. Many famous researchers, such as Charles Darwin in his book *The Descent of Man*, mentioned tool-use in monkeys (such as baboons). Both wild and captive elephants are known to create tools using their trunk and feet, mainly for swatting flies, scratching, plugging water-holes (so the water doesn't evaporate), and reaching food that is out of reach. A group of dolphins in Shark Bay use sponges to protect their beak while foraging. Sea otters will dislodge food from rocks (such as abalone) and break open shellfish. Carnivores (of the order Carnivora) can use tools to trap prey or break open the shells of prey, as well as for scratching.

Corvids (crows, ravens and rooks) are well known for their large brains (among birds) and subsequent tool use. They mainly manufacture probes out of twigs and wood (and sometimes metal wire) to catch or impale larvae. Crows are among the only animals that create their own toys. Tool use in other birds is best exemplified in nest intricacy. Warblers manufacture 'pouches' to make their nests in. Some birds, such as weaver birds build complex nests. Finches and woodpeckers may insert twigs into trees in order to catch or impale larvae. Parrots may use tools to wedge nuts so that they may crack it open (using a tool) without launching it away. Some birds take advantage of human activity, such as seagulls which drop shellfish in front of cars to crack them open.

Several species of fish use tools to crack open shellfish, extract food that is out of reach, cleaning an area (for nesting), and hunting. Octopuses gather coconut shells and create a shelter. They may also construct a fence using rocks.

The key to identifying tool use is defining what constitutes a tool. Researchers of animal behavior have arrived at different formulations.

In 1980, Beck published a widely used definition of tool use. This has been modified to:

The external employment of an unattached or manipulable attached environmental object to alter more efficiently the form, position, or condition of another object, another organism, or the user itself, when the user holds and directly manipulates the tool during or prior to use and is responsible for the proper and effective orientation of the tool.

Other, briefer definitions have been proposed:

An object carried or maintained for future use.

— *Finn, Tregenza, and Norman, 2009*

The use of physical objects other than the animal's own body or appendages as a means to extend the physical influence realized by the animal.

— *Jones and Kamil, 1973*

An object that has been modified to fit a purpose ... [or] An inanimate object that one uses or modifies in some way to cause a change in the environment, thereby facilitating one's achievement of a target goal.

— *Hauser, 2000*

Others, for example Lawick-Goodall, distinguish between "tool use" and "object use".

Different terms have been given to the tool according to whether the tool is altered by the animal. If the "tool" is not held or manipulated by the animal in any way, such as an immobile anvil, objects in a bowerbird's bower, or a bird using bread as bait to catch fish,[7] it is sometimes referred to as a **"proto-tool"**. Several studies in primates and birds have found that tool use is correlated with an enlargement of the brain as a whole or of particular regions. For example, true tool-using birds have relatively larger brains than proto-tool users.

When an animal uses a tool that acts on another tool, this has been termed use of a **"meta-tool"**. For example, New Caledonian crows will spontaneously use a short tool to obtain an otherwise inaccessible longer tool that then allows them to extract food from a hole. Similarly, bearded capuchin monkeys will use smaller stones to loosen bigger quartz pebbles embedded in conglomerate rock, which they subsequently use as tools.

Rarely, animals may use one tool followed by another, for example, bearded capuchins use stones and sticks, or two stones.[9] This is called **"associative"**, **"secondary"** or **"sequential"** tool use.

Some animals use other individuals in a way which could be interpreted as tool use, for example, ants crossing water over a bridge of other ants, or weaver ants using conspecifics to glue leaves together. These have been termed **"social tools"**.

Borderline examples

Play: Play has been defined as "activity having no immediate benefits and structurally including repetitive or exaggerated actions that may be out of sequence or disordered". When play is discussed in relation to manipulating objects, it is often used in association with the word "tool". Some birds, notably crows, parrots and birds of prey, "play" with objects, many of them playing in flight with such items as stones, sticks and leaves, by letting them go and catching them again before they reach the ground. A few species repeatedly drop stones, apparently for the enjoyment of the sound effects. Many other species of animals, both avian and non-avian, play with objects in a similar manner.

Fixed "devices": The impaling of prey on thorns by many of the <u>shrikes</u> (*Laniidae*) is well known. Several other birds may use spines or forked sticks to anchor a carcass while they flay it with the bill. It has been concluded that "This is an example of a fixed device which serves as an extension of the body, in this case, talons" and is thus a true form of tool use. On the other hand, the use of fixed skewers may not be true tool-use because the thorn (or whatever) is not manipulated by the bird. <u>Leopards</u> perform a similar behavior by dragging carcasses up trees and caching them in the forks of branches.

Use of bait: Several species of bird, including <u>herons</u> such as the <u>striated heron</u> (*Butorides striatus*), will place bread in water to attract fish. Whether this is tool use is disputed because the bread is not manipulated or held by the bird.

PLAINTIFF: During my consultation with the anthropologist mentioned before, how rock piles and stacks could be utilized became the central question, I also researched hunting and animal behaviors and found that small animals, rodents in particular are attracted to piles of rocks, and will congregate in such places. The anthropologist when asked by me if it were possible for primates like the Sasquatch to construct such structures to attract rodents as a supplementary food source responded that yes it is indeed a strong possibility. They are very likely highly intelligent creatures and could do such things.

The link to a possibility such as this lies in the witness testimony when the logger Glen Thomas states that when the large male dug furiously and came up with apparently a nest of rodents, that the three creatures divided among themselves and devoured before becoming aware of the loggers presence and leaving quickly makes the possibility of making the piles and stacks very plausible.

PLAINTIFF: I would now like to introduce the second type of behavior in the form of marking of terrain. The testimony in this case is from an interview for an article in Sports Afield Magazine from the early 1960's. The gentleman whom the article is about was involved in an incident that establishes the evidence found in the wilds today. I would like to enter this account as Item 12A.

Item 12A

"The story is titled "Long Hunter – Alaskan Style" by Russell Annabel. The story is about a mountain man named Tex Cobb, who spent years trapping in Canada and Alaska. Here is an excerpt from Patterson's book.

The Denna people liked him, Tex Cobb. No sentiment was wasted on either side, but he and the tribesmen had a live and let live understanding that was rare in those days. He stayed off their trap lines, and they stayed off his. If an Indian had a salmon net in an eddy, Tex found another eddy, and vice versa. Due to the fact that the Indians trusted him, we became involved with what today would be called, I suppose an abominable snowman. I have since heard and read a great deal about the abominable snowman. I have seen the photographs of those tracks in the snow on a Tibetan mountain, and to me they are simply the tracks of a man with gunnysack or some cloth wrapped around his feet as protection from the cold, climbing slewfoot because the slope was steep and he had no crampons. But when I was a youngster roaming the North with Tex, we had never heard of the abominable snowman. We had, however, heard much about Gilyuk; the shaggy cannibal giant sometimes called the big man with the little hat.

Our adventure with Gilyuk occurred while we were camped in a pretty spruce park on Yellowjacket Creek, south of Tyrone Lake. We had spent the entire summer on this mountain – girt Nelchina Plateau, wandering about in aimless nomad fashion. Tex said we were prospecting and looking for fur sign. Maybe we were. He always had to have an excuse for enjoying the country, a commercial excuse if he could think of one. Anyway, it was now late September, the beautiful time, no mosquitoes, the land ablaze with color, the fish and the meat animals summer fat, the caribou horde gathering, and we were footloose and free as perhaps men can never be again. This morning Tex was making coffee, and I was down at the creek cleaning a mess of grayling for breakfast, when six Indians filed through the timber. They stood for a moment solemnly regarding our four horses. To them a horse was a rarity, a mysterious animal. They called them McKinley moose, because McKinley was the only president they had ever heard of, and the horses were as big as moose. I followed them to the camp.

"Have you eaten?" Tex asked them in Denna.

They said they had eaten. Chief Stickman was with them. I had seen him once before, at Eklutna Village. A squat, square – faced man, very dark, with long hair and quick – moving obsidian eyes, he was the Denna boss of this entire area, and his reputation was bad. But now he had trouble that he couldn't handle. He told us about it, and as he talked, he kept standing first on one leg, then the other, balancing himself with the moccasined sole of the free foot against the knee of the supporting leg. I don't know whether it was habit or a medicine trick to ward off evil spirits, or both, but it was disconcerting. He had come into this area two days ago, he said, with some of his people to kill and cache caribou for winter use. But they had discovered that Gilyuk, the shaggy giant, was hanging around. They found his sign yesterday. And of course everybody knew that Gilyuk wasn't interested in caribou. Gilyuk ate men.

"What kind of sign" Tex asked.

"We will take you to see it," Stickman said. "It's not far."

After breakfast we followed the Indians upstream a couple of miles to a burned flat on which a nurse crop of aspen and birch had grown. In the center of the flat stood a ruined birch sapling. It had been about four inches through and maybe ten feet tall. Something had twisted the sapling as a man would twist a matchstick. The wood had separated into individual fibers; the bark hung in tatters. Stickman and his hunters stood back, while Tex and I looked the site over. Moose often ride a sapling down to get at the tender upper twigs. So do caribou. But no moose or caribou had done this. This had been done by something with hands. It had happened yesterday, because the leaves of the sapling had not yet completely wilted. It wasn't the work of lightening – no burns. A freak whirlwind hadn't done it, because trees and

118

brush a few yards distant were undamaged. The hard ground showed no tracks. We found no snagged hair on the brush. Absolutely nothing except the incredibly twisted birch sapling. It was without question the eeriest sight I have ever beheld in the wilds.

Stickman said, "It is Gilyuk's mark. We have seen it before."

I wish to make clear that to the Denna people Gilyuk was no legendary creature their grandfathers had told them about. He was a reality, and they spoke of him as they spoke of bears and wolves. They saw his sign, and they saw him. He was a shaggy giant who wore a little hat and ate men. "We want to ask you to camp with us until we have killed our caribou," Stickman said. "Gilyuk doesn't molest white men. Perhaps he will not molest us if you are in the camp."   Stickman had already told us that he was bivouacked on the shore of a pothole lake two hours to the eastward.

Tex said all right, we would move to his camp in the morning. As he was still looking at the twisted sapling, his green eyes narrowed in thought. I couldn't take my gaze off it either.

Stickman said, "Thanks, Kosaki," a strange word of respect, held over from the Old Russian Cossack, and we parted company with the Indians.

Next morning I brought the horses in at daybreak. We ate, broke camp and were putting on the packs, when here came the Indians, all of them – all, that is except Stickman. An old man told us Stickman was dead, he said. Gilyuk had taken him. The chief had got up in the night and gone down to the lake, perhaps for water, but nobody knew. A squaw with a birch – bark torch found his red flannel underwear on the gravel beach. It had been torn off him. There may have been tracks, but the entire hunting party had swarmed over the beach, and by daylight no tracker on earth could have made sense of the jumble.

Well, until the day of his own death last July, while on a sentimental journey to a fateful spot in Cook Inlet, Tex was convinced that the cannibal giant Gilyuk killed Stickman. When asked if he believed in the existence of abominable snowmen, Tex would reply that he didn't think there were any around in Alaska nowadays, but that they had existed, at least one of them, a couple of decades back."

(I wished to use this story for two reasons, first is to demonstrate the time frame and second that the markings left by the "Gilyuk" or Sasquatch can still be found today. This story provides us a historical context not only in this particular account, but that the Native people knew of this historically. The description provided in this story gives us enough information as what to look for.

The first time I discovered this type of evidence was in 1991, Jack Livingston and I were investigating the Washougal River watershed, which is south of Mount Saint Helens in southwest Washington State. This area for years previously seemed to be the hub of Sasquatch related activity in that region. Stories of hairy giants in that region go back as far as recorded history of the area, and my investigations led me to this particular place. The area is very deceptive in terms of appearance. Reaching the watershed itself is very difficult because the river has to be forded first and cannot be done at just any time of the year. Snow covers the region through the winter and during the spring water levels can change in minutes making crossing treacherous. Summer and fall are the times for access to this place.

The lay of the land is also difficult to navigate, although today with global positioning systems a person could navigate the area with little trouble. Jack and I had to make five separate attempts at getting to the center of the watershed, we looked through the creek bottoms easy enough but the ridge tops was what I wanted to look at. The climb is approximately twenty two hundred feet up through all sorts of underbrush. As a side note I should mention that Jack Livingston to his credit is the only person who has ever gone more than once into an area through brush accompanying me on investigations. Difficulty usually takes a back seat to me when I am trying to search a location especially if I believe I will find evidence. I had a reputation for dragging unsuspecting people who at first were enthusiastic about ventures only to end the adventure exhausted and usually beaten up by the underbrush and adverse weather conditions.

On the fifth attempt to get to the ridge top, we began to find trees sharply broken. I measured each one we found and all were within an inch or two of eight feet from the ground. Broken completely over with no other evidence of having been damaged. The breaks were freshly done within a week or so of our finding them and this was in mid July. We wondered about weather being behind the strange breaks but ruled that out since they all were within thick stands of trees of similar size and protected from winds. The trees themselves were two to three inches in diameter and snapped over just like a person might do to a pencil.

We found usually one tree broken in the same fashion at about a one hundred-foot interval, and we counted about ten to fifteen as we proceeded along the ridge top. We did not complete the trek to the end of the ridge but would have likely encountered more of the broken trees along the way.

These trees were not mangled in exactly the same fashion as that example in the Tex Cobb account, however there is probably some variation between how each individual creature may do this, and tree type as to how the destruction of the tree in question may look.

The photographs I have included clearly show how unnatural these breaks are and that they stand out clearly from weather breaks, diseased breaks and damage from another tree falling on them. The next example I have is more dramatic however and conforms much more closely to the example from the Tex Cobb story.)

PLAINTIFF: I now wish to enter in the record photographs showing this kind of marking to trees. This sort of marking is entered as "Territorial marking" I will enter them Items 13A through 13L.

Item 13A

First tree I discovered at approximately the 2200 foot level in elevation near the Washougal River watershed.

Item 13B

Same tree wider perspective.

Item 13C

The author next to another example.

Item 13D

Another example from the eastern United States.

Item 13E

Near Mt. Rainier Washington.

Item 13F

Same tree different perspective.

Item 13G

One more perspective of the same tree near Mt. Rainier.

Item 13H

Twisted tree Northern California.

Item 13I

Twisted tree Northern California. This was in the center of a small grove of the same type/age trees. I found this in mid-July none of the other twenty or so trees had any damage to them.

Item 13J

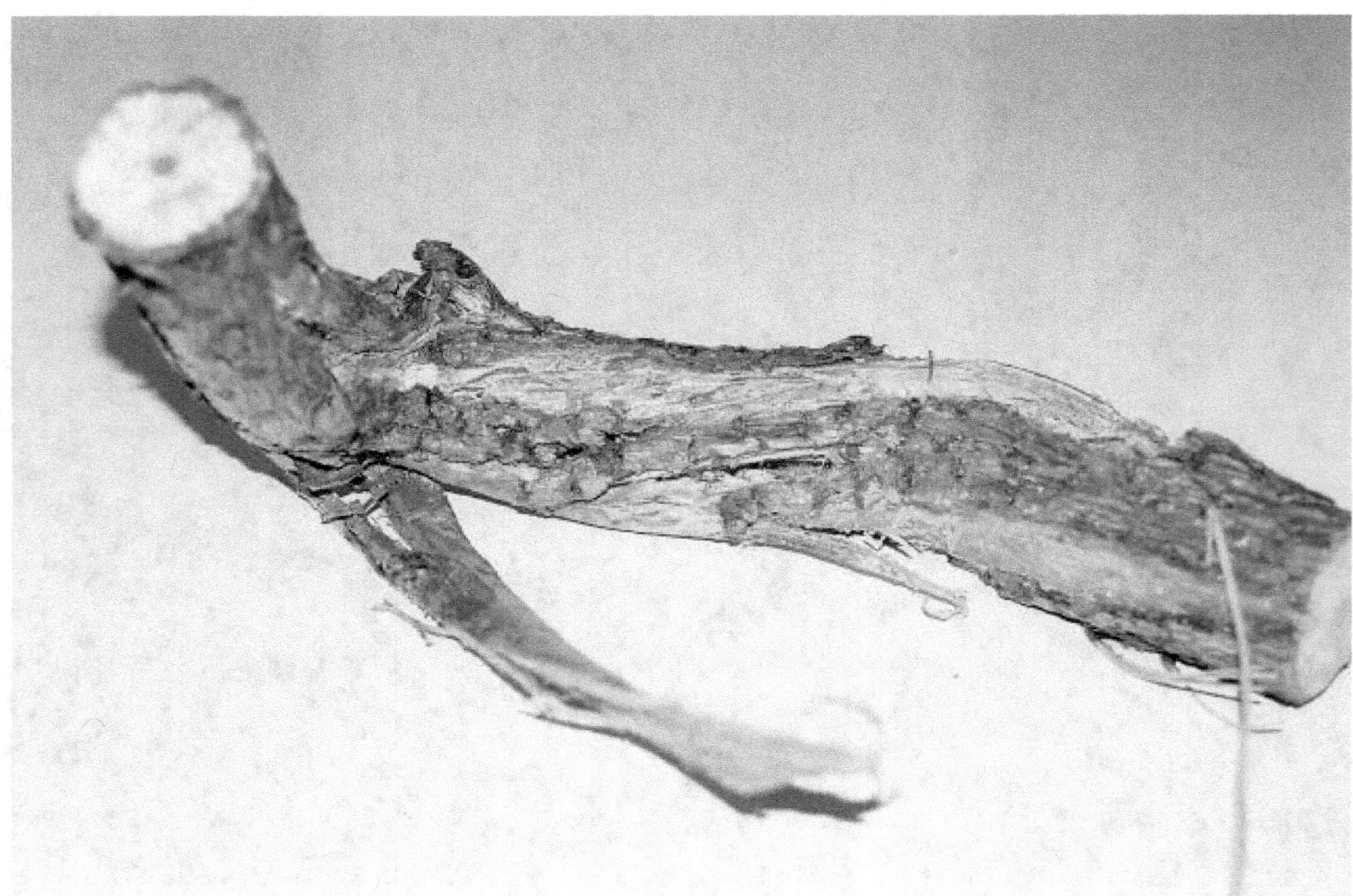

Same tree in item 13I, note the twisting, gaps in the trunk were one quarter in width and one could see easily through the trees trunk.

Item 13K

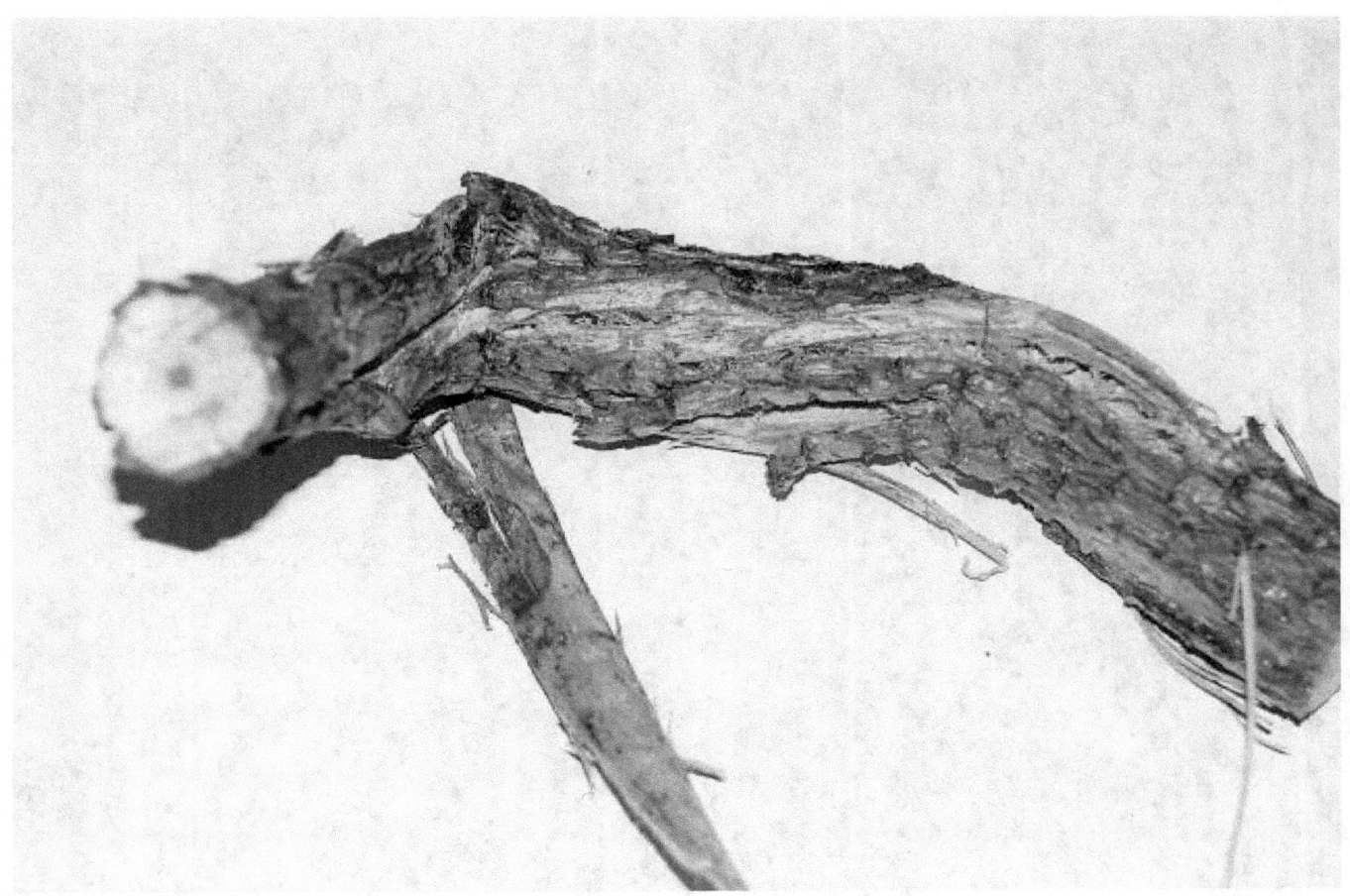

Different perspective of the same trunk measuring three inches thick.

Item 13L

One more example of a twisted and torn tree in California.

PLAINTIFF: I would like to enter the following items of evidence into the record being possible markings made by Sasquatches. It has yet to be proven, and to date the popular "structures" have yet to be associated with other sign such as footprints to connect Sasquatches with said structures, in this case it is possible that the creatures could have made some although the reason is yet unknown but could be of navigational use in wilderness areas. The items will be entered as Items 14A through 14D.

Item 14A

Discovered by a Native American gentleman this is many miles on tribal lands far from any human access.

Item 14B

Different angle, same object.

Item 14C

One more perspective same object.

Item 14D

This is very unusual, it could be the product of weather however. If artificially constructed, what could the purpose be?

PLAINTIFF: I have one more item to introduce into evidence, it was in direct connection to purported Sasquatch events and activity near the town of Yacolt Washington in 1989. One morning dozens of sapling trees were pulled out of the ground along a trail that the creatures reportedly traveled each day, this was not seen previously nor afterward and is unknown to this day why it was done. The item will be introduced as item 15A.

Item 15A

Ralph Garrish holds two saplings of many pulled up.

DEFENSE: Your honor, stacked rocks and broken trees? These could simply be the product of human activity and weather.

PLAINTIFF: In the case of the rock stacks and piles, it has been entered into evidence eye witness testimony of said creatures doing this behavior. The additional sites where these structures have been discovered are in every case very remote accessible only by cross country trekking on foot, no trails or other man made access are miles away from these locations.

In the case of the broken trees, Native American sources, as demonstrated by the Tex Cobb account show what is found today. The damage done purportedly by a Sasquatch is quite different than any weather related damage, it often found recently damaged during calm clear weather conditions. Trees damaged by other sources such as bears display a number of different characteristics including claw marks and in the case of human caused damage there is accompanying too marks on the bark of damaged trees.

JUDGE: The court will keep an open mind councilors, please proceed.

PLAINTIFF: I would now like to enter into the record feeding and feeding related behavioral evidence, entered as items 16A through 16G

Item 16A

Purported "baiting" site

Item 16B

Same tree slightly different angle.

PLAINTIFF: Photographs 16A and 16B show what is claimed by researchers in the Adirondack Mountain region of New York State to be a possible "baiting" site created by one or more Sasquatch creatures. It is believed they do this at times to draw additional prey animals to the location to conserve energy tracking down single prey. This particular tree has had an adult deer hung in it on two separate occasions covering a three year time span. The deer was measured hanging at a height of eleven feet above the ground.

DEFENSE: Your honor this is preposterous, this is nothing more than the work of a mountain lion!

PLAINTIFF: Not true, enter exhibit 16C and 16D into the record.

Item 16C

Mountain lions (Cougars): Opportunistic hunters, mountain lions typically hunt alone from dusk to dawn, taking their prey (primarily deer) from behind. On average, a lion will kill a deer about once a week. They also dine on coyotes, raccoons, rodents, elk, feral hogs, and even porcupines. They may drag the meal to another area and cover it with dry leaves, grass or pine needles to protect the food from other animals and to reduce spoilage. A mountain lion may return to feed at the site over a period of several days.

Feeding Areas (caches)

Cougars usually carry or drag their kills to a secluded area under cover to feed, and drag marks are frequently found at fresh kill sites. After killing a large animal and having eaten its fill, a cougar often will cover the remains with debris such as snow, grass, leaves, sticks, or soil. Even where little debris is available, bits of soil, rock, grass or sticks may be used to cover the carcass. The cougar may remain in the immediate vicinity of its kill, guarding it against scavengers and eating it over a period of six to eight days. (Meat becomes rotten quickly in the summer and male cougars have to patrol their territory. Often these males will make a kill, feed until full, leave to patrol the area, and return to feed on the carcass days later.)

(From the Washington state department of fish and wildlife.)

Item 16D

Eastern Cougar
Puma concolor cougar

New York Status: **Extirpated**
Federal Status: **Extinct**

Description

The cougar is known by many common names, including puma, mountain lion, catamount, and panther. Next to the jaguar, it is the largest North American cat. Weights range from 80-225 pounds (36-103 kg), averaging 140 (64 kg). Length varies from 5-9 feet (150-275 cm); this measurement includes the 26-32 inch (66-82 cm) tail. Males are larger than females. Cougars have long, slender bodies and small, broad, round heads. Ears are short, erect and rounded. The short fur is usually tawny (brownish red-orange to light brown), more tan in the summer months and grayer during the winter. The muzzle, chin and underparts are a creamy white. Black coloring appears on the tip of the tail, behind the ears, and at the base of the whiskers on the sides of the muzzle. Immature cougars are paler, with obvious dark spots on their flanks.

Life History

Females mate every two to three years and produce a litter of two to three cubs. There is no set breeding season, however most births are in the spring. At six months of age, the cubs weigh 30-40 pounds. They leave the den at this time, accompanying the female to her kills and occasionally hunting with her individually. A young male may leave at one year of age, but most cubs remain until they are nearly two. The average life span for cougars is about eight years.

Prey species include deer, elk, occasionally domestic livestock, and any smaller mammals which opportunity makes available. The preferred meat is deer. Cougars kill about a deer a week. Cougars are solitary, territorial hunters.

Distribution and Habitat

The original distribution of the cougar was across lower Canada in the north to Patagonia, South America in the south. It was the most widely distributed land mammal in the Western Hemisphere. It was found in a variety of habitats, including tidal marshes, deserts, mountainous terrain and deciduous, coniferous and tropical forests.

With the exception of Florida, the cougar has been considered extirpated from states east of the Mississippi River since the 1900s. In the west, it is still quite common in wilderness areas of the Rocky Mountain states and British Columbia.

Status

Cougars have been extirpated from much of their former range, especially in the east. In the west, it continues to be found from southern Canada south through Latin America to Patagonia. Florida has cougars in the Everglades and Big Cypress Swamp.

Cougars are considered big game in many of the western states. There are limited legal harvests in these areas that do not threaten local cougar populations.

The remaining population of cougars in Florida is federally protected as an Endangered species. Western cougars appear secure; the relatively vast amount of wilderness available to them will assure their continued survival.

Source: New York State department of conservation.

PLAINTIFF: Mountain lions commonly referred to as cougars A: are not present in the area in which photographs 16A and B were taken, and B: this is not mountain lion behavior as stated on two different state game and wildlife websites. Now it has yet to be proven that the creatures known as Bigfoot or Sasquatch do this however this was not done by humans, and there can only be one other source which is what is reported by the local inhabitants reporting this. It may that a different behavior is being exhibited, but we contend that this was indeed done by a Sasquatch creature.

PLAINTIFF: I will now enter items 16D,16E, 16F and 16G into the record. Feeding by the Sasquatch takes numerous forms as they are said to be omnivores meaning they will eat most anything, most often said to consume prey animals but diet is supplemented by vegetation. The following are a couple examples.

Item 16D

Close up of leaves stripped not bitten from plants.

Item 16E

Often areas of vegetation measuring 30 feet across or more are attributed to Sasquatch feeding, stripping leaves in large areas.

Item 16F

Manzanita berries are said by Native American sources to be a favorite of the Sasquatch during summer months where available.

Item 16G

Food and Feeding Habits of Deer

- Deer eat a wide variety of plants, but their main food item is browse—the growing tips of trees and shrubs. In late winter and early spring, deer eat grass, clover, and other herbaceous plants (Table 2).
- Deer also eat fruit, nuts, acorns, fungi, lichens, and farm and garden crops if available.
- For their first few weeks of life, fawns thrive on milk, which is more than twice as rich in total solids as the best cow milk.

- Deer eat rapidly and, being ruminants, initially chew their food only enough to swallow it. This food is stored in a stomach called the "rumen." From there it is regurgitated, then re-chewed before being swallowed again, entering a second stomach where digestion begins. From there it is passed into a third and then a fourth stomach, finally entering the intestine.
- **Feeding Areas**
  In areas where many deer live, a noticeable "browse line" appears on trees where the deer have repeatedly reached up to eat low-hanging twigs and branches. Similarly, the tops of shrubs may be browsed, leaving only a few inside branches extending upward. Browsing seldom occurs more than 4 feet above the ground, except in areas with deep snow.
- Browsing by deer can usually be identified since twig ends deer have browsed have a ragged appearance, while those browsed by rabbits, porcupines, and other rodents have a neat, clipped appearance. This is because deer lack upper incisors and canine teeth, and cannot nip off twigs. Instead they must press foods between their hard upper palates and their bottom teeth, and jerk their heads up to tear it free (Figs. 5 and 6).
- However, when deer browse new growth they leave a clean, blunt stem-end, where the tender shoots break off. The height of the clipped plant will then be the indicator of what species ate it. When browse and other green foods are no longer available, deer strip bark from young trees.

(Source: Washington State Department of Fish and Wildlife.)

PLAINTIFF: Deer are commonly referred to as "nibblers" meaning they typically do not graze like cows, they walk and take bites from plants as they move, believed to be a form of defense from predators as grazing would expose them to a greater chance of predation. However when large areas of plants such as black caps, etc. are found, which is seldom it has been attributed to Sasquatch feeding as large quantities of leaves are often stripped as by hands grasping the stalks of the plants and pulled off them rendering the plant "leafless".

PLAINTIFF: I wish now to enter evidence into the record of purported Sasquatch scat. I will also enter bear scat for comparison purposes. Items 17A through

Item 17A

Bear scat (black bear) Due to the black bears varied diet, the scat comes in different forms. Most commonly, the scat is tubular and segmented and often in piles. If the diet is full of moisture, it may be more amorphous. Often the seeds, fruit skin, berries or fur is visible in the scat. When firmer, the scat generally measures about 1.25 " to 2.25" in diameter and between 5" to 12" in length.

Typical example of bear scat.

Item 17B

Grizzly scat, generally 2 to 2.5 inches in diameter and up to 15" long.

Item 17C

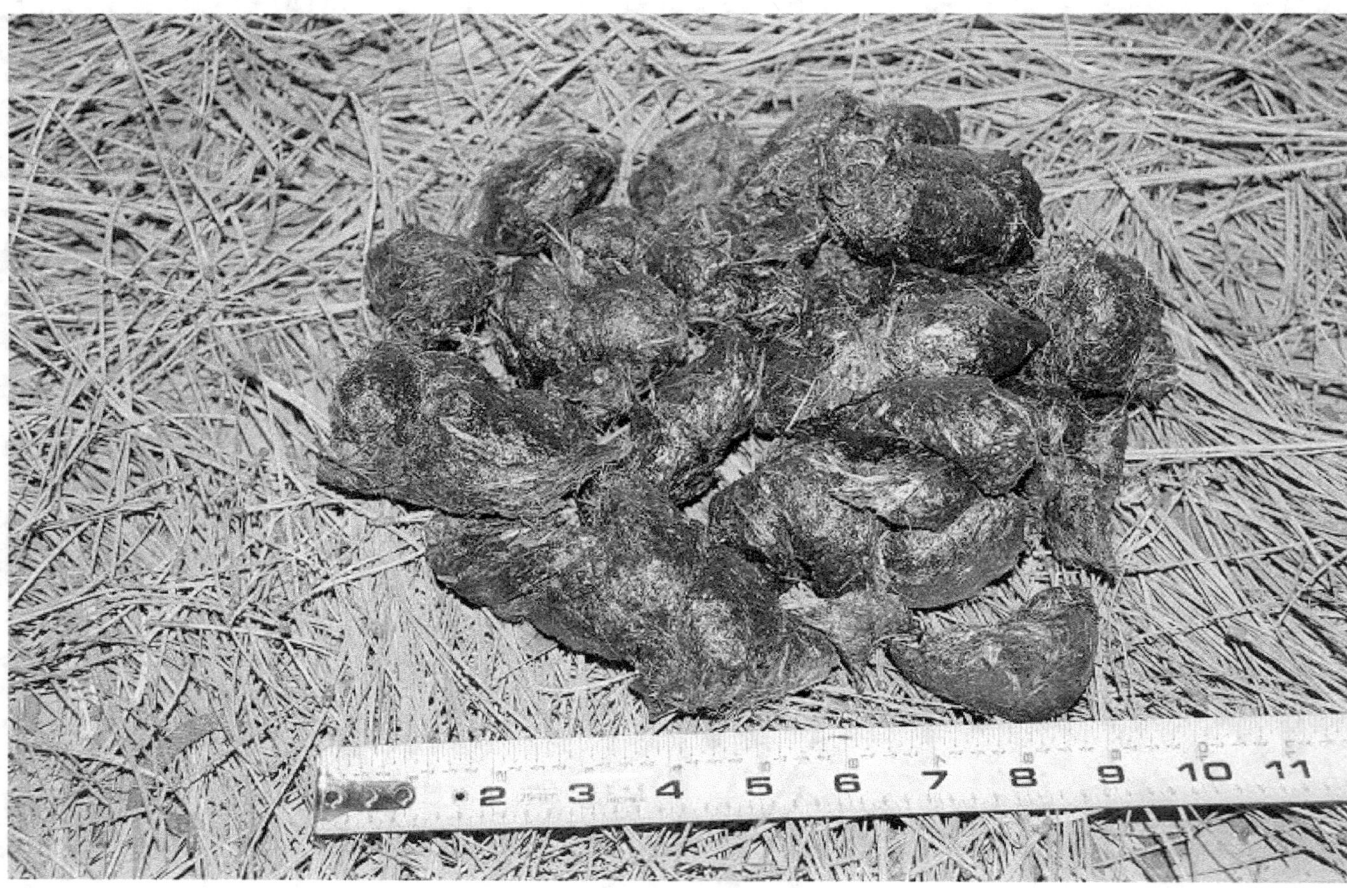

Sasquatch feces, segments are typically 2" to 4" in diameter and in this case measured over 18" across pile. Volume equal or exceeding that of a 1200 pound horse. This is an example of Sasquatch scat in pile form.

Item 17D

Sasquatch Scat example from Northern California in tubular form.

PLAINTIFF: I have shown many photographs of purported Sasquatch and bear scat to the forensic anthropologist previously mentioned. When he studied photograph Item17C and others similar from locations of heavy Sasquatch activity, he stated that the obvious presence of large amounts of deer hair and protein marked by coloration indicated a heavy meat died often characterized by Sasquatch diet and hunting behavior.

Black bear, which most often share habitat with Sasquatches display more varied diet than the Sasquatch, however they compete for the same food sources the only difference is that bear would also be on the Sasquatch diet.

PLAINTIFF: Your honor, I have two additional items I wish to enter into the record that are part of the hunting/feeding behavioral evidence I submitted as items 16A through 16G. May I enter these into the record now?

JUDGE: I will allow it, enter them as items 16AA and so on.

PLAINTIFF: thank you your honor. I would now submit items 16AA and 16BB into evidence.

Item 16AA

This was discovered near a ranch during Sasquatch activity nearby, the deer had been killed and hung over the barbed wire fence. No domestic or wild animal would approach it.

Item 16BB

Goats were repeatedly killed by Sasquatches on this farm, they were seen attempting entry to the goat enclosure and estimates of 30 or more were taken or killed. This one was mutilated and dragged toward the home, not away as most wild animals would do.

PLAINTIFF: Your honor I would at this time like to enter into evidence a witness statement (interview) and the photographs he subsequently took after his encounter with a Sasquatch. (NOTE: the interview vocabulary is a bit off at points, the discussion was very animated so my apologies for any errors in the text) The evidence will be entered as Items 18A through 18Y.

Item 18A

Dan Roberts testimony:

Canadians are a little less apprehensive to talk about the subject of Big Foot than their counterparts down here are less paranoid. So yeah so growing up how was the subject treated. Well I had like I said to you earlier my dad is a park ranger so I grew up kind of in the provincial parks system and stuff like that. And my dad had actually done a paper on Sasquatch when he was in school for the forestry school and so he had like I think it was the Patterson Gimlin book laying around the house and a couple other books on Sasquatch so I had considered it and watched the documentaries and really hadn't really thought too much about it really as a kid but you know it just grew up out in the woods and my dad was an open minded guy that obviously had considered it. So now he you told me once for he's sort of an expert in his field. He handles all the bad bears. Yeah he's the problem wildlife manager and as well does all the search and rescue. So he's a park ranger a conservation officer in the southern Alberta area and forest and I guess he'd be the elbow sheep area and we were in the spray Lakes area before that. So yeah he's done. He just retired this year so I think it was 35 years of search and rescue and wildlife management. So yeah he's got lots of knowledge. Now he's an expert tracker and all that right.

Search and Rescue tracker for sure and a room I recall from our conversation we had before you really impressed me with your knowledge about tracking and wildlife so that's pretty much where you gathered that information from right? Yeah just Second-Hand I mean I grew up hunting my whole life. We lived in the provincial parks. Hunting was something that we did every year and all the time we were out going in the you know like looking for grouse and just cruising around. So yeah Hunting tracking and like I said He's got 35 years of search and rescue training as well and then they are on top of that. They train their search and rescue personnel to train their search and rescue volunteers. So he's gone to the schools where they train border patrol. And then there's like a tracking school that they actually send the conservations off the conservation officers off to and then they use that to train they're tracking volunteers. That's really impressive. So OK now let's go ahead. Now you'd never had any big foot encounters or anything growing up is that right. As far as I know I don't think I had. I mean there's always you know like when you're out in the woods some weird things happen especially when you're a kid you've got a big imagination. But Sasquatch was as far as I know I've never seen anything. Nothing you could really put your finger on. So the first time you really noticed anything. How long ago was that? Would have been spring, and I think it would have been 2004 or 2003. We're tree planting up in northern British Columbia.

We had a contract off of a forestry access road that's a Gundi and it's off of the Alaska Highway north of kilometer 101 and between kilometer 120 mile marker 101 and 102 and 127 somewhere in there. But yeah it's a fairly large basically wilderness access point for service oil and gas logging. And then we had a contract that was all helli (helicopter) planting. So we are on a road access highway remote access service road and then driving out to a launch point and then flying. We had it was about a 30 minute helicopter ride to our pieces. So when you're talking remote to the launch areas. How many how many people do you think really go to a place like that. I mean it's not it's not when we say remote around here it's like you know 20 minutes. It's one of those funny things we're like. I really don't know if any other Americans or Alaskans really understand the magnitude of the remoteness of some of the lowest population densities in the world. And the thing is even like people aren't living there they're working there for the most part. And so someone had gone in and logged that block and so had built the roads. There's people around but there's not very many people,That's for sure Very few. There's no settlements or towns, the closest settlement is actually a gas station camp called Wano and then there's North of that there's another gas station hotel type thing that's pink mountains so there's nothing around you. So when you drove to this point where you flew to the helicopters How long did it take you to get to that?

I guess that might give people an idea of just how remote this is,We were probably another 45 minutes up the highway and then off of the highway on the gravel service roads it was probably another hour to hour and a half depending on how we drive to our camp. And then from the camp we were north another 20 to 25 minutes to the Helli staging points. And then like I said another 20 minute flight out. That's a long distance when you're talking. Those driving times just to get to your camp and then to the launch point were you. You loaded into helicopters and it was about a 30 minute flight. Yeah 20 or 30 minute flight I mean by the time you're all staged and loaded to go, you know it was summer and you could fly a long ways and 20 or 30 minutes you can fly a long wait at least 100 kilometers. Right So, everybody should understand this listening where you went was one heck of a long ways away from anywhere. It's important because people say and I think this myself you know when people find things you know Bigfoot wise you know you have to factor in what are the possibilities that other people were in the area and could have possibly hoped something. So yeah. And it would have been one elaborate joke.

You know I mean like we were there the first day and on the cup block like they would have had to been waiting for us. Sure. And how would anybody know you were going to go do you. Yeah I mean there were like the foreman would have been there you know and there's not untold stories of people messing with each other and in trouble and in camp so I had my first thought actually seeing the sign. So when you got there. Tell us sort of how what you were doing and how that happened how that whole situation unfolded. So they've established the cache of trees basically hidden under a tarp and then we've divided the cut blocks into sections. So we were lucky that we flew out the first for our group and landed at our cache with a short walk up to it. So we get in there and we carry bags and like a little short spade shovel for tree planting and then we'll bag up with usually somewhere between two and 500 trees depending on the size of the tree and the weight of the plug you know. Right there they vary quite a bit. So you bag up with basically as many as you can carry. And then you start along the perimeter and then fill back in towards your trees so that you're trying never to walk across a cut block without planting trees and making money because we get paid per tree. So we are always privileged to be out there first, you bag up you get at it right away.

Me and my best friend loaded up and we started up the tree line along the edge of the cup block and I basically got like two thirds of the way up this slope and it was a really good incline with like a little bench and then another good incline and then the tree line kind of like looped back around on the on this slope overlooking the valley and back down to our cache where we had landed with the helicopter. So I made it up to about the bench and then you know nature called I'd had a couple of cups of coffee and at that point I was like I got to find a nice spot. And I just sort of walked off along the bench and came to a spot where there was kind of like a knocked over root ball like tree to block me from the whole cut block so nobody could see where I was sitting. And then a nice little you know log. Good view. I looked over and right in front of the log where I was going to sit down there were black ants, and they had just had brought up this really fine loam like soil. You know just perfect dirt clay mixed right to the top of it and in the middle of this anthill was stamped footprint, like absolute perfect. It was like a flower the soil you know what I mean.

So the consistency ate perfectly took the impression of a track that was about as big as my booted foot but wider with bare foot you know five toes, I can even see like the creases. That sounds maybe like a juvenile me that is you know growing up in the bush all the time I used to walk by and thump them kick the anthills you know and just you know as a kid. This is why I say you know we used to do that. It was like someone had deliberately walked up and kicked these ants. And then there were there was absolutely no repairs done to the anthill the ants were still running around in distress on the first that it was that fresh like someone had just done this and then off through the grass just the long the bench there's the dew kind of on the grass and you could just see where the vegetation had been laid out in a double pathway going off up the bench and then into the trees. And so as if there were two individuals there was definitely two people walking side by side or two individuals. Yeah you know it kind of makes you wonder you know somebody walking barefoot steps into an anthill especially out in the middle nowhere. And what are your thoughts on that. I mean what came the first thing I thought was like that. Like who is who is out here. You look at it and I was like I just see the ants looking around or running around on and I was like man that's fresh.

I don't know who is who is out here, Like I just flew in here and I find this no one should be here. That was the thing that really spooked me because from where I was sitting I deliberately picked a spot where I could see the entire valley and they had watched me fly and get up and walk up the hill and had left. You know what I mean like they'd just left . They were right there. That was the thing that spooked and I kept going. Needless to say I couldn't to do my business anymore I wasn't feeling all of that. My partner he is kind of a city boy and I'm like come look at this man. I'm like I don't think you're getting a good look over there two people just walked out and he's like wow what do you think was here. And I'm like a god damn Sasquatch you know like joking around that time the hair on the back of my neck was like standing up. But you started thinking in terms of Bigfoot immediately because like I said it didn't belong there, no one was up there so what could have made that print? It was like I have a short foot like a nine foot my tread is five. Like super wide. And I was looking at it and like it was impossibly wide for the for the length of it. You know I mean like it was bigger in all around. Every measure of a booted foot track you know,right?

It was not very big in length but the proportions were very strange. You know I growing up with my dad he'd always be like oh look at this you know pointed things notable people's tracks like I always see that he drags his heel like his shoes patterns ward off on that side. So you know he says one of those things I would look at and I was like this is explainable. And then the freshness and then looking over and just seeing the clear distinct like the sun was coming up over it and it was just perfect two pathways in the dew and the vegetation bent over and they just went up on the hill above us. And it makes you wonder it would make me wonder about you know the timing. You flew in this into this location from quite a ways away. And what are the chances that you know you go to do a nature call and then right near where you happen to pick are these tracks and then it also made me wonder like what are they doing there. Like why. Why are they sitting there watching? You know I mean. Right. They're looking out and you know also that I started to think of like all kinds of stuff and the funny thing is I told my dad I was like I have seen the tracks like an unexplainable barefoot human tracking them in the wilderness like the wilderness that most people don't understand like wilderness. And he's like it was a bear. No it wasn't .

I'm not one of those guys is going to mistake a bear track for Bigfoot. When you've grown up from that and learned animals Yeah you know even people who aren't that knowledgeable. If you've seen bear tracks and you see something that's not bear tracks I mean it's really difficult to mistake their tracks and Sasquatch tracks.

Yeah my dad and I did actually talked, later on we had talked about it he thought that like I don't know there's two different and species mostly in these forest the black ants and the red ants in the red ants cut like little twigs and make their nests out of that where the black ants make their nests out of the soil he kind of in his mind that vision like an impression indistinguishable impression in an anthill made out of twigs you know and was like oh you're just paranoid. He didn't realize the clarity of which you said it was the consistency of cornstarch or like flower to show dermal ridges. The cracks you could see like this one actually had the had dermal ridges running laterally along the foot along the edge of its foot like any cracks right. And it was perfect like perfectly in the impression and the track was no less than 20 minutes old because the ants hadn't even like stopped running around to fix things. They were still running around the they rebuild their nest for an hour. They start repairing it and you can see in this fine of like substrate you can even see the ant tracks. You know what I mean like that's how it's like cornstarch and so fine you could see where they had moved around. Everybody has different opinions about footprints. It really depends on the medium the tracks are left for sure and most often in the forests aren't really great for leaving footprints.

Yeah I guess I mean the thing is like after that I had like I said I started to just I fully truly believed in Sasquatch because I'd seen the tracks and I'm a hunter. When you see a sign there's game and you know sign can't be faked. It could be fake but that one would have just been such an elaborate one. That's the thing it's the conditions you know the context of the situation does not lend itself to or even anyone else's or mistaken identity. You know I mean some hermit in the woods is unlikely right. So I had definitely believed in them and then I guess the next time I actually saw something that I just absolutely thought back to the immediate idea was this isn't a person. I was working in the oil field in that same region along that water on Alaska Highway just north of Pink Mountain. When I was on the west side of the Alaska Highway instead of the east side towards Alberta so skyway just pretty much only road up there. The Gagny road goes back east towards the Alberta border and then I was on north of Wanto I was on the east side of the road just drilling. Actually it was my first oil and gas job up there. So first time I've actually been back to the region since that summer.

You know eight years or so or whatever it was it would have been so yeah almost ten years since I was there and I was just I was working nights so I got up and decided to go for a walk in the afternoon and I didn't have any bear spray or anything like that so I was just kind of sticking close to the rig and walked away from that rig towards the north and it was just walking through the trees. On the other side but there was a stream that had kind of come up to that same area so I had seen I'd walk through that area a little bit before just kind of on the road in and around the trees just stretch my legs and it seemed that's kind of where the animals are coming. Going through there to walk through that area got about 80 yards away from the oil rig you could still hear it working in the background, and just cut a line of tracks. Bipedal tracks looked like booted feet in the duff moss you could just see in that really perfect underneath the pine forest is really not much that grows just a big blank Duff.

Finches are the ones that are out there you know but I had thought that because I was following his tracks and I could see he had plucked out one of them, I don't know what they're called. I didn't even know they were edible tell you the truth but they're like a brown Woody mushroom and you could see the hole that it left in the duff moss like that where the mushroom was. And you know and like I said I didn't even know they were there and edible mushroom but you could see that he had picked one out so it was like picking mushrooms and I started following them and just out of boredom walking along through this track way and he's just moving like straight towards like I had no idea what was back behind this area or anything like that you know I'd be walking through the bush which is funny because you know if you're picking mushrooms you kind of like wander around right and now let me ask before we go any further. Was the spacing between the feet like the person or whatever was in a hurry or I mean in other words were they further apart or was it closer. I know when I if I'm in the forest I'm looking for something I take much shorter steps you know because I'm looking around and yeah you're 100 percent right on that.

It was kind of strange because you could see that they were like moving like I was walking in their steps and it was a good stride like you would have had to been like I said looking for something but then stopped and picked a musher Yeah. Something that I've done when I'm hunting is like you come across your brother's tracks or your hunting partner and you're walking along them and you can see where they like stopped and looked this way and stop and look away and have a little snack here and you know you can kind of see what they were doing as they went along. But this guy is moving at a clip straight through the forest. Stop. Picked a mushroom turned you know and you could see he was walking along and every you know five ten strides would stop. Like when you turn to well back you take like a 45 degree angle step. You know I mean that back step look. So he was walking along and I could tell he was looking around and then just started like moving the track spacing out a little further and he would just step over things that I couldn't step over you know anyway it would have been something like a log that was down there. So it's an indication that whatever whoever or whatever it was had much longer step than me running through the bush and just lofting over things. But then at the same time being able to like turn back around you know I mean like I would have been running to make that same stride length.

So it was like it would turn but it was looking around look behind me. So yeah. then it came up to the edge of an old cut block and then tucked in behind a tree and you could see where someone had stood there for a bit. The most impressions was just these Duff Moss impressions like it wasn't like I was making later. This is for sure a bipedal Sasquatch you know . Strange but you know. But you know you mentioned to me when we first talked about this about doing a behavioral profile based on the kind of impressions you yeah like in search and rescue when you're looking for someone and they're hiding from you or you can tell when they're walking around looking in or you know what I mean are or like looking back on their back trail. You know you can kind of tell what you say like profile of someone and there's something and so I guess depending on how the angle of the foot is where the weights distributed distribution such that kind of gives you an idea of what it was doing. Yeah like I said if when you're looking backwards like you can see and the hunters tracks a lot they'll do that. You'll see him walking along and then they'll look and then there's one track. Lots of times people look over their right shoulder and that that tracks you know this way and it points in the direction that they're looking.

So you can see someone come along on a track way to a cut line and they looked here they looked there or whatever it was. This guy was going straight through the duff moss like a in a straight line like he knew where he was going. But you know the same time stopped but didn't pick mushrooms and clearing a larger gate than was comfortable for me to walk on and stepping over things that I would have walked around like he knew I was going walk straight to it while looking around still looking around checking and then stopped at a clearing and then waited there for a while and then walked off into the cut block and then I couldn't. There was no more tracks like it was just perfect conditions for those Duff Moss impressions you can get a clear look at what someone had done with their feet as they went through there. And that goes back again like we mentioned before unless the conditions are just right and the forest you're lucky to see Prints or even to make out in any kind of animal for sure. And like I said I wasn't like oh God it was a Sasquatch it could have been a big guy walking around who was maybe looking to find the best place to pick mushrooms and just happened to see you. And you know what I mean. So there was this part of those ones where I was, I had seen up in that area and had seen a very unusual track that you know and then yeah the proximity is fairly close. You know probably four or five hundred kilometers.

And that's fairly close I mean that's for these things in that area because there's not, It's well within, I mean in terms of speculation anyway you know you can certainly put it in that basket and say well maybe the same habits same habitat same region. So it's certainly a possibility. Yeah. It was just you know kind of cool to be back in that area just go in the bush. And you know it's been years I wasn't even thinking about it and even when I didn't see it I didn't realize it you know like I was like wow I was like Who's this guy. I was wondering with how is this guy doing, Where is it going. And they just walk off into a cut block. On the other side of that there's nothing to the east of that you know we were the furthest east portion of this energy project. So someone just walked across the highway or walked across the service road picking mushrooms then stood at the end of a cut block and then walked off into the wilderness.

I had gone back to the same area where we were drilling on the same area Alaska Highway back towards Gundi road we were actually just north of the Gundi road that same road that I had been on years before and were going up to New Energy Project hadn't worked in that area with that oil company or whatever so we were just kind of new to the area and I always bring my fly fishing gear and sometimes my shotgun and some hunting stuff depending on where we're at. It's just one of those things I especially in the summertime the fly fishing which is amazing up there Arctic grayling like every cast but we can't we came along and there was like we were proposing 20 through 127 kilometers from Dawson Creek which is near the Alaska Highway. So that's about 100 kilometers away from like one of the best. Like the city Fort St. John that's in the area. And then we were West on the 127 road and. And we've got a kilometer 26 there's this like huge flights and beaver ponds and just a big creek that kind of like flowed through the whole area and then you just go up this huge slope on this single lane bridge that sloped it like something ridiculous like a 15 percent grade. You know mean like so dangerous. And as we were driving across it you can just see right down to this big pool where the creek turned and hit that bank that the sloped bridge went up big swirling pool and then came underneath of us and my partner we were on the radio. And he goes that's you. That's your visual buddy. There it is.

We're like OK sweet so took a couple days getting them set up and he was kind of green and so took a bit getting comfortable and stuff like that and then finally I was able to break off. And best thing about working out there is like we work from 7 till 7 but in the summertime it's like 11 sometimes. So you have lots of free time still daylight so I've finished my shift packed the truck up and I didn't actually notice there was a shortcut road that I could have taken. I would have made my driving time like a quarter but I drove all the way back around the ridge to the to the fishing hole and parked on the uphill side of the turnoff on either side because it's a single lane bridge for the logging trucks and energy trucks and everyone you know you have to call your kilometers or else you can get killed in a spot like that it's like I said its super dangerous. So I parked on the uphill side which I think is in in hindsight the only reason that I had had any sort of sighting whatsoever is because I parked in a really funny spot and walked into the whole scene from a completely different path than what most because there are people like you said in the area and that particular spot there was a hunters camp probably another two or three kilometers downstream. And then there's an abandoned house. I think it was a hunting camp or something at one point and it was like a fairly large two story place that was just abandoned no windows in it whatsoever. And I guess that guy had released a bunch of horses into the area. So there's wild horses run around there.

But I think that's kind of what was bringing him in because like I said I parked on the top of this pull out, walk down this super steep ridge which was kind of like a access point and all underneath the bridge on the uphill side was just a big cliff. So I walked across the river and then on the down river side hopped off the bridge climb down through the like the boulders the erosion control and down to the bottom tied on fly. And then I just took a couple of casts from underneath the bridge and you know what looked like a little log there and it was just a log jam it immediately snagged into my fly. So I just was reeling in all right well I guess I'll just walk up this fishing hole and fish there. And it was you know it was within line of sight. So it was you know under you know it's hard to remember. You know guesstimate distance from memory but I would say it was under 100 yards probably in that 60 to 80 yard range relative. So I was just reeling in and then you know walking up towards the beach and like I had already tied a fly and cast for a minute there. So I was under that like 80 yard range. I was walking up reeling in. It's like a Grebe almost looks like a loon the pointy bills red head little crest on them and they came flushing up off the water.

Because the day before I had fished closer to the rig on that same stream and I had come across like tracks of within 500 meters on this one beach I came across a boar grizzly that would have been like in the range of 3500 pounds to the tracks, well it was nine and a half ten inches on the heel across the heel in the mud. You know I mean like just a massive northern grizzly here. That's a big bear. I've seen two black bear tracks that were well within. a 400 pound very large 400 pound and then a whole pack of wolves like 12 to 15 wolves. And one of the largest Wolf tracks that was larger than my hand. And I think that's because of those horses those wild horses that had been kicked loose and. There was an abundance of them running around just like back then all these predators.

And like when you're in that kind of area you don't just get a chuckle out of these guys they throw their iPod on in their ear buds and then they're you know like you get your heads on a swivel like carry a can of bear spray in the view can't bear spray. I mean that's usually what's going to save your life. But you know that the shotgun, I think it just reassures me. I Carry them. I used to feel pretty safe carrying my tool and we loaded with buckshot and slug, the books even say use this silly old trapper combo. And so I had already seen you know how densely populated this area was with predators the day before and like I've seen some of the pictures like I can send you the pictures the little grizzly bear tracks the wolf tracks like I was just shocked to the size of these wolf tracks like you could make out the alpha that walked through the pack itself and was you know like almost twice as heavy. You know what I mean like into that to the two hundred fifty pound dog and that's something you know I think people here in the U.S. don't understand they think that you know animals are you know are friendly are afraid of us and all this but you know up your way you understand a little bit better that you know that's an extremely dangerous environment. You have to really pay attention to what's going on and you run into these like juvenile grizzlies that have never seen them before. And they have a way with you. They're the biggest thing around and especially the juveniles are so dangerous because they've never seen people before and b sometimes they're having a tough go of it.

So just getting into it I had parked on the uphill side walked in tight on broke off a fly and you know it took a few minutes that I was walking upstream looking upstream reeling in. And like I said it was probably in that 60 yard range and I just seen those in McGann's come up downstream. And I thought huh I wonder what flushed those ducks.

And as I was thinking that I just seen what I my mind thought when I first saw it just it was just huge brown movement and it was moving. You're thinking grizzly right away I was whoa. And then boom that spooked me as it was like it was flying like flying along the riverbank and I just seen it through the trees and then it would break into this stand right on the edge of the big slope was a really dark stand of timber like spruce timber. So it was kind of willows like a kind of a flat's of willows and then into this really big stand of timber and I just saw it moving along the riverbank and the sun was like I didn't really didn't think, it was a Sasquatch. I just seen the sun behind it a huge mass moving at huge incredible speed along the riverbank and I was I was like shit that was a big bear and I thought I was like whoa. I dropped the fishing rod and I was looking upstream and it spooked me out because the only spot where you could see I was standing kind of underneath the bridge when I first tied on.

There was a track line that came out like and I'm seeing noticeable huge tracks that came out of the bush walk to the edge of the water which was the only line of sight from where I was standing to where it was and then up and then I just you know you started immediately see what you're looking for as I was looking for bears. I saw there you know it was Big Brown. It was moving fast and you'd already seen it run. Yeah I saw. You know I was already looking for him and then I just was like looking at it and I was like looking at the height of the willows you know they were like when I when I started the other side you know I'm five eight not very tall but they up to my chest so I was thinking like you're looking at it only there was like height you know only huge and I'm looking at the tracks I'm just like it doesn't look right. So I just took the safety off and I was like bye. No I'm going in there to take a look now. You know I'm like I'm going in. The there was a beach area of sand that I was kind of like walking up towards this bend in the river. But along the outside of the beach was a really thin strip of Bruce and pine and brush and there was kind of like I didn't notice at the time but there was like a ATV track that went along that side of the brush on the other side was an opening meadow and in a pool I would actually where you could see people had pulled out come into this spot and clearly fished it before.

There was trash and there was horse tracks and there was ATV tracks and it went kind of along this beach road to the point where the you know the trees stopped and the river was or it was not much more than a creek or any kind of pinched out and there was a crossing there. And then the Rapids and then this big pool and then the stream kind came down. So it dogleg ran at that spot. So it had come out of this thin strip of trees walked out to the beach to look down to where I was. It must have heard me or seen me or something. I think it must have heard me and I walked down and looked and then walk up and around the corner as I was you know taking those first few bass and must have crossed the stream as I broke the fly off. I think it was running because the tracks were so fresh they were still filling with water.

That's how clear it walked into that silty sandy mud right up to the edge of the water from across the gravel through the sand into the water and it peaked from the waterline over the kind of the bank to where I was standing and that's I believe the only reason that it made any of those tracks because it walked out of where it was perfectly concealed and could have walked down a hard packed track crossed the creek without anyone knowing it had been there had someone come in the normal way. I know that it had because it was running and it flush those ducks up and when it flush those ducks out man and it covered that gap that remaining it was 35 40 yards from the crossing where it had flushed the ducks up like the little rapids and there was the little pool the start of the pool and then ran about 30 yards and it covered that like and it was like Usain Bolt dream like that. Like I don't know how many people I've actually seen like a full boar grizzly run but they are faster than a racehorse and it had that kind of fast like you know unlike it's amazing for yeah they're scary man they kick up the duff behind them when they're running. They do that they do that zero to racehorse speed and three strides are scary fast.

Yeah but it had it had covered that ground in that kind of time like you're talking like the three second or two second 40 to uncover and for the you know four as like you know what the linebacker you know can run and this thing doing a like to that's how fast like a bear can do it. Race horses it's you know the thing. And I was just looking at these tracks and they are clear like clear as day. You can see where the foot pivoted in the middle and it looks like someone walking on their hands almost the way it like grasps the sand and there's a fold in the middle of the sand.

I'm was staring at just in particular it just struck me as unbelievable because you could see like the toes spread out the mud was squished up between the toes you could actually see hair imprinted around the fringe of the track on the heel on the heel is just amazingly wide. And then there's this double dimple looks like a heel impression rate dead center of this track. You know it was just did you did you measure there 12 inches.

I didn't see any of the like this was a different fishing spot the night before I had gone down to the creek that was same creek but close to the rig so I didn't know this was probably only 10 kilometers downstream but I have driven all the way around on all the service roads back to this spot where the bridge was when I said sure I had been able to just drive straight through that creek crossing that I was on the day before.

And then just cut cross country 10 kilometers. I was at that spot but I learned that afterwards. I say yeah. Just so I see these tracks. They came out and I'm like this is Sasquatch. You know what I mean I'm thinking Ha. Like finally I'm going to rub this in my dad's face. Pretty hard to dissuade anyone from knowing it or thinking like this one. I was like I just seen this sucker. You know what I mean like I just you know yeah you know I was just I was like You know I was like this thing is fast. And this thing is like fast and I'm looking and it's only like you know from the stand of trees that I've seen it run into to where I'm standing is across this creek that's no more than 15 yards across. You know I am I'm standing there looking into the spot where I seen this thing running. Looking at its tracks and you were pretty close with it. Yeah like it under 20 yards from where you are. And I just I was like oh I got to know if that's what I seen running. You know what I mean. So I like I started following these tracks and I could see it walked up to the creek looked downstream at me and then walked up the path or like up the stream bed along the rocks you can see it in the sand and the impressions.

And then it came to the creek crossing and you could see literally where it flushed the ducks up and it crossed the stream and then crossed the opening on the other side which was 20 feet and then there was only one wet foot impression in the center of that. So it made like 10 feet and then up onto the bank did you have any impression why it would have just taken off running all of us. Because I was walking upstream and it flush those ducks. And it was already you could see it had turned and was walking sneaking because there were Flatfoot impressions and there was a stick laying on the beach and this thing said its foot down almost touching the stick. So it had spotted me and started to sneak away and then it flushed the ducks and it must have looked up as I went in and just felt like it was only like this thing ran and it covered this like 40 yards. And like I said like two seconds from the time the ducks flew up. All I seen was a flash.

I got to the point where I seen that it had hopped of out of the creek you could see the wet foot impressions on the stones.

And then there was a wet foot impression on the dirt bank like it had hopped across the wash out the river bank and up onto the or across the stream bed and up onto the riverbank you know the wet foot on the stones and one wet footprints on the on the dirt flat foot perfect you know footprints like you could see ribs punched into the soil even then and then the water like water dripping off of someone running into the trees in the direction that I had seen the movement going to and I was not abode because I seen how fast it covered that ground greenery and like it was lightning. So I just turned round and I walked back to the to the spot where it'd come out. And I was looking you know holding the shotgun and bear spray looking into the end of the spot where I'd seen it go just looking for movement you know looking for anything. And then right that's when like a whistle that we are I don't think it whistled at me but it whistled like straight up. So it didn't just keep going it was still, just went into the trees and stopped. That's what spooked me out because I was like man he's in there there's like he would run up a huge cliff face. The noise it made was Dee Dee Dee Dee Dee Dee. And that's pretty typical but it was like deep like baritone like you much bigger than what it was like the first impression of a chickadee and I was like oh my god he's whistling at me. And I was like yeah oh whistle back and I started to whistle my mouth just sort of went dry as the whistle started to come out of my mouth, I just had this vision of like a basketball sized River stone just bashing me in the back of a head.

I've never felt terrified until it ends but that was that's when people like oh I was terrified I didn't know what that meant to me and then I was like Yeah I know. I was terrified like until you hear the terror It just crept up from the back of my head and I ran like sprinted out of there. And the funny thing is I think it would have been different had it kept going and you wouldn't of heard anything but the I think the fact that it stopped in was doing something. And then you know that's what I was like He's whistling to me and then I was like oh my god he's whistling to his buddy.

Item 18B

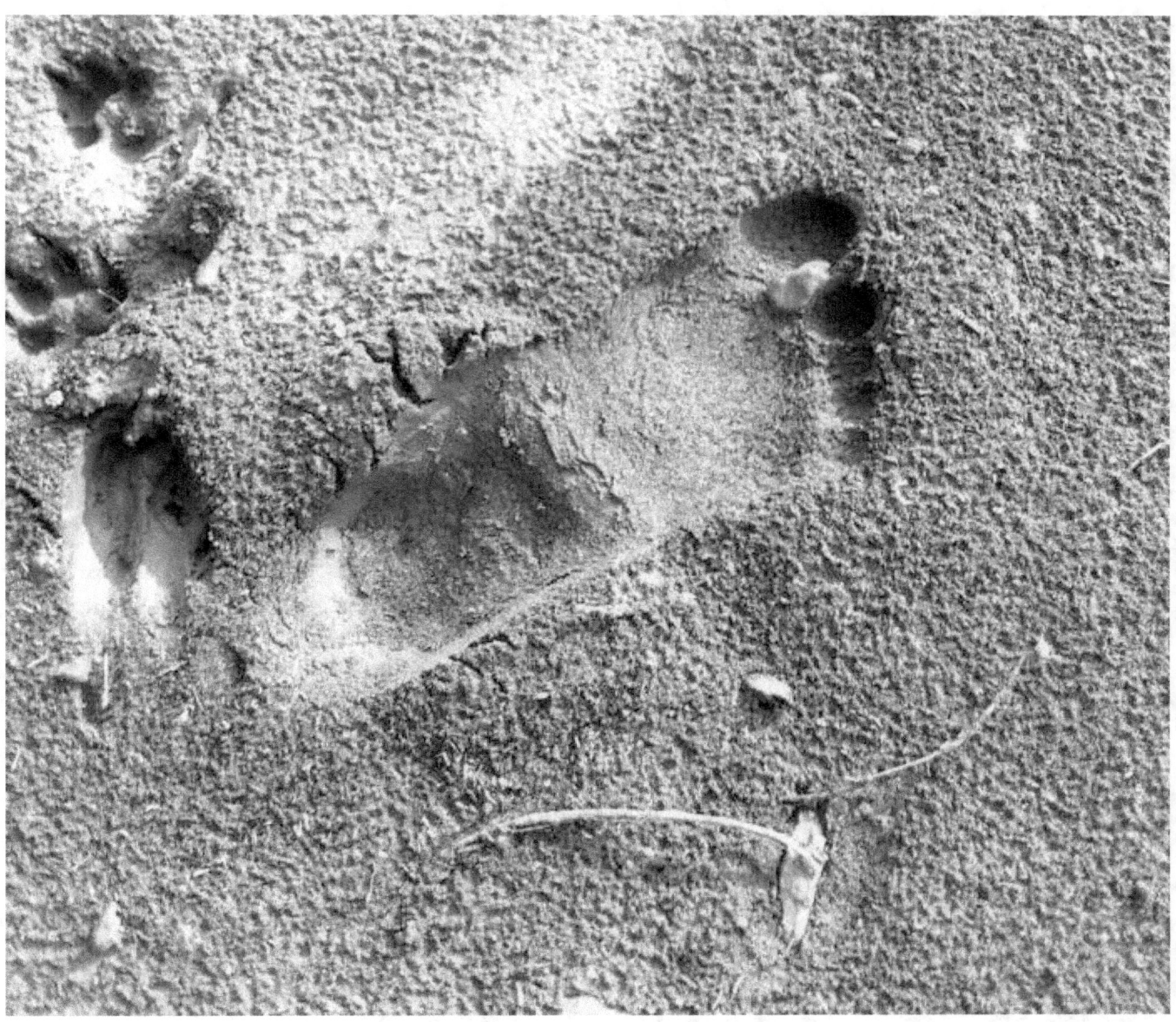

Photograph Dan R.

Item 18B

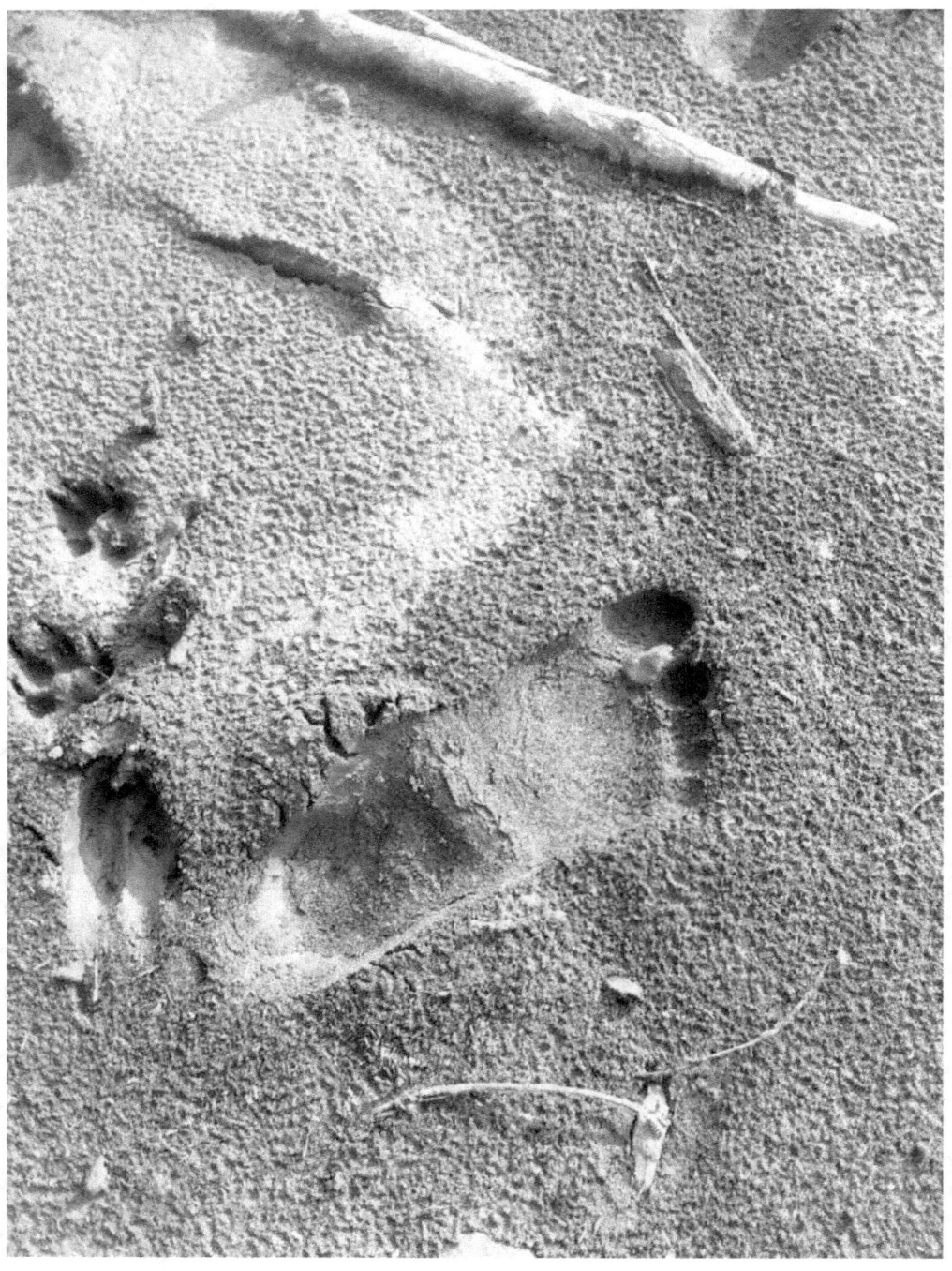

Wider perspective, same photograph.

Item 18C

Dan's footprint left, Sasquatch right (juvenile Sasquatch)

Item 18D

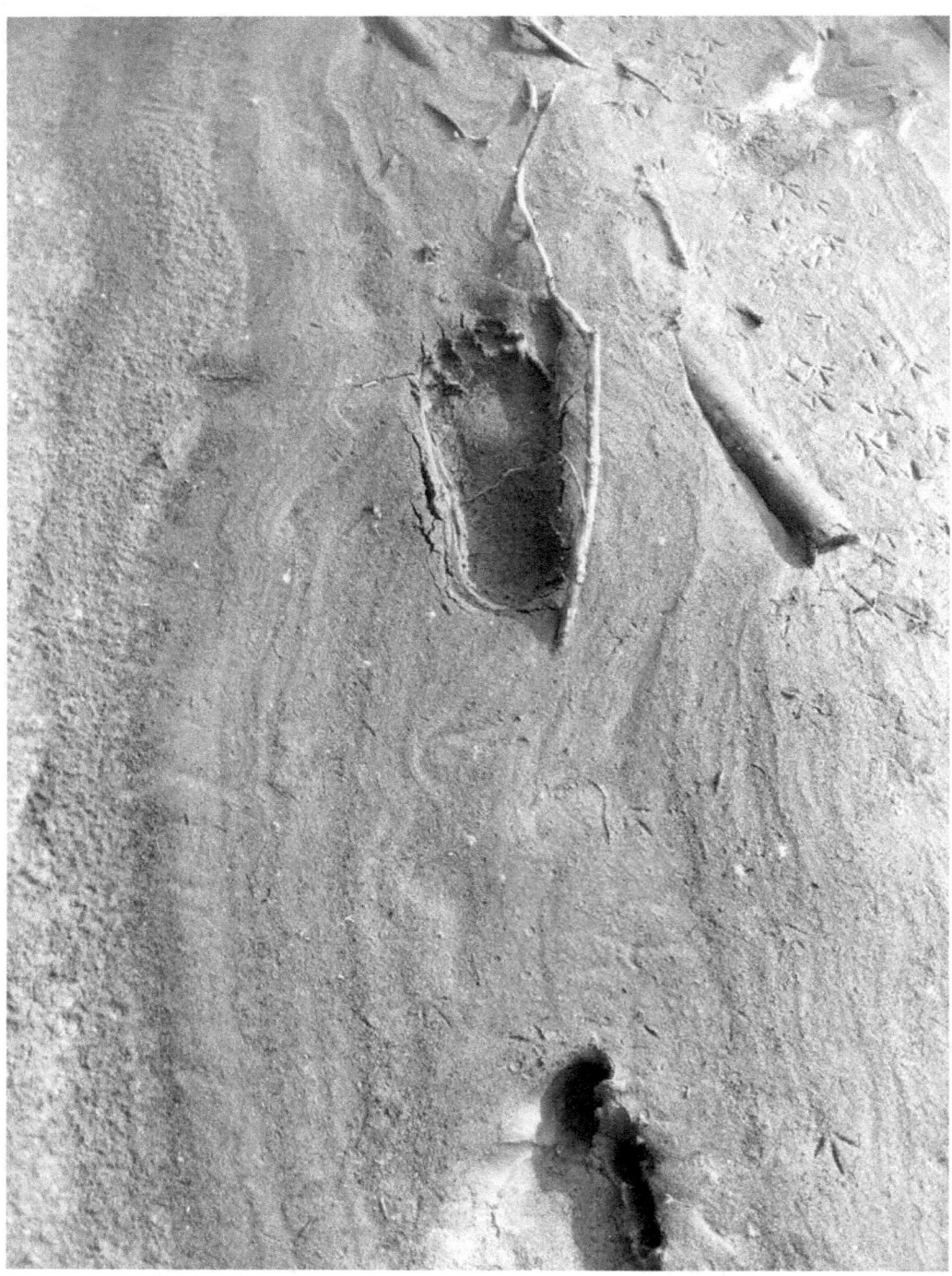

Sasquatch footprints consecutive impressions.

Item 18D

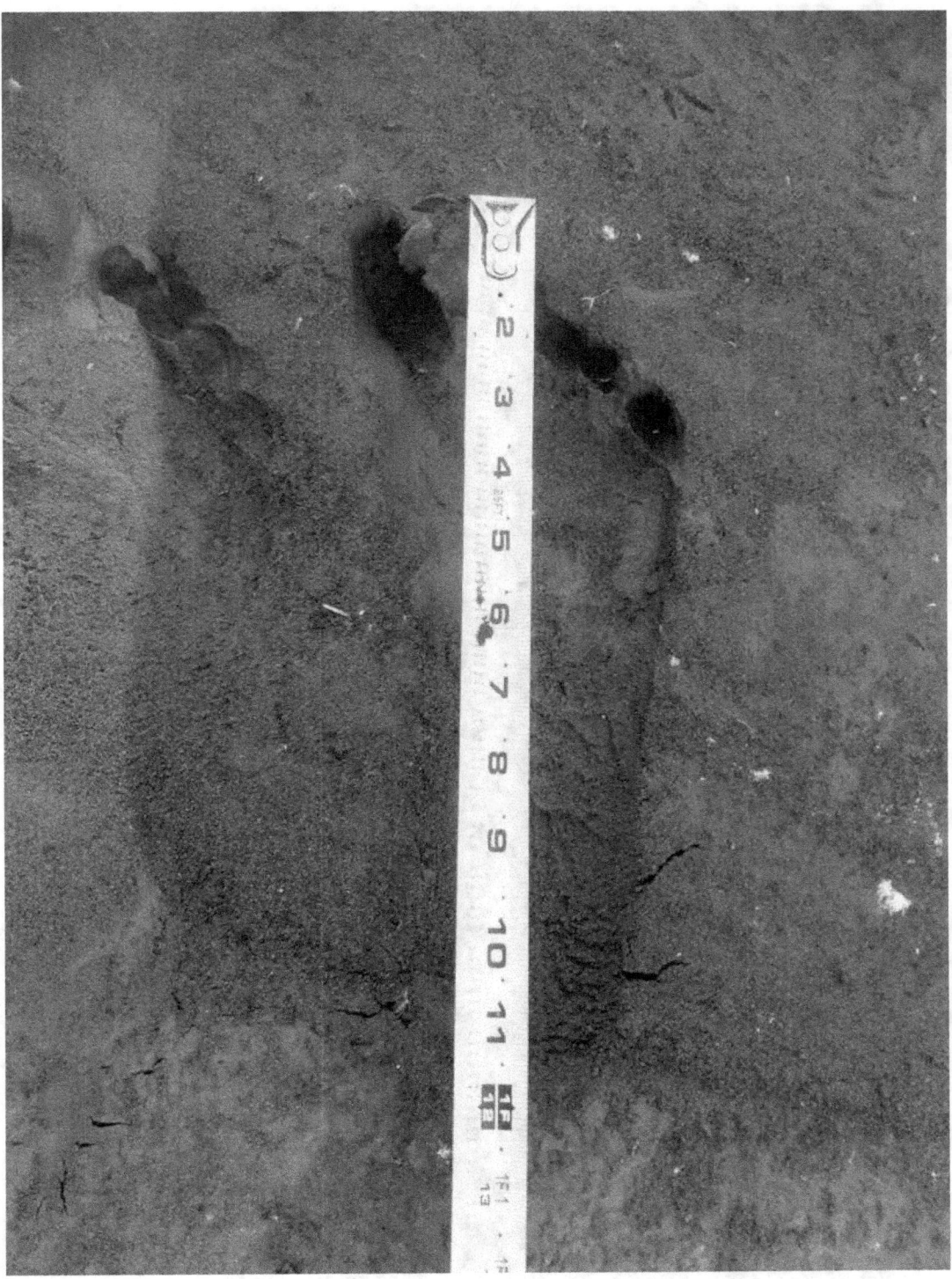

Measurement of the tracks.

Item 18E

Dan's hand next to one of the prints for scale.

Item 18F

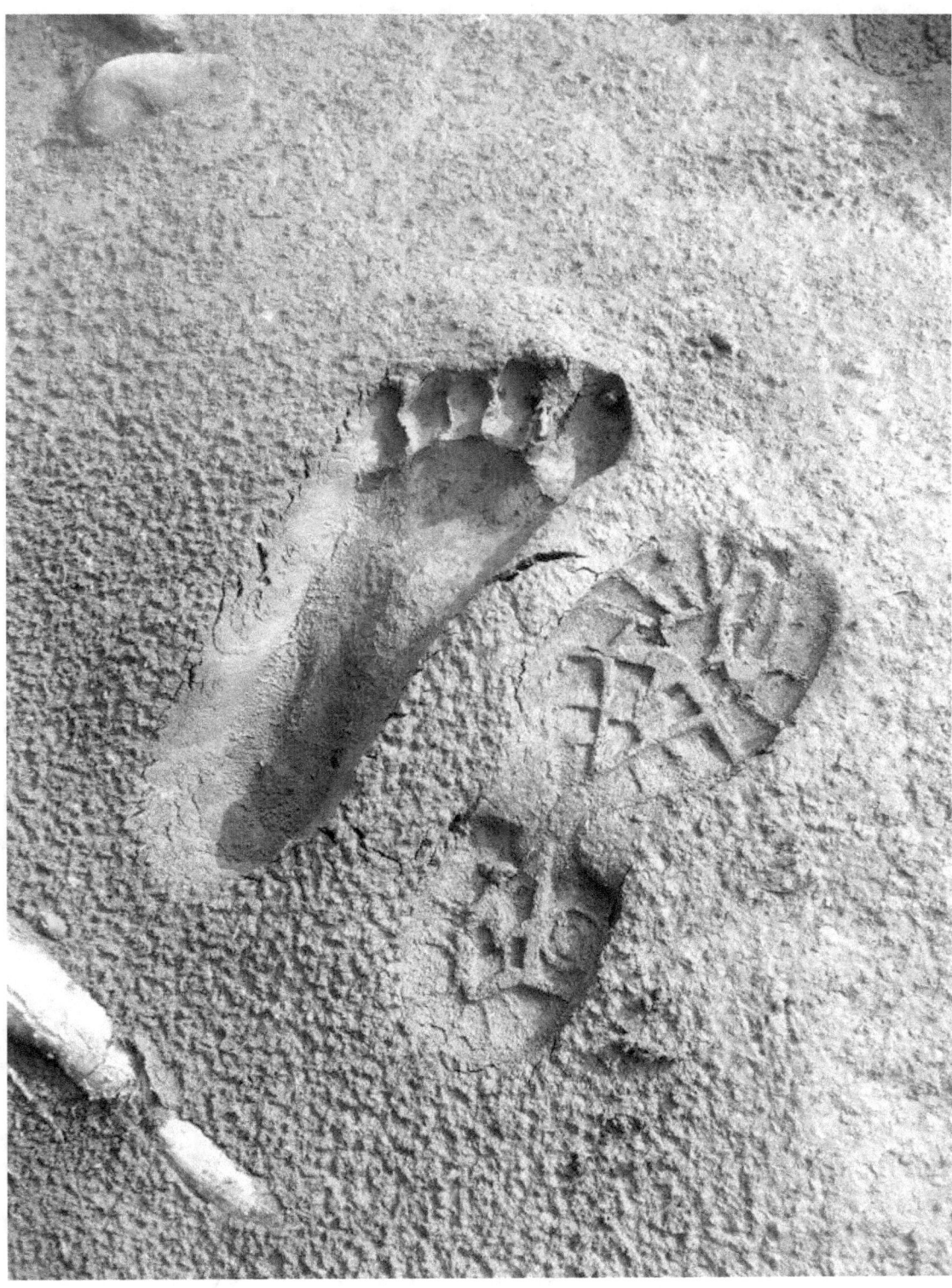

Dan's boot print next to Sasquatch track.

Item 18G

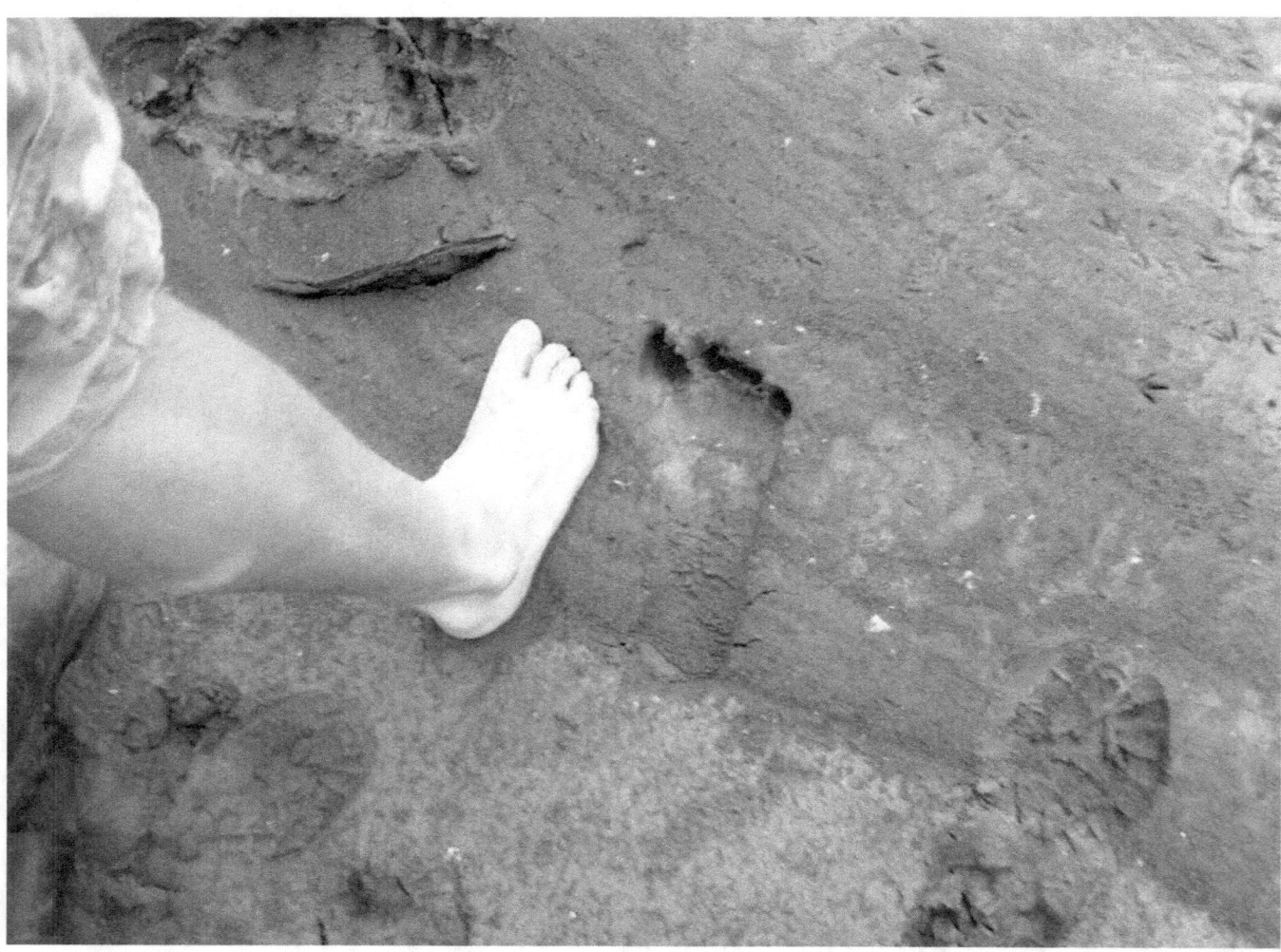

Dan's foot next to a Sasquatch track for scale.

Item 18H

Another photograph of Dan's foot next to Sasquatch track.

PLAINTIFF: I will now enter into evidence footprints of Sasquatches from Canada and across the United States to demonstrate similarity of impressions covering a large area in both space and time. Some of the impressions are of varying age and decomposition and various types of soil they were made in. They will be entered as Items 19A through 19

Item 19A

Carbon River Washington State.

Item 19B

Photo taken by moose hunters in Canada.

Item 19C

Second print from Canadian moose hunters. (same line of footprints)

Item 19C

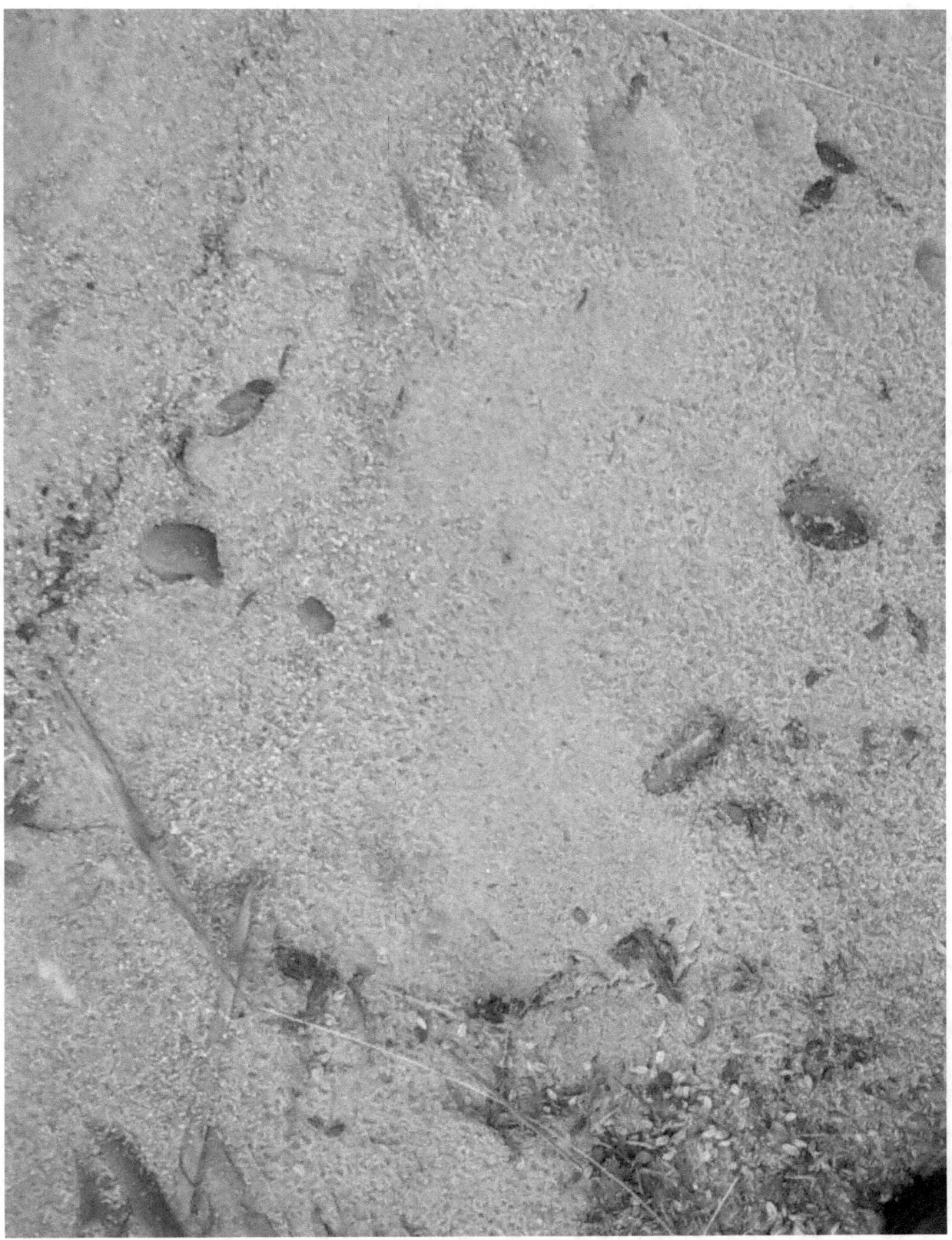

Third print found by Canadian moose hunters. (same line of tracks)

Item 19D

Older weathered 18″ track Skamania County Washington.

Item 19E

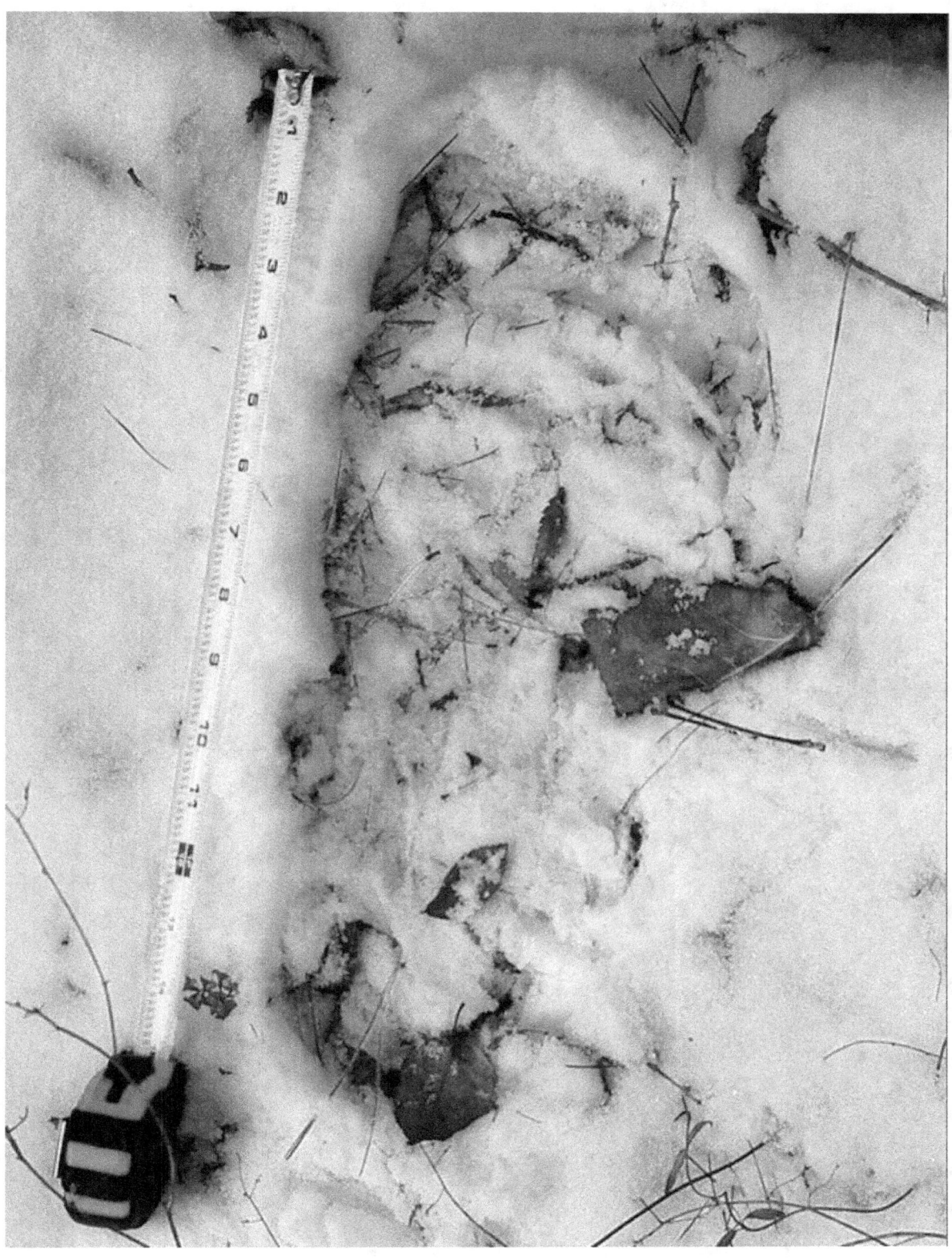

Footprint in snow (credit Bobby Woods)

Item 19F

Photo courtesy Gail Beatty

Item 19G

Photo courtesy Gail Beatty

Item 19H

Track line in snow, courtesy Gail Beatty

Item 19I

Weathered footprint

Item 19J

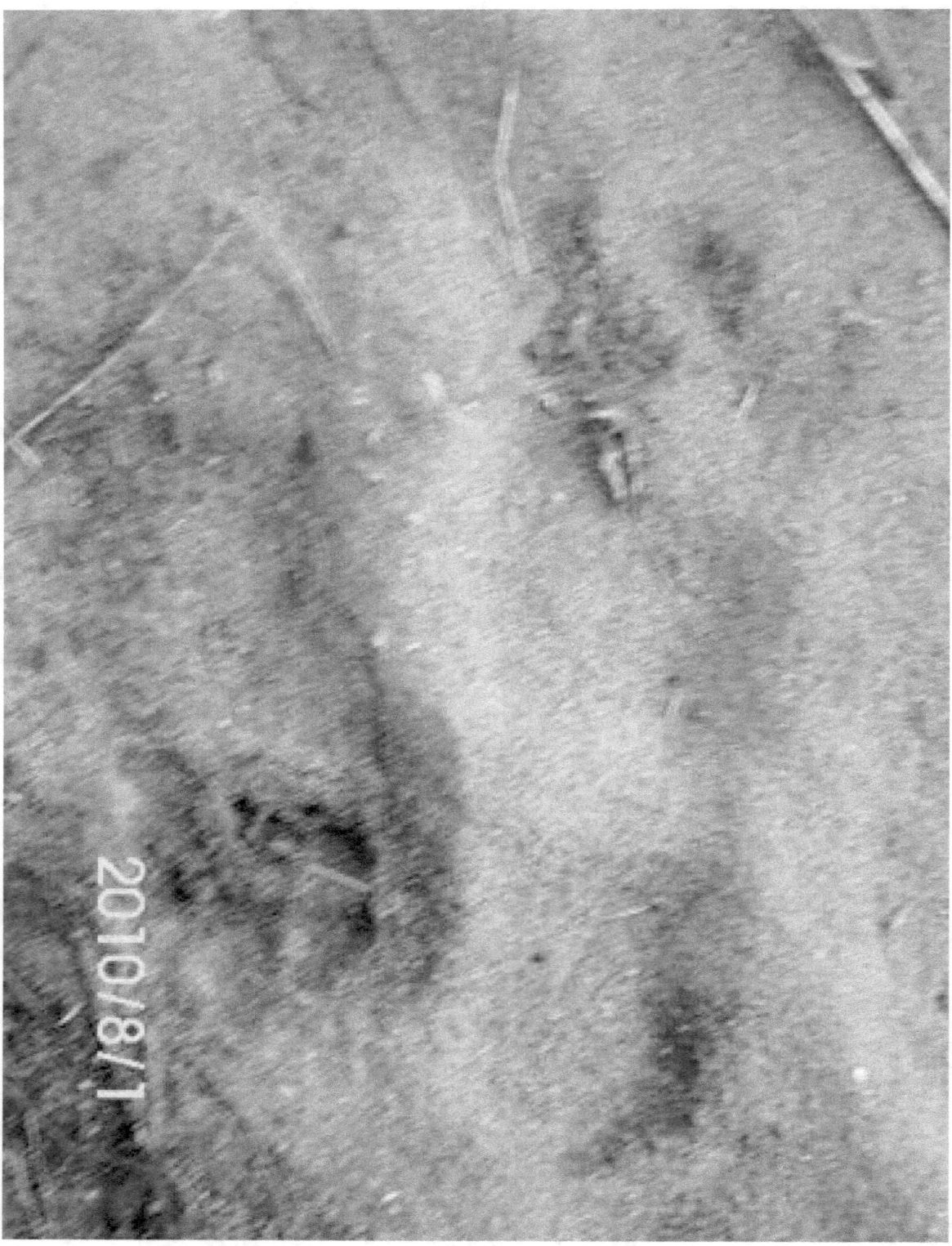

Footprint in sand. courtesy Susan Rankin

Item 19K

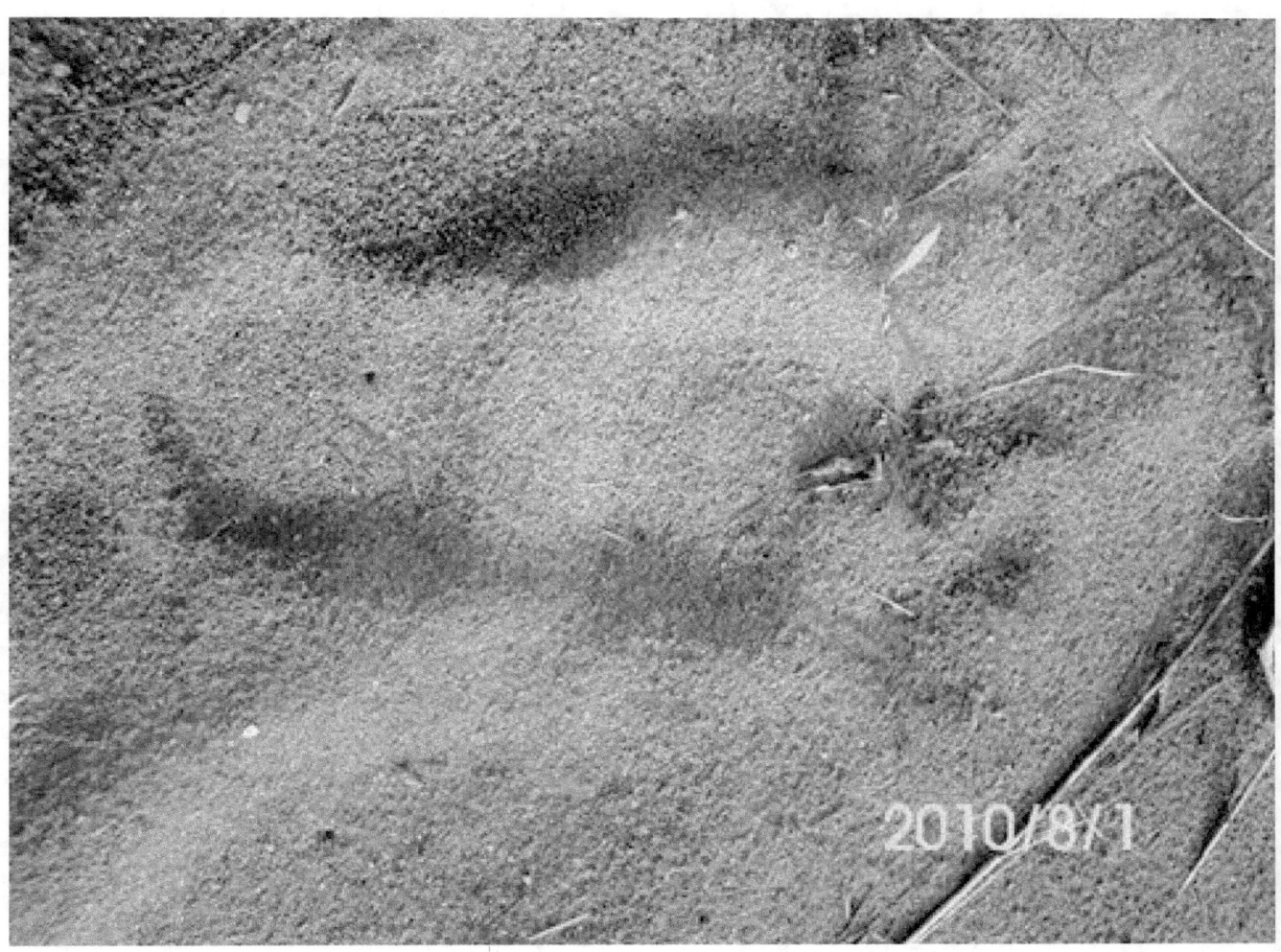

Same footprint courtesy Susan Rankin.

Item 19L

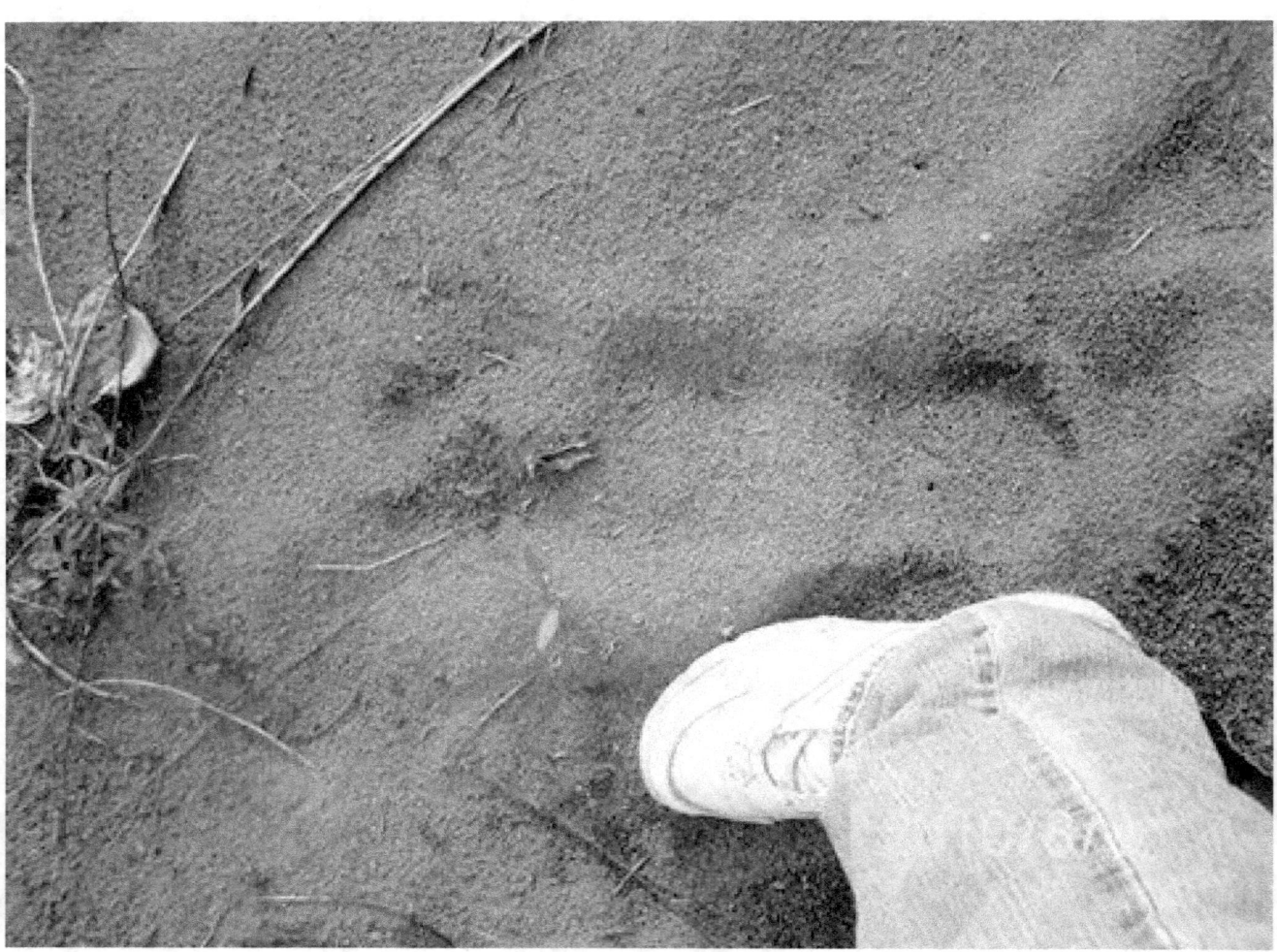

Susan Rankin with her foot next to track for scale.

Item 19M

Close up of toe impressions. Courtesy Susan Rankin

Item 19N

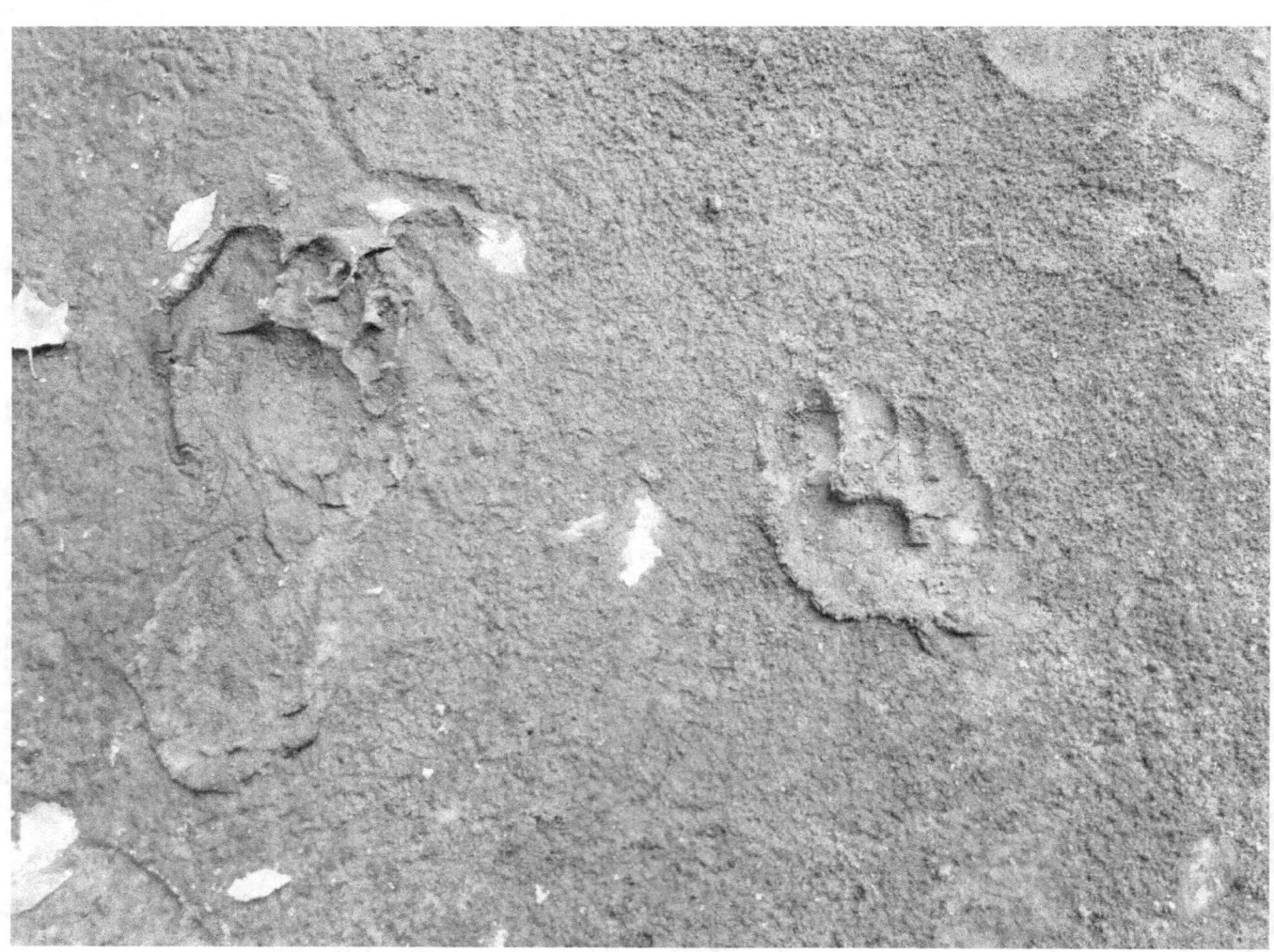

Sasquatch footprint left, bear track right.

Item 19O

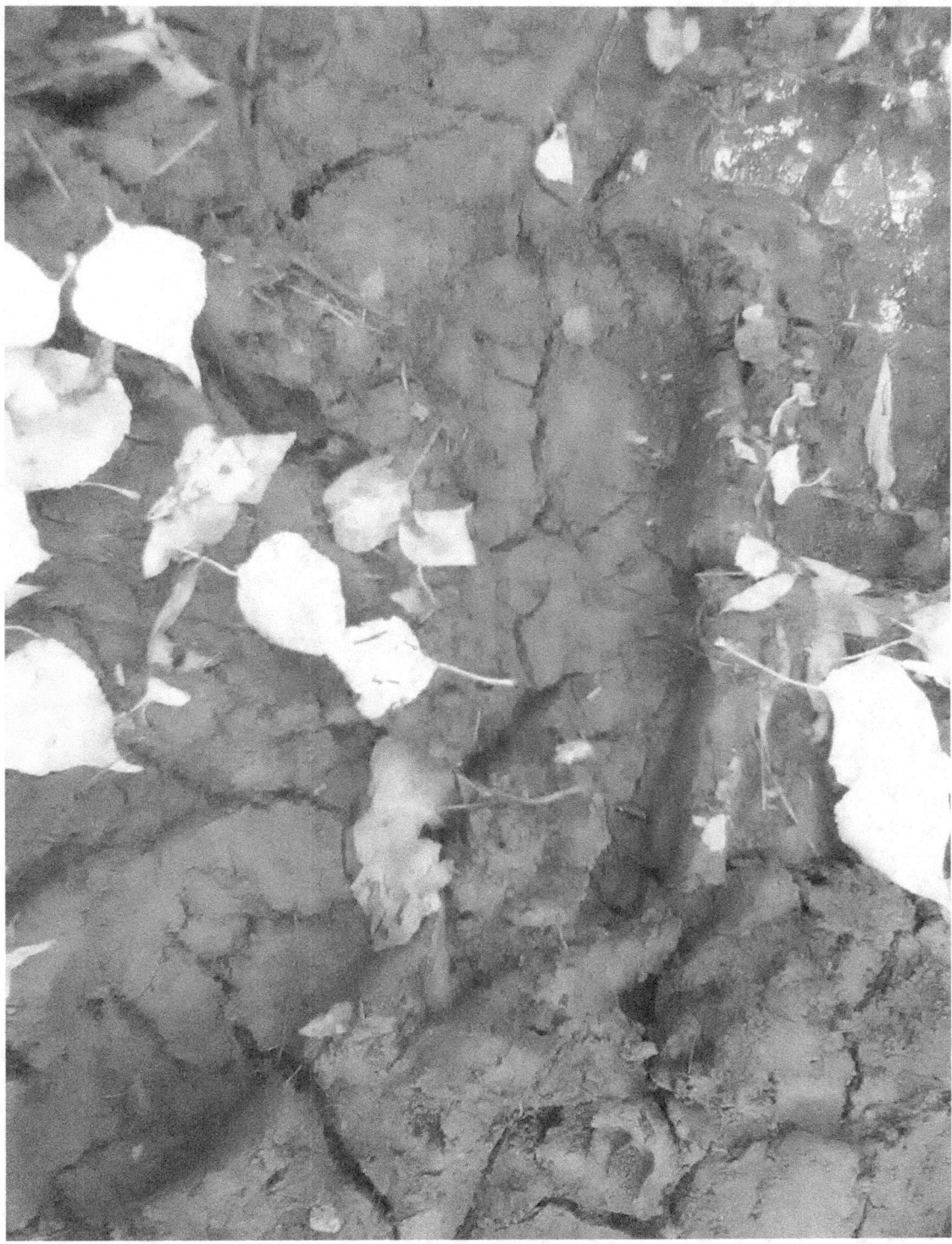

Partially destroyed track in mud. Courtesy Mark Birchette

Item 19P

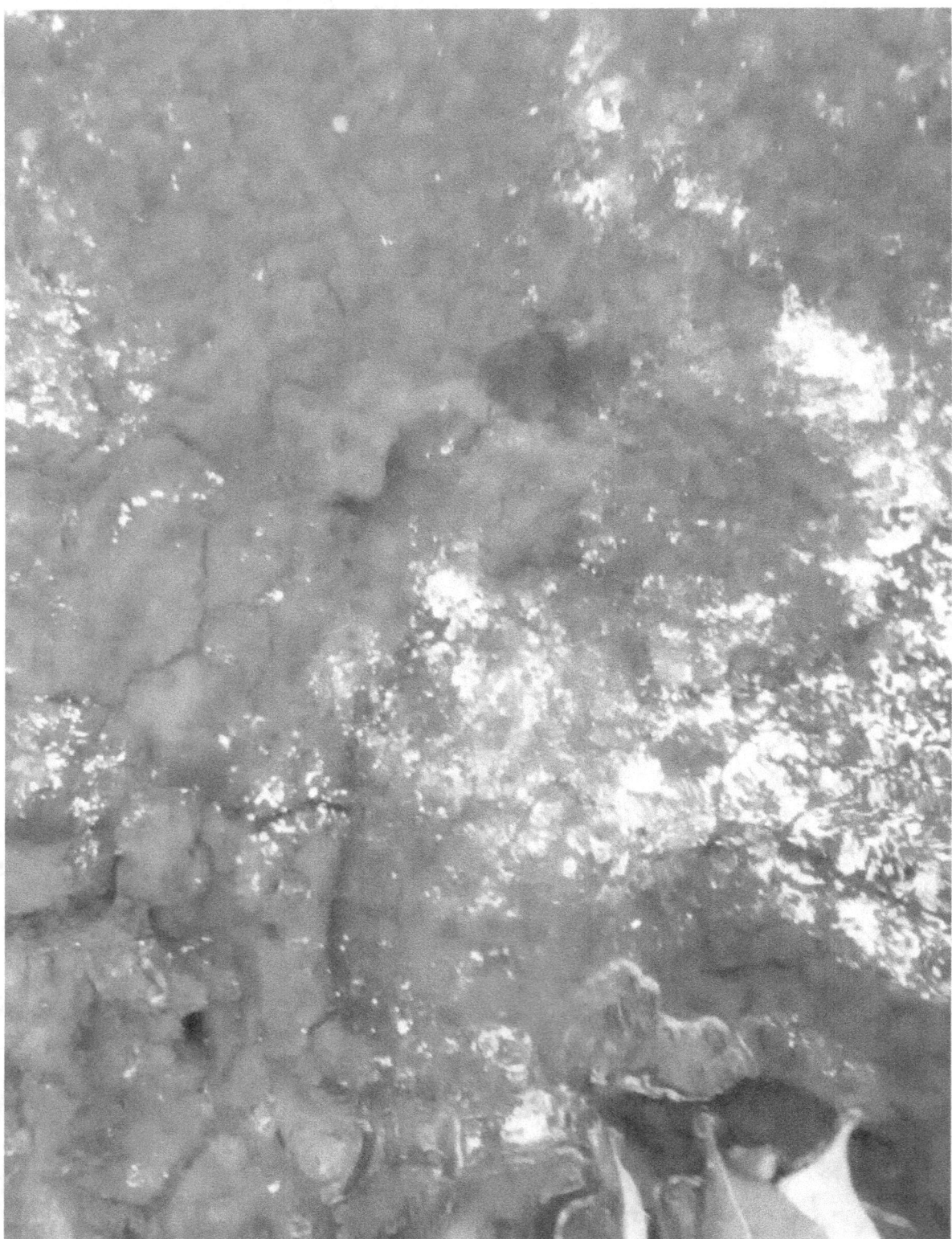

Same line of prints (in water) courtesy mark Birchette

Item 19Q

Line of juvenile tracks near Happy Camp California (Jim Karl photograph)

Item 19R

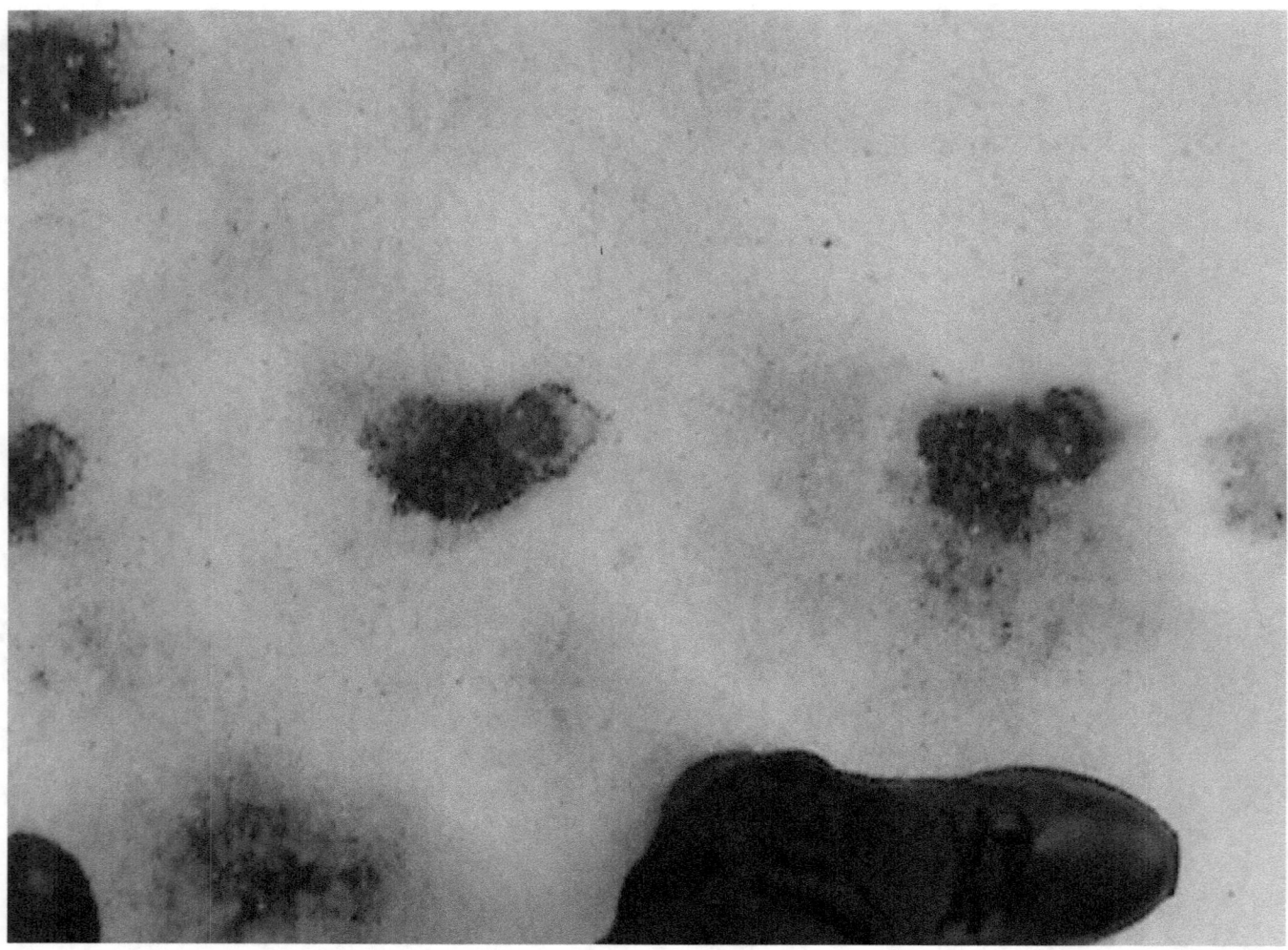

Close up of Jim Karl tracks.

Item 19S

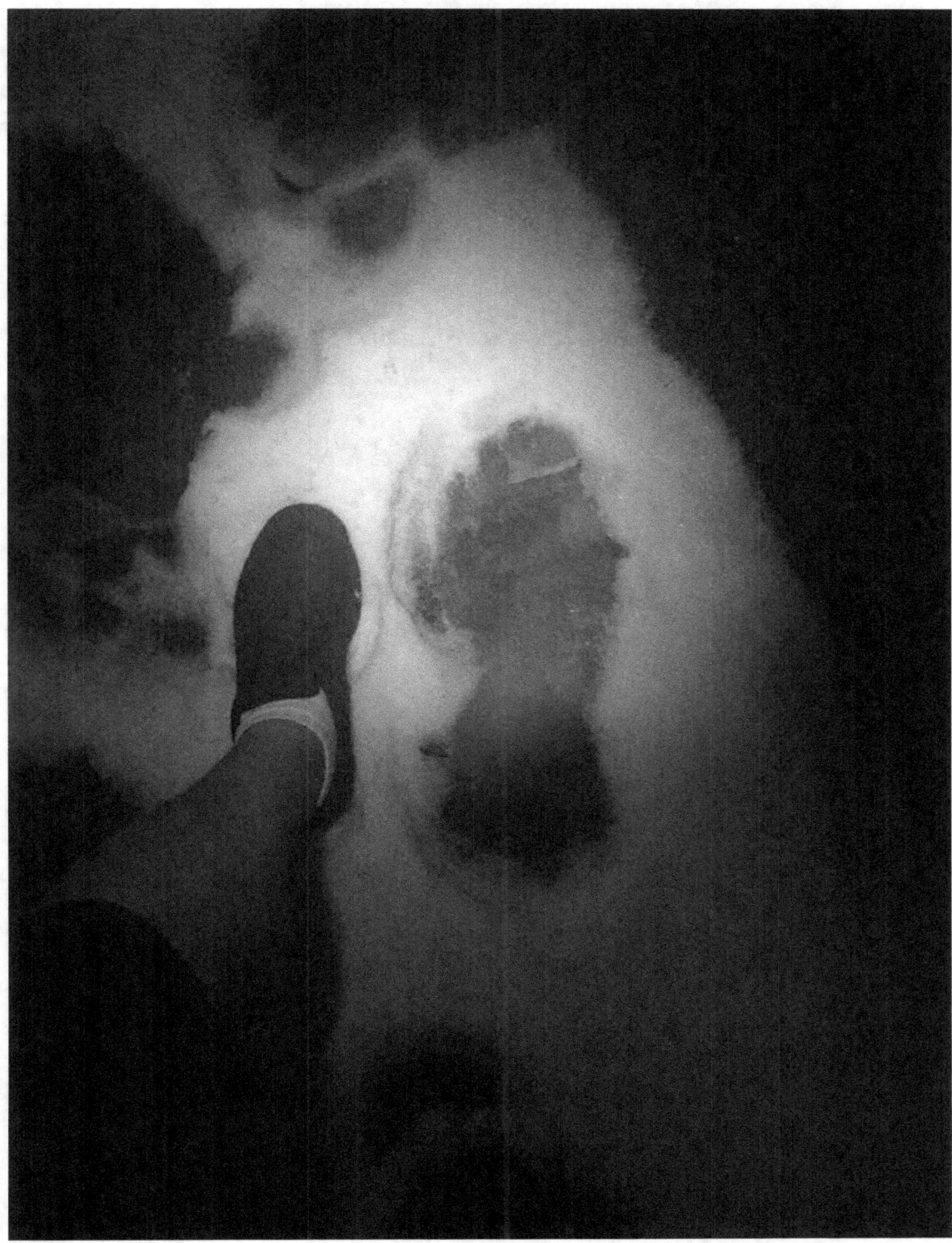

Melting tracks in snow, courtesy James Gibson.

Item 19T

Infant Sasquatch footprint, courtesy Wynn L.

Item 19U

Footprint from Iowa

Item 19V

Footprint from Utah.

Item 19W

Another print from Canadian moose hunters.

Item 19X

Another track in the line of prints found by Canadian moose hunters.

Item 19Y

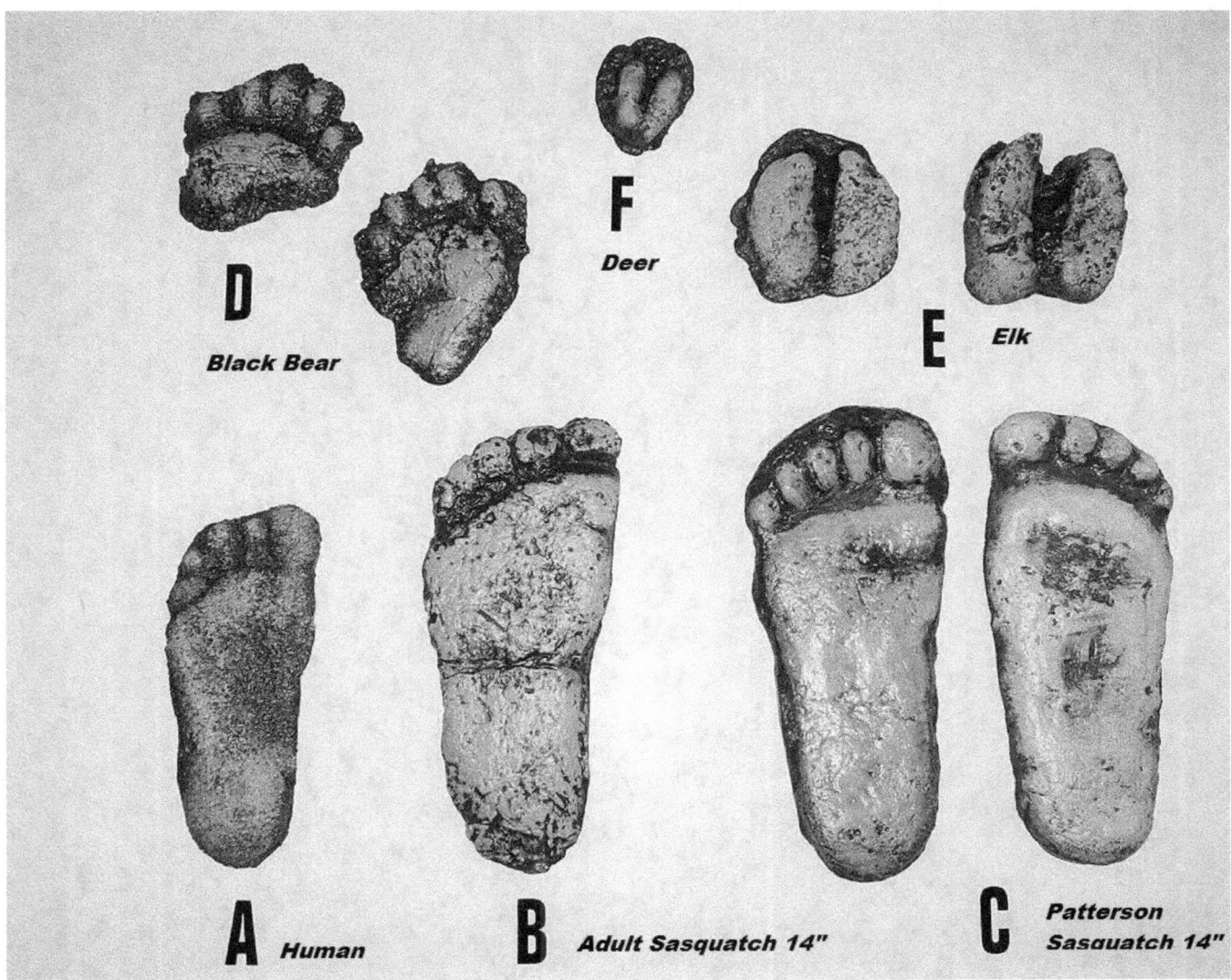

Comparison of 2 different Sasquatches, human, black bear, elk and deer to demonstrate size perspective.

PLAINTIFF: I wish to enter into the record some black bear footprint photographs for distinction between them and the items in 19A through 19Y. They will be so noted as items 20A through 20

Item 20A

Front and rear footprints of a black bear, Mt. Adams Washington.

Item 20B

Bear track from Northern California.

Item 20C

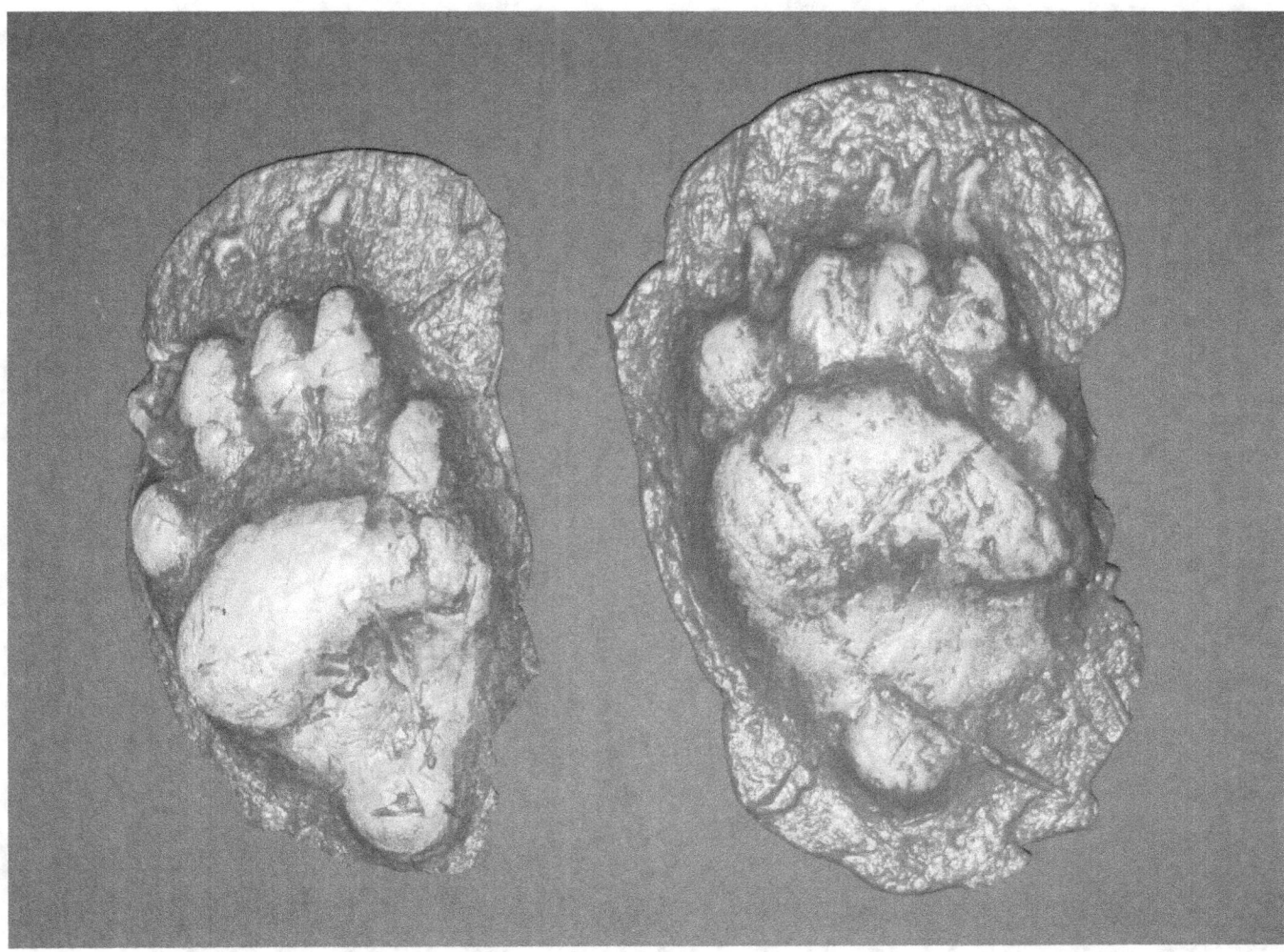

Plaster casts of black bear tracks by the author, Northern California.

Item 20D

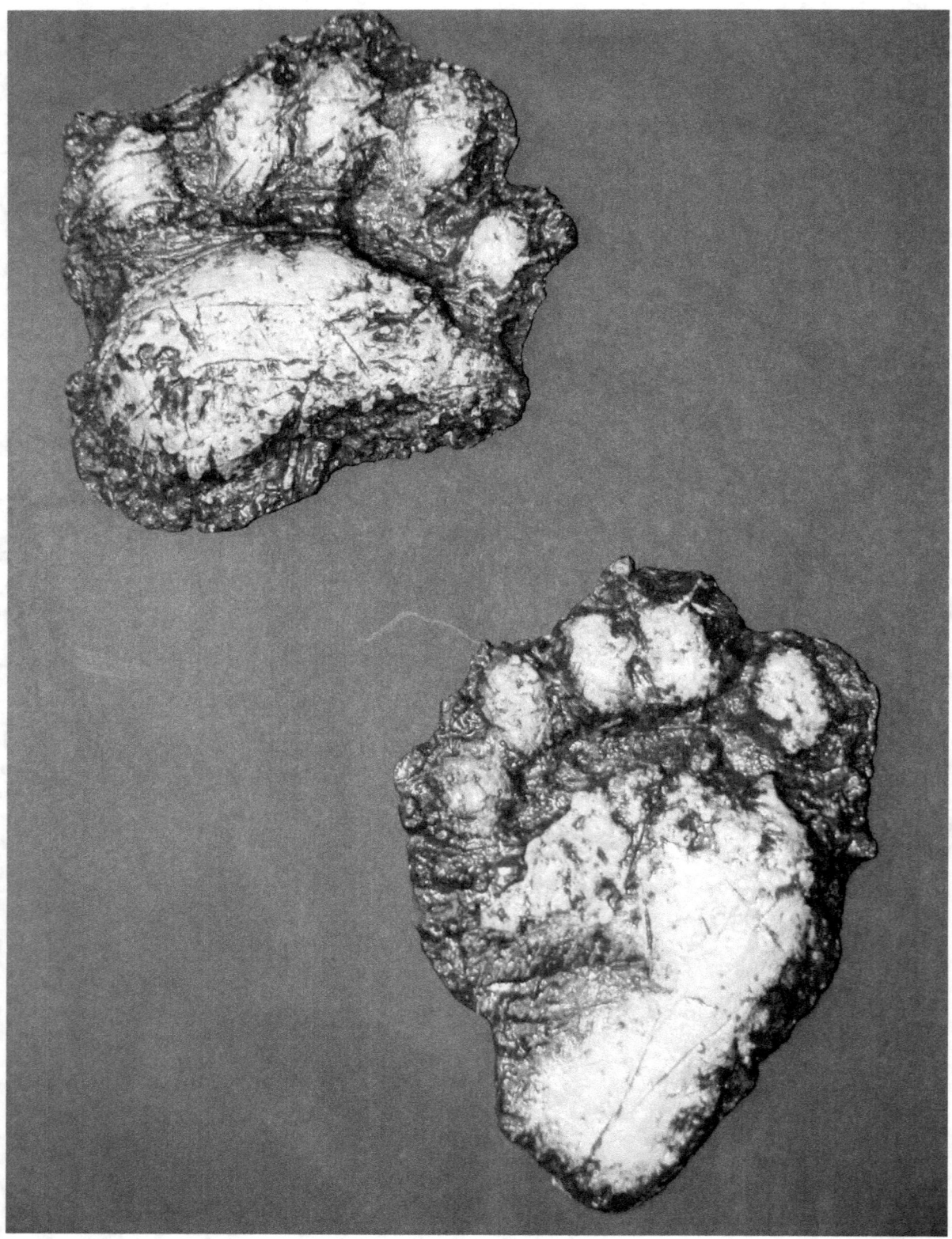

Plaster casts of black bear tracks, front and hind feet by the author, Northern California.

Item 20E

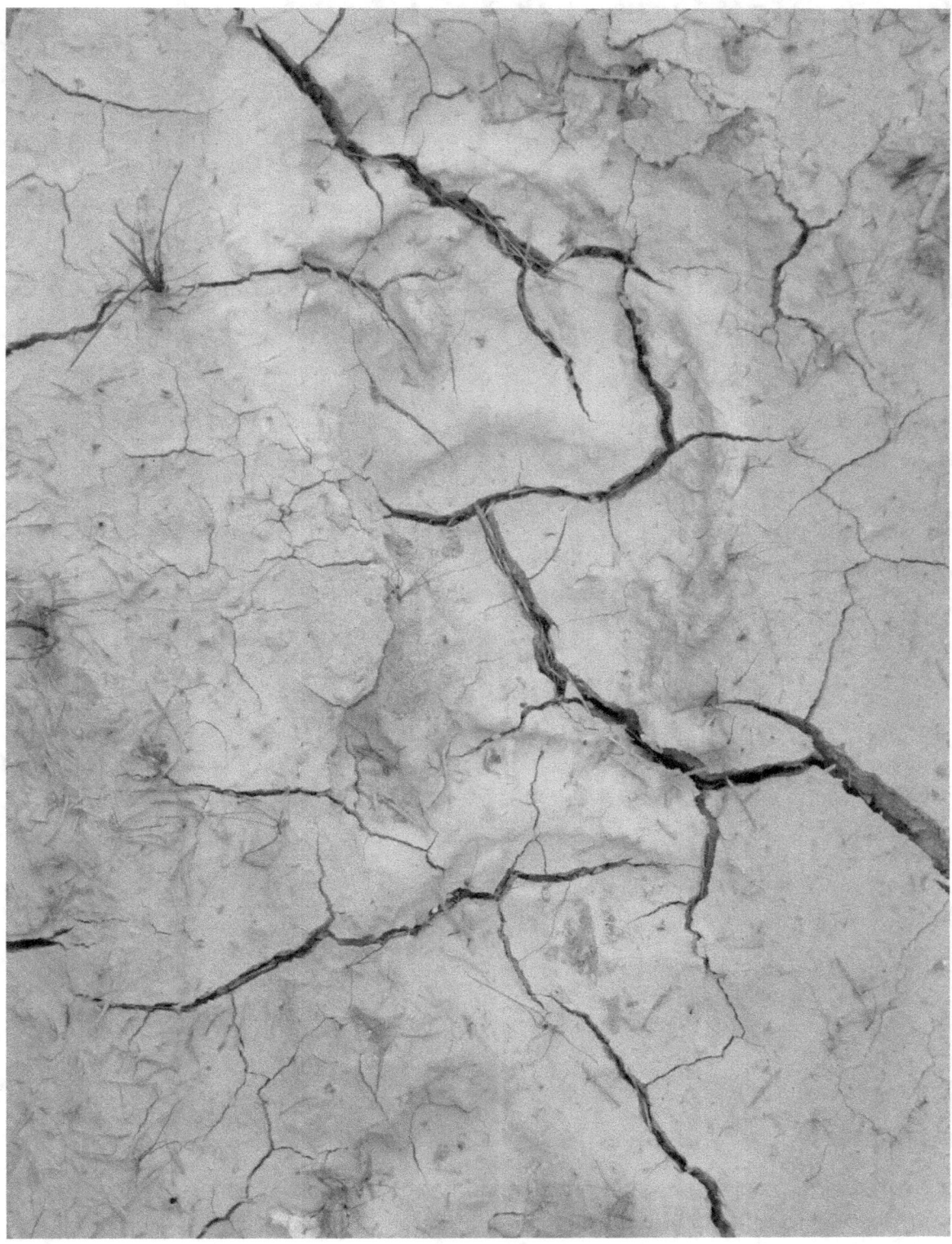

Three overlapping footprints from a black bear, overall length 17 inches. Photo by the author.

Item 20F

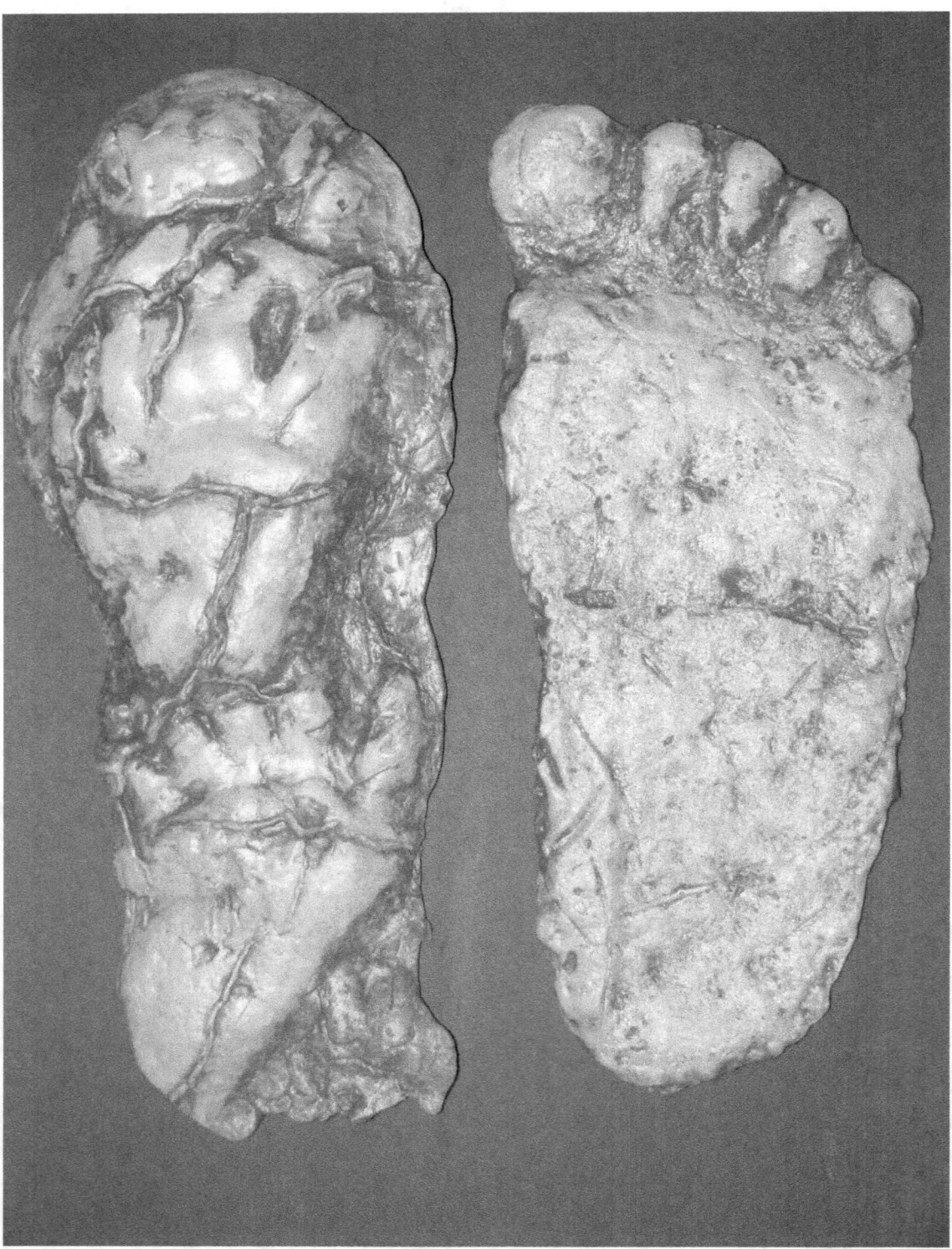

Plaster cast of overlapping bear tracks alongside Sasquatch track, both measure 17 inches and both cast in Northern California within two miles of each other. These are not easily confused with the other as overlapping bear tracks normally occur only every fifth set of prints in a line. Photo the author.

PLAINTIFF: I would at this time like to enter evidence of hand impressions into the record. I will enter them as items 21A through 21

JUDGE: Proceed council.

Item 21A

The first recorded hand print impressions come from Ivan Marx, an outdoorsman and photographer. Marx became a hoaxer in later years and was totally discredited. Anthropologist Grover Krantz wrote the following regarding the hand prints, two of which Marx found in 1970 in eastern Washington.

By Grover S. Krantz

Two plaster casts have been obtained of handprints of the reputed Sasquatch. The prints measure more than half again greater than normal human hands and are relatively very broad. The thumb is non-opposable and there is correspondingly no elevation of the thenar eminence. Characteristics of these handprints, as with associated footprints, suggest their makers were gigantic hominids.

The sasquatch, or bigfoot, is an often reported, but thus far unverified bipedal primate which supposedly lives in western North America. Descriptions by eye-witnesses are of hairy, man-like forms eight or nine feet tall. The most tangible evidence of the species until recently has been their human-like footprints which have been measured, photographed, and cast in plaster in large numbers.

During the summer of 1970, handprints of two of these animals were photographed and plaster casts of them were made by Ivan Marx, a game guide in northeastern Washington state. Marx loaned the original casts to the writer who then made latex molds from them in order to produce exact duplicates for further study. The copies are illustrated here rather than the original casts so that they would have a uniform color.

The authenticity of these casts is impossible to demonstrate by any direct means. That they were not faked is strongly indicated by the fact that these are only the best two out of several prints that were cast, and that photographs of many more were taken. For a hoaxer to have made them all would have involved a considerable amount of difficulty.

The two good prints described here are both of left hands which were imprinted flat into soft ground showing all digits and outlines of the palms. The longer print shows all digits somewhat flexed and their tips were well indented into damp ground. It measures 292 mm. in actual length to the end of digit III, but the hand would be closer to 300 mm. long if fully extended.

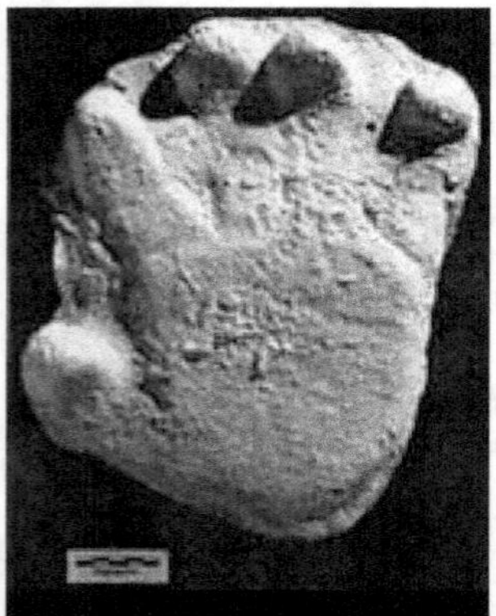

Fig. 1. Plaster cast of handprints of sasquatch from northern Washington. This is the longer of the two handprint casts.

Its palm is 174 mm. wide at the distal ends of the metacarpals, thumb excluded. The shorter print is more nearly flat with a length of 265 mm. and a breadth of 185 mm. Only the second digit of this hand is slightly flexed. Other dimensions not given here can be taken by the reader from the photographs, Figs. 1 and 2.

Footprints corresponding to the long hand are almost 500 mm. long (19½ inches). The shorter hand is reportedly associated with 432 mm. Footprints (17 inch), cast copies of which are also in the writer's possession. It can be seen that the size ratio of hand to foot is similar to that encountered in man.

The hands which supposedly made these imprints can be compared and contrasted with those of recent man in several particulars. Most obvious is their immense size — in linear dimensions they are more than half again greater than an average European's hand. My own hand, of average proportions but quite large, measures 205 mm. in length and 95 mm, in breadth. The sasquatch hands are thus 46.4% and 29.3% longer than mine, and 83.2% and 94.6% broader, giving a mean of over 63% greater in these two dimensions. This is at least commensurate with claimed stature estimates.

The hands are relatively very broad. My own hand has a breadth which is 46.4% of its length, while the corresponding figure for the long sasquatch hand is 58.1% and for the shorter hand it is 69.8%. The major difference between the two is in their finger lengths. Actually, the short hand has a larger palm, both in length and breadth, while the third digit appears to be only 33% of the total hand length if the measurement is correct. In the long hand, that digit clearly makes up 42% of its length, a quite human proportion.

The fingers are well separated from each other and the divisions between their phalangeal segments can be seen in several cases, especially in digits II and V of the longer hand. The fingers are all relatively broad, especially at their tips, and are nearly the same size as one another within the same hand. There is very little decrease in length and breadth from digit III to digit V as in man. This relative unifomity in finger sizes is interestingly matched by a near uniformity in toe sizes as well.

Finger positions are also somewhat unusual, and in the same way in each hand. Only digit V is clearly extending in a straight line from its metacarpal. The other three fingers fan out considerably so that digit II appears to be strongly abducted toward the thumb from what should be its more normal, or human, position. In other words, the long axes of all four fingers meet at, and radiate from, a point at the base of the palm, not in the center line of the hand, but rather on its edge under the fifth digit (the hypothenar eminence). The significance of this is not evident.

Probably the most unexpected feature indicated for these hands is the apparent non-opposability of the thumb, which is clearly evident in both individuals. In the short hand the palmar surface of the thumb is quite flat and is in the same plane as all of the fingers. In the larger hand the thumb flexion parallels that of the other digits in digging into the ground. Still, these thumbs both separate from near the base of the palm and extend out to the side in a quite human direction.

Fig. 2. Shorter sasquatch handprint cast.

The thenar pad, or eminence, at the base of the thumb is virtually non-existent. In this eminence would be found the major muscles (abductor pollicis brevis, opponens pollicis, and flexor pollicis brevis) which in man pull the opposable thumb in various ways across the palm. Since in this case the thumbs do not oppose, it is consistent that the thenar area is not thickened. It would require someone quite familiar with the anatomy of the human hand to make the connection between a non-opposable thumb and an absence of a thenar eminence. This tends to support the authenticity of these handprints. Ivan Marx has no known training in human anatomy, and no other person could have planted the many impressions without leaving his own track for Marx to observe.

On the larger handprint, along the distal segment of digit II, there can be seen a series of parallel ridges and furrows. These run perpendicularly to the long axis of the finger in a position corresponding to human fingertip prints of the arch type (Fig. 3). The ridges are almost 2 mm. apart and are more closely spaced toward the tip of the finger. This spacing is considerable, being just twice the amount found in the ridges of my own fingers at the same location. One could suggest another possible explanation of these ridges: that they are the grain in the piece of wood from which this hand was carved. If this were the case, the ridges should be narrower than the furrows, however, the reverse is the case here as with human fingerprints.

A transverse crease can be seen in the palm of the longer cast under digits III to V. Other palm creases are vaguely indicated, but their identification is uncertain.

There are many other irregularities in the cast's surfaces which cannot be identified in terms of human anatomy. Most of these irregularities no doubt resulted from unevenness in the dirt into which the hands were pressed, and also from various particles which fell into the impressions before the casts were made.

Both hands give the appearance of being very flat in palms and fingers with all margins turning abruptly. This may result from callus formation which is especially prominent around all of these margins. The same kind of abrupt edges occur in the footprints associated with these hands. The larger individual shows less of this callousing in both hand and foot.

In most respects these handprints show about what might be expected if one grants the reality of the creatures reportedly seen making the gigantic footprints. The only totally unexpected trait is the non-opposable thumb. The hand strongly suggests one designed for digging into the ground and for raking berries from bushes rather than being primarily for manipulating objects. Flexing all five digits in the same direction would best facilitate the suggested functions. Heavy callousing, including along all margins, would also be expected to follow from such uses.

Fig. 3. Tip of digit II of longer handprint showing ridges and furrows.

Another peculiarity, not indicated in the illustrations here, is the evident rigidity of the hands. I have examined three different casts of imprints by the same left hand of the larger individual, and photographs of still more mpressions of both of his hands. In all cases the fingers and thumb are in very nearly, though not exactly, the same relative positions and degrees of flexion. Photographs of more imprints of the shorter hand indicate the same thing. In contrast, their footprints (from numerous casts and photographs) often show variations in toe positions. Unlike in man, finger mobility is not greater than that of the toes, and is possibly less.

A final item of interest is the relative length of the thumb which differs between the two hands. The shorter one has a relative thumb length which is comparable to man's. The longer hand has a relatively shorter thumb, even after a liberal allowance is made for unflexing it. No figures can be given with any accuracy because the proximal measuring point is too vaguely located. This contrasts markedly with the finger lengths; the short hand having both the shortest fingers and the longest thumb. Such a high degree of individual ariation might be expected to occur in a very sparse population of any large mammal. The casts illustrated here are available for examination be serious investigators by contacting me in Pullman, Washington.

An interesting problem is created by the publication of this description. Future reports of handprints, with photographs or plaster casts, might be suspected of being faked if they show all the characteristics described here. However, any experienced hunter or game guide should have no difficulty recognizing imprints from a live animal as opposed to impressions made by solid, rigid forms.

Item 21B

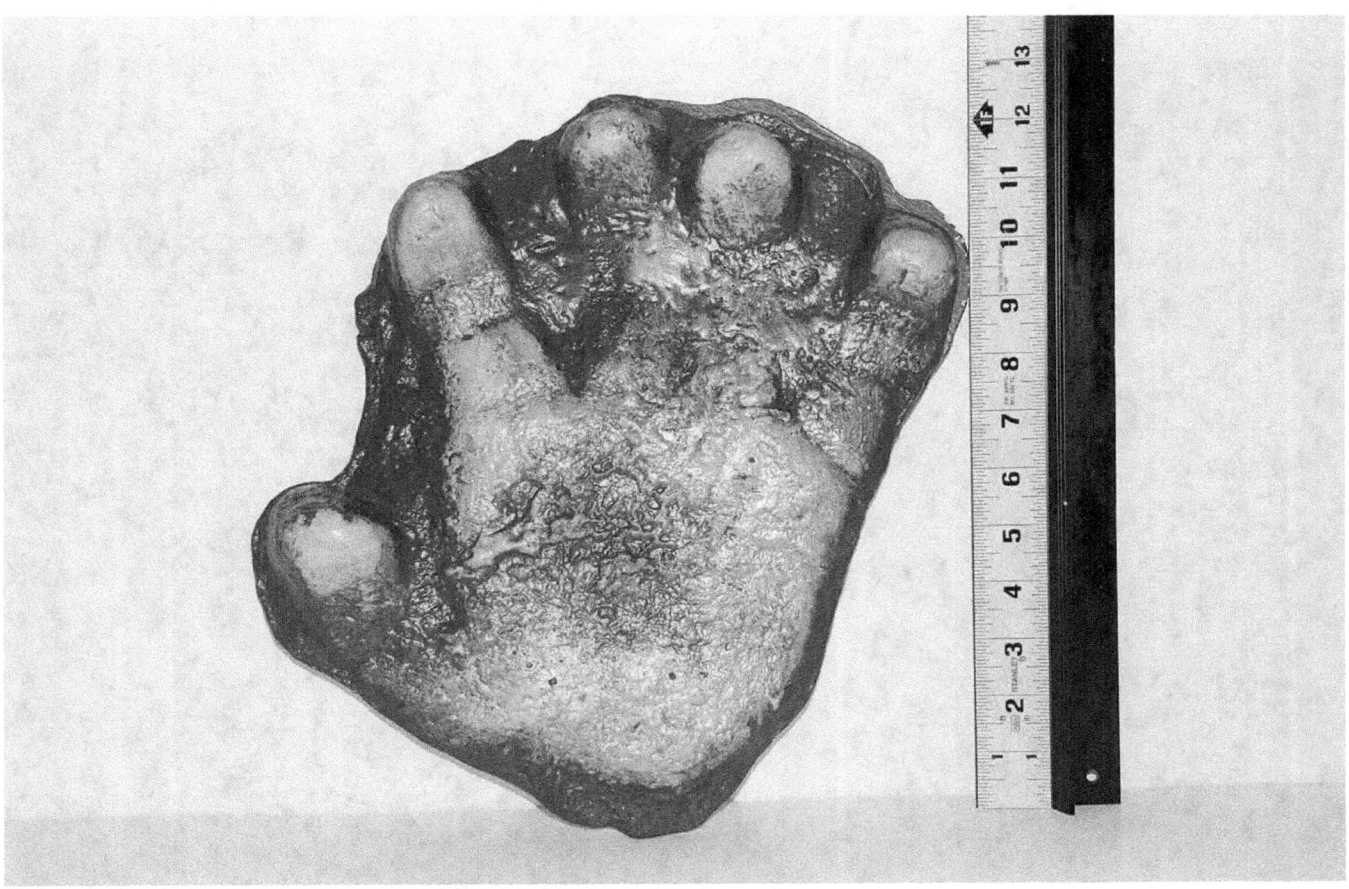

Plaster cast of one of the impressions Ivan Marx cast.

Item 21C

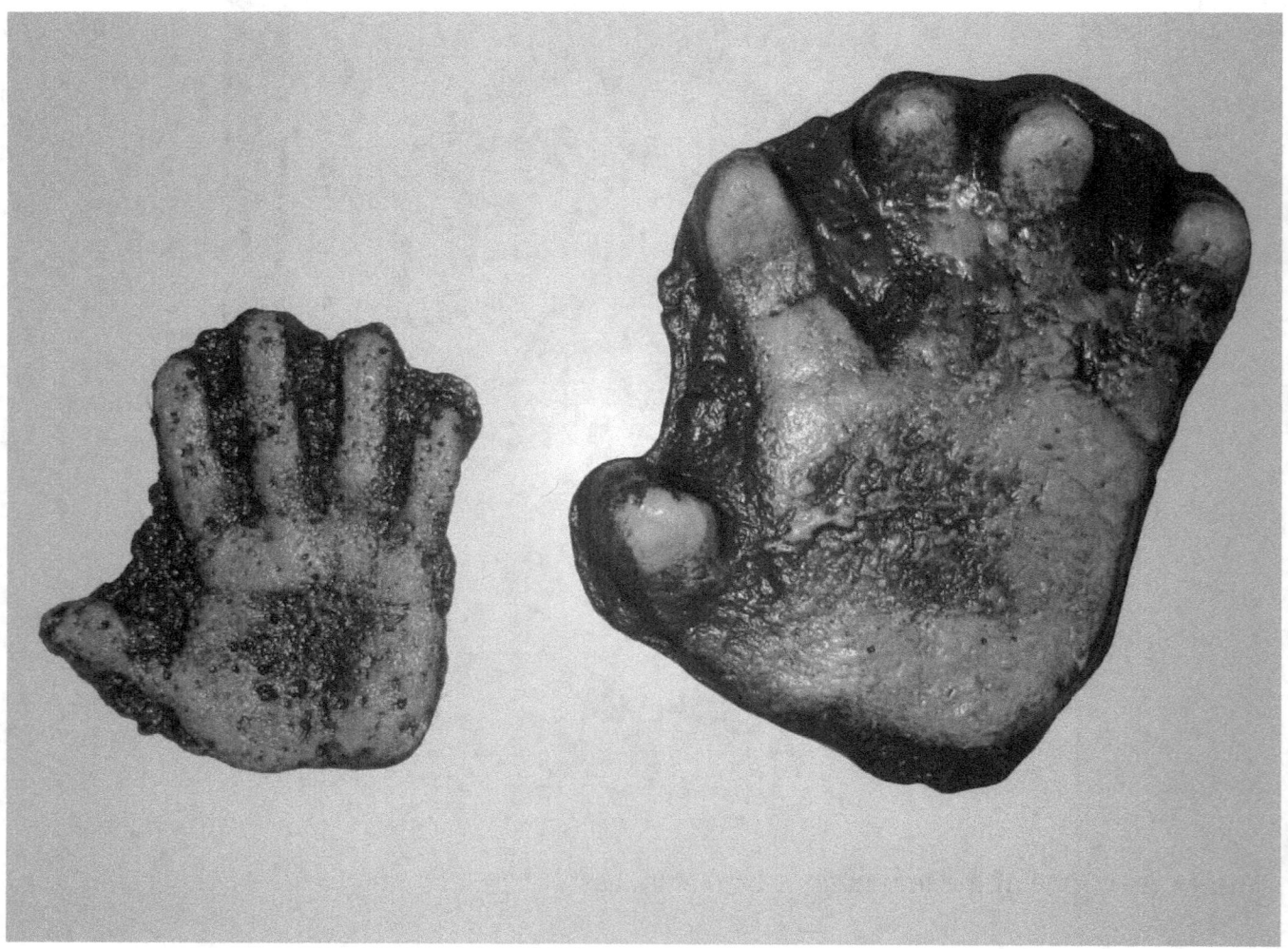

Plaster casts of a human hand left, and the Marx Sasquatch hand right.

Item 21D

Dave Gibson statement regarding hand prints on his car.

My wife got me up at 5:30. She heard, and then saw, a Sasquatch outside our cabin. She also found this small hand print on the back of our car. I don't know what it is about our car, but they seem to love to touch it. This one is obviously a juvenile and small. It also trashed a bunch of small trees next to our cabin on Sunday night. It seems like both prints that I've found, the Sasquatch hands are very cupped, not flat like a human print.

Item 21E

Courtesy Dave Gibson

Item 21F

Courtesy Dave Gibson

Item 21G

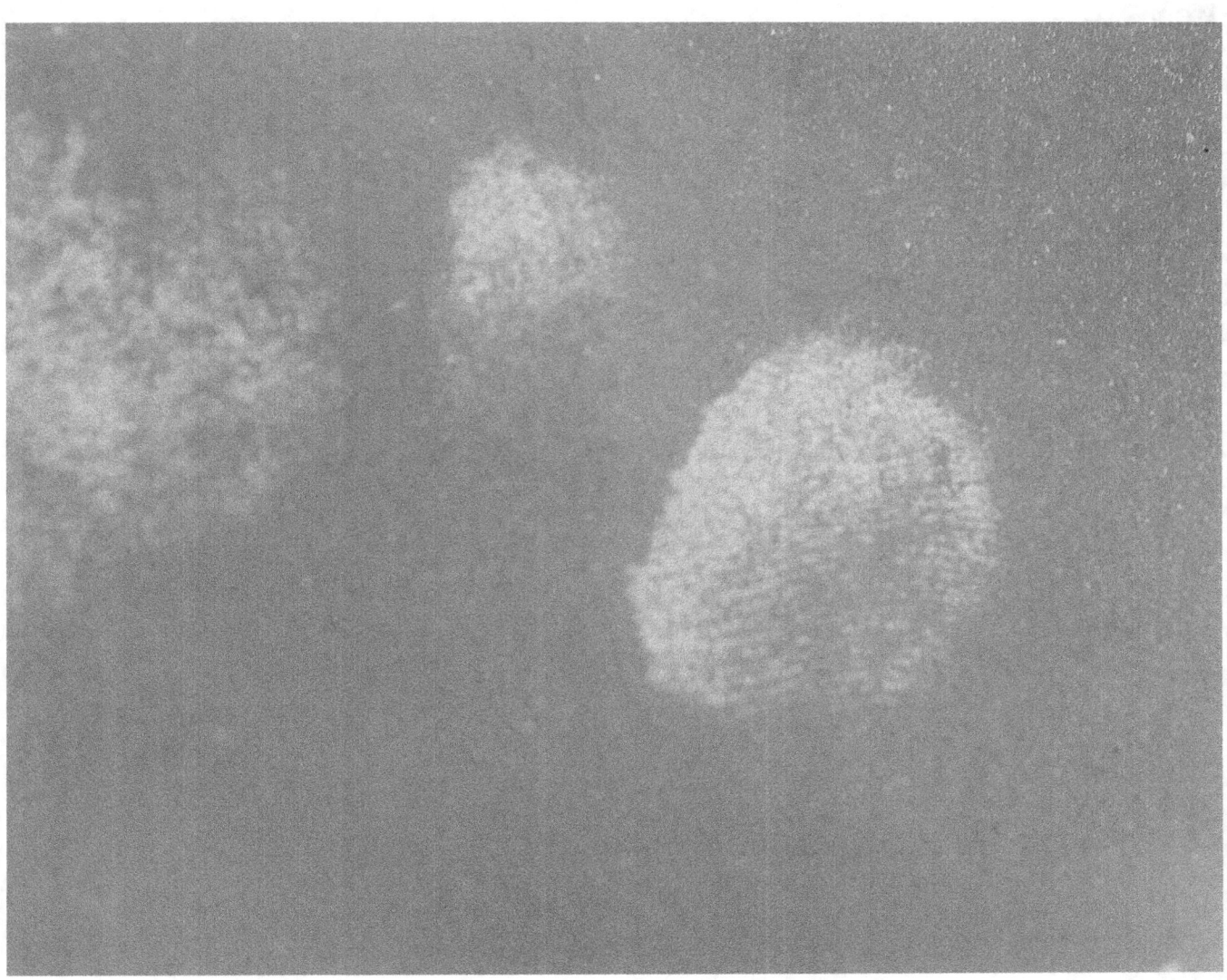

Courtesy Dave Gibson

Item 21H

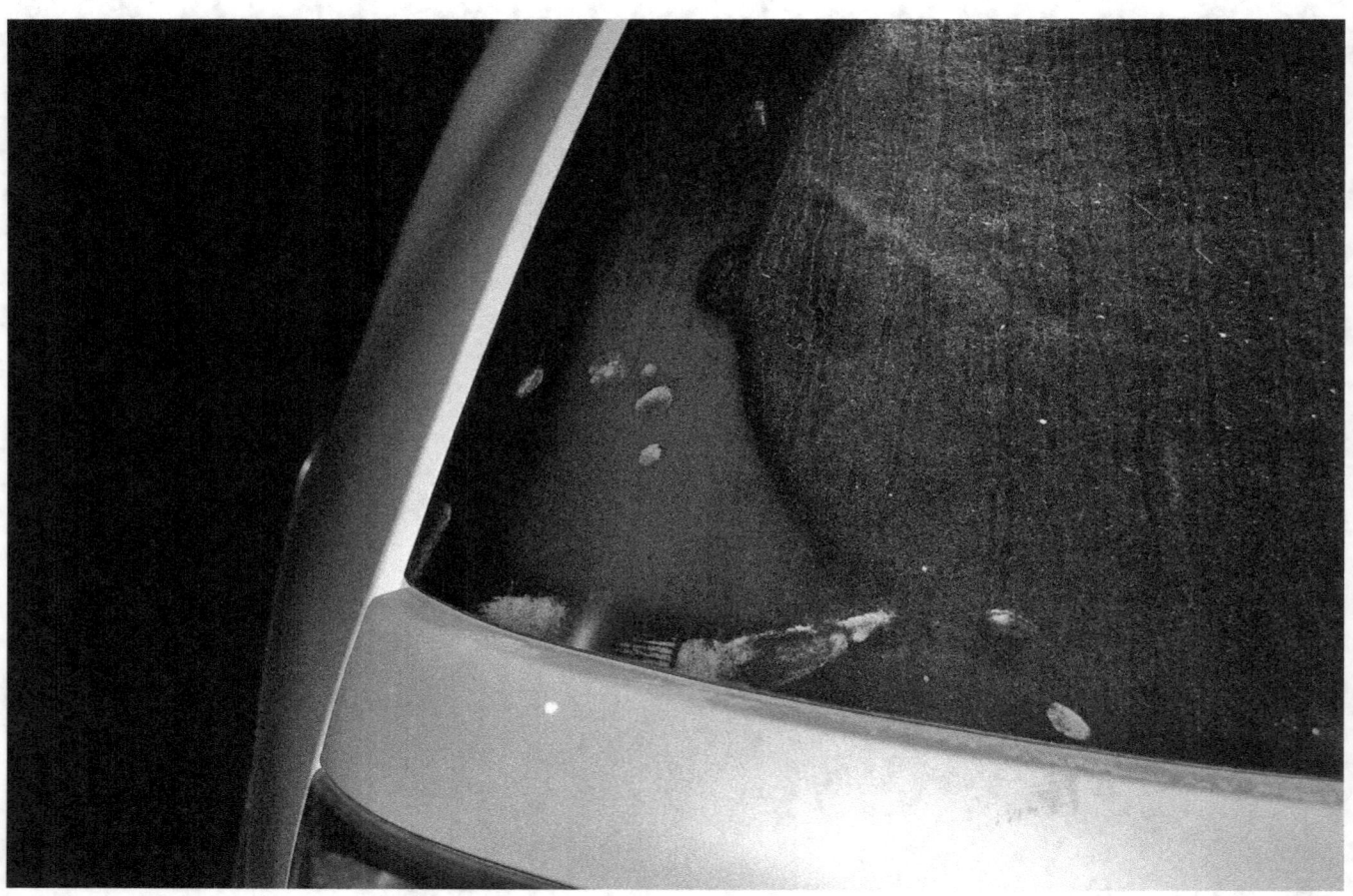

Courtesy Dave Gibson

Item 21I

Courtesy Dave Gibson

Item 21J

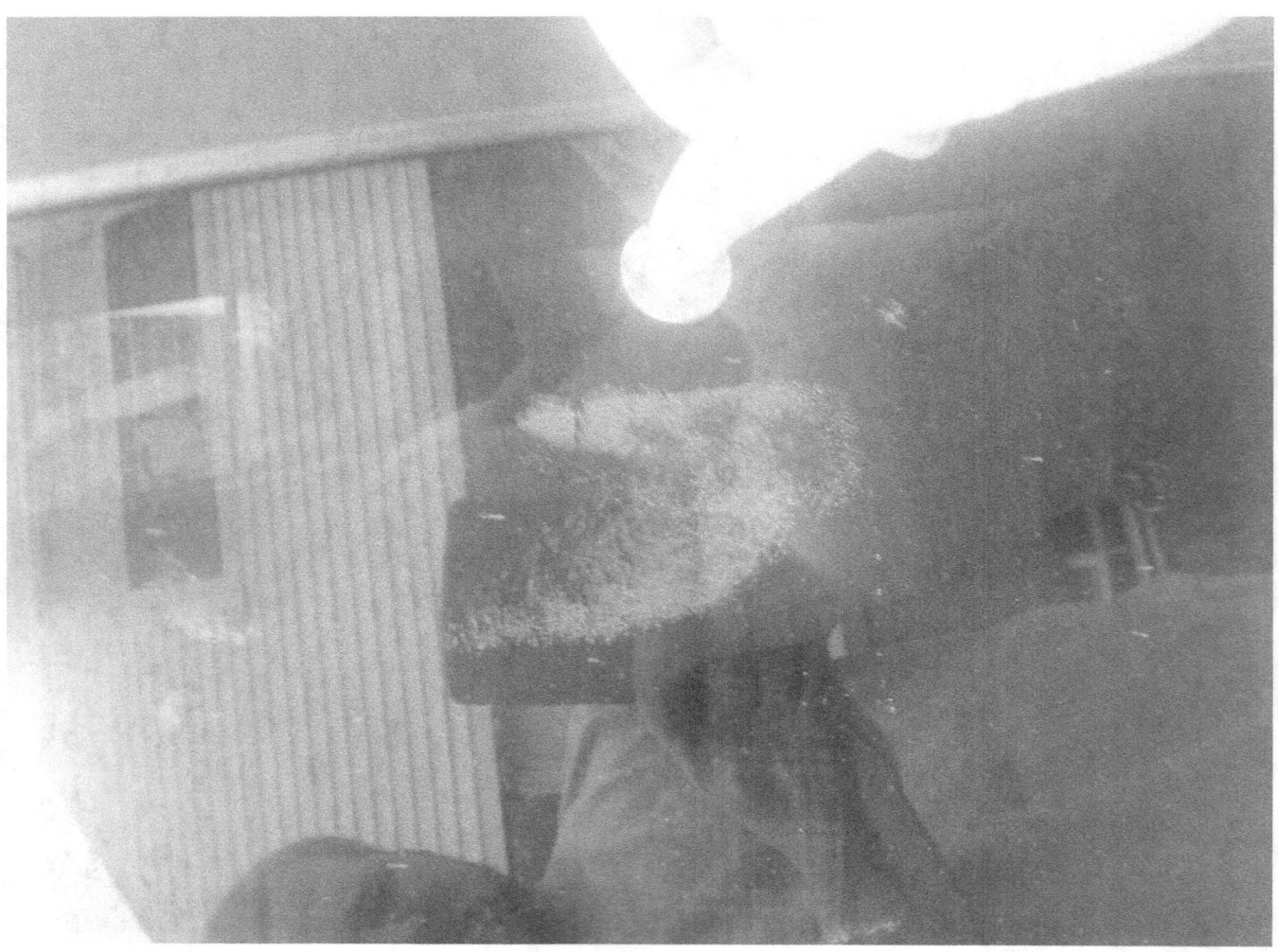

Sasquatch hand impression left on truck window. A veteran crime scene investigator working for a large city prepared the print, before he could lift the print it rained losing the print. He did remark that it was nothing like he had ever seen in his long career.

Item 21K

Another perspective of the print in Item 21J

Item 21L

The following is testimony from a witness in a southwestern state:

There's a creek, named Talala Creek which is really close to town. I've heard that Bigfoots will travel the creek lines, etc. The experience I had was either a chimp or Bigfoot. The reason I suggest it's a chimp is because back in the 1940's or so, someone in Talala had a chimp as a pet. A few years ago, around 3pm on a sunny clear day with maybe a few scattered little puffy clouds, my Mom and I were walking out looking for my sister's cat. She was talking and I was looking around and I noticed this huge black hairy thing sitting on top of an abandoned house (it's over or about 100 years old and its entire block that it sits on is wooded; although now the new owner is clearing it out so whatever lived there is now gone) facing away from me. I was shocked! I couldn't interrupt Mom to tell her and by the time I got a chance to talk it went silently over the roof without making any noise whatsoever! This entire block was full of lots of trees and high tall weeds, bushes etc. Birds were always nesting and singing but that day it was dead quiet. This house sits inside the town limits which surprised me that something like this was inside because there were neighbors all around it. So Mom never saw it. I didn't have my camera with me that day and I've kicked myself ever since, and when I walk past that house, I still feel my eyes drawn up to the roof. Since that day, I take my camera when I go for a walk. I must mention that this roof was metal and sharp pointed - meaning it wasn't flat or sort of flat like today's roofs are - and so it seemed content to sitting up there. I also saw that when it went over the side (this house is a 2 story house and I've been in it about 3 years ago) that its bottom was white and hairy. About 2 weeks later, I was walking around that particular block on a Wednesday night, it was dusk and as I neared closer I could hear what sounded like to me monkey sounds. There was a trailer nearby and so I thought that perhaps their TV was on loud. As I neared their house, I noticed their door and windows were all closed. The monkey sound continued by to my right (the trailer was to my left) and I got scared. Then just as abruptly, the sounds stopped. I walked quickly and didn't bother to look in the trees that lined the area. Sometimes I wish I had because maybe I'd seen the face, but then I would've been even more scared. So after a few feet of walking away, the noises started up again. (Sorry to be so long.) About the same time, my sister who lives just down the street from this block was babysitting; the kids told her that they saw a monkey in the trees. She didn't believe them until I told her my story. Now my dad owns this property where they saw it and I live now next door to my sister.

There are some more weird events that I'm not sure are related to Bigfoot, but I can tell you those later to see what you think. Well, there is one instance; my brothers live across from my parents where I used to live until I moved out. I heard this noise twice (my brother heard it from inside the house) I was outside at dark and felt something watching me from my brother's 5 Russian olive trees near a streetlight. I heard this noise that sounded like a cross between a pig squealing and a horse being dragged down - that's the best description I can give - it scared my brother's chickens and caused one to lay her eggs prematurely in the barn.

No smell. No tracks. But other weird events happened. I don't want to take up too much of your time now, but I'd love to tell you when you have some free time. My brother's doubt in Bigfoot, basically it's just my sister and I that believe. It's hard telling these stories because people ask me "What have you been drinking?" I find it weird because I'm a Pastor's daughter and wouldn't make up a story like this, especially when we live near Nowata and further north to the Noxie monster.

I just talked to my sister to see if she remembered the year, she said it was in 2007. They moved into their house in 2004. She reminded me that in 2006 around 6am one summer night she was awakened by a high shrill whistle 2 different times.

I looked up the time I heard the weird noises because I was taking photos in the dark of a spider at the end of my mom's porch and it was Sept. 2011. Do you think the strange noise I heard could've been a Bigfoot?

Just about maybe 3 Fridays ago around 3am my youngest brother was leaving for work (all 3 of my siblings leave about the same time because they work at the same place) he told my sister he saw light green eyes or gray eyes about 3-4 feet high near some trees starting at him and then it turned its head and was gone. He didn't know what it was, but it was in the same area as the weird pig noises on his property. Not to confuse with the monkey noises because that was on a different block and a different year.

The same time frame that that noise happened at my brothers, with the chickens something had picked up my brothers white bucket (without handles) that had much in it and carried it across their lots without spilling it and I took photos of that because it was too far away u felt for a raccoon or whatever to pick it up and carry it without spilling it. There was also what looked like finger marks on the inside as though someone out something was scraping the bottom"

Item 21M

Closed and covered containers next to the witnesses home as described in testimony.

Item 21N

Bucket taken away from storage location.

Item 210

A second bucket carried away from witnesses home, emptied of food contents.

Item 21P

Finger markings inside bucket.

Item 21Q

Same bucket, different perspective.

Item 21R

Contents of bucket scraped.

Item 21S

This and the following photographs show the side of a hand scraped away the top covering soil to expose the soft clay underneath, there appear to be 4 finger marks, the one on the right is long and not as easy to discern. This was discovered in Northern California near a very active place Sasquatches inhabit and scat and footprints are often found.

Item 21T

Item 21U

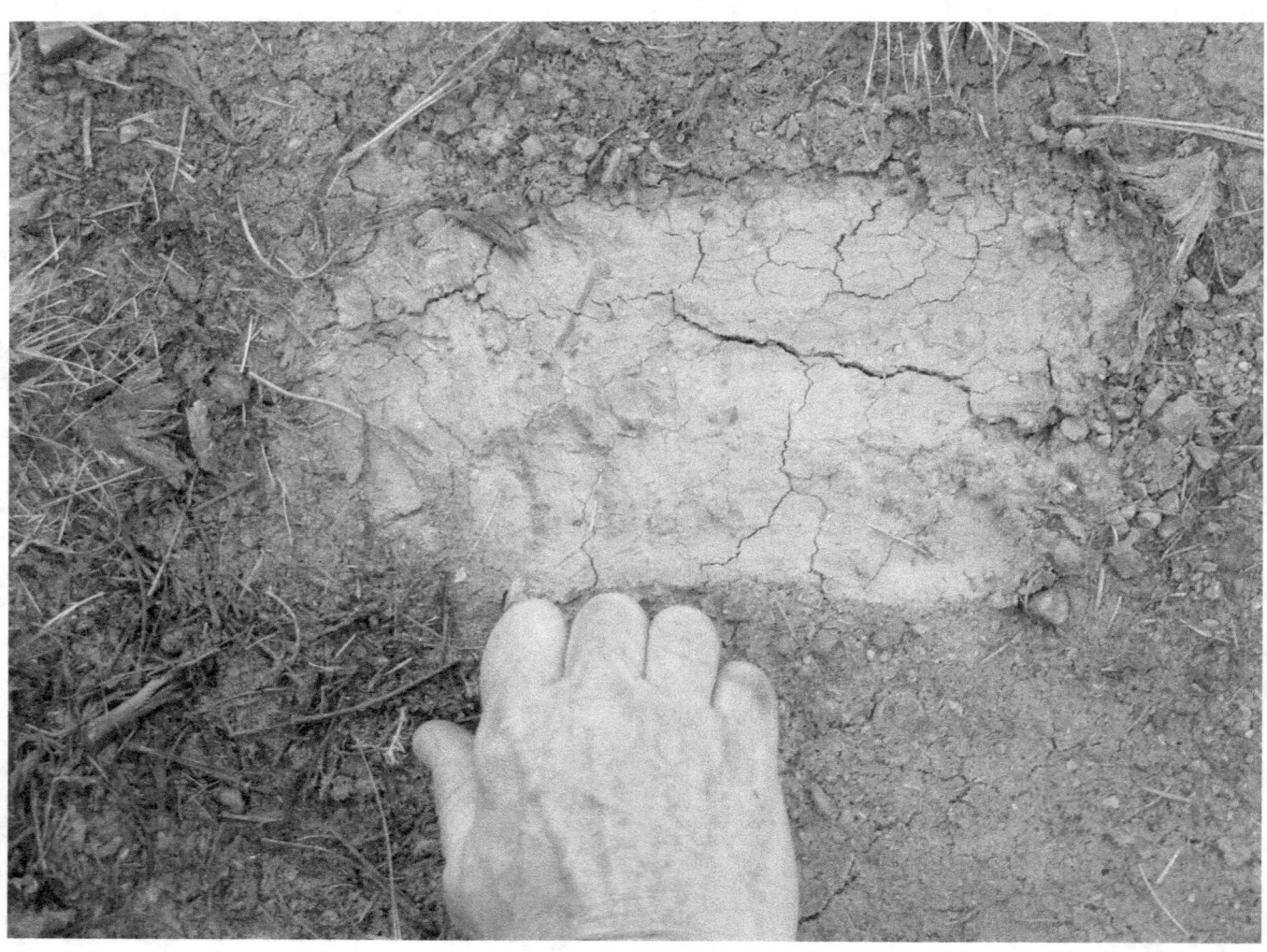

Item 21V

Item 21W

Hand print discovered northern Nevada by a Native American gentleman.

Item 21X

Second Sasquatch hand print found by Native American gentleman and his children in a very remote region of northern Nevada.

Item 21Y

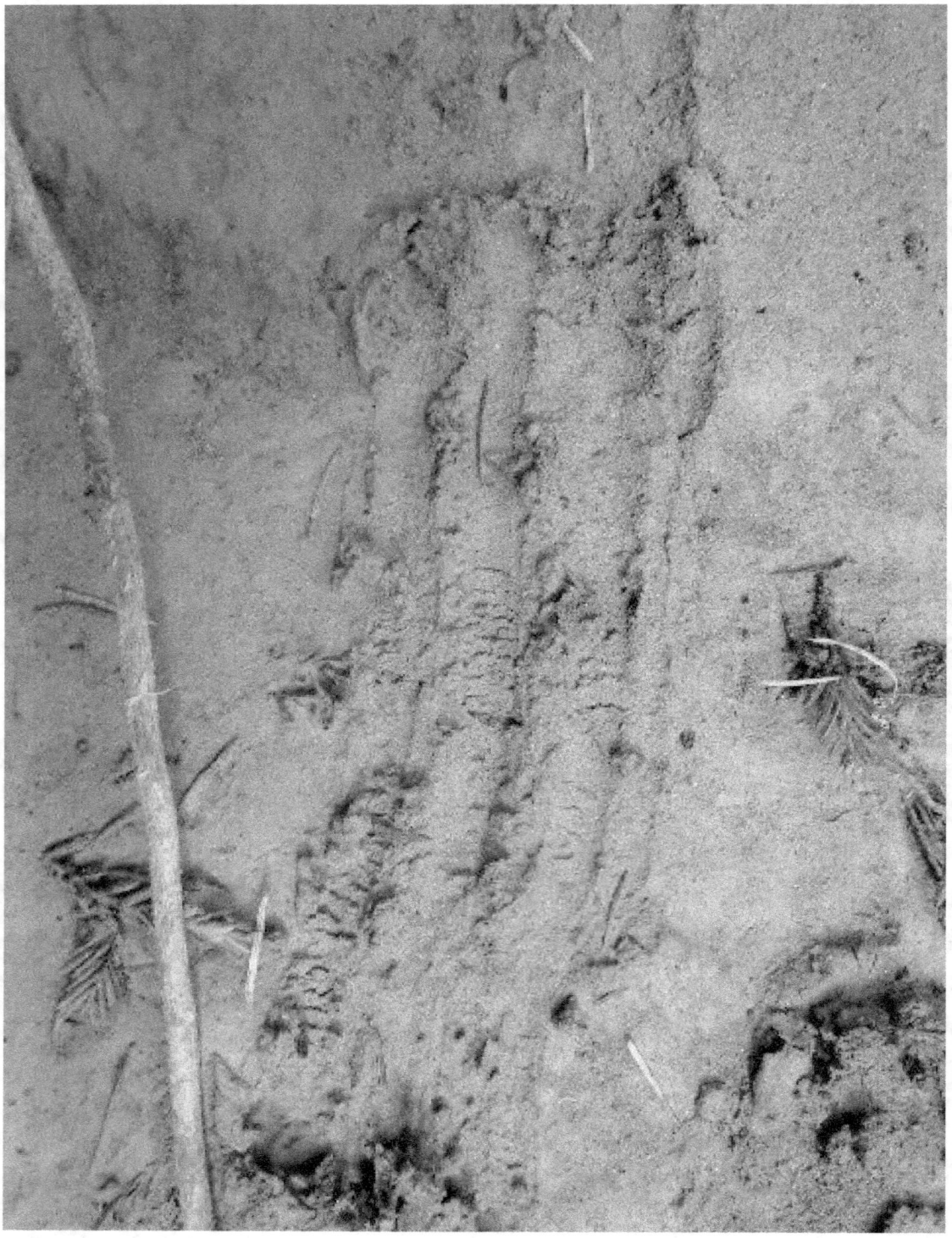

Sasquatch finger drag marks in soft clay, northern California.

Item 21Z

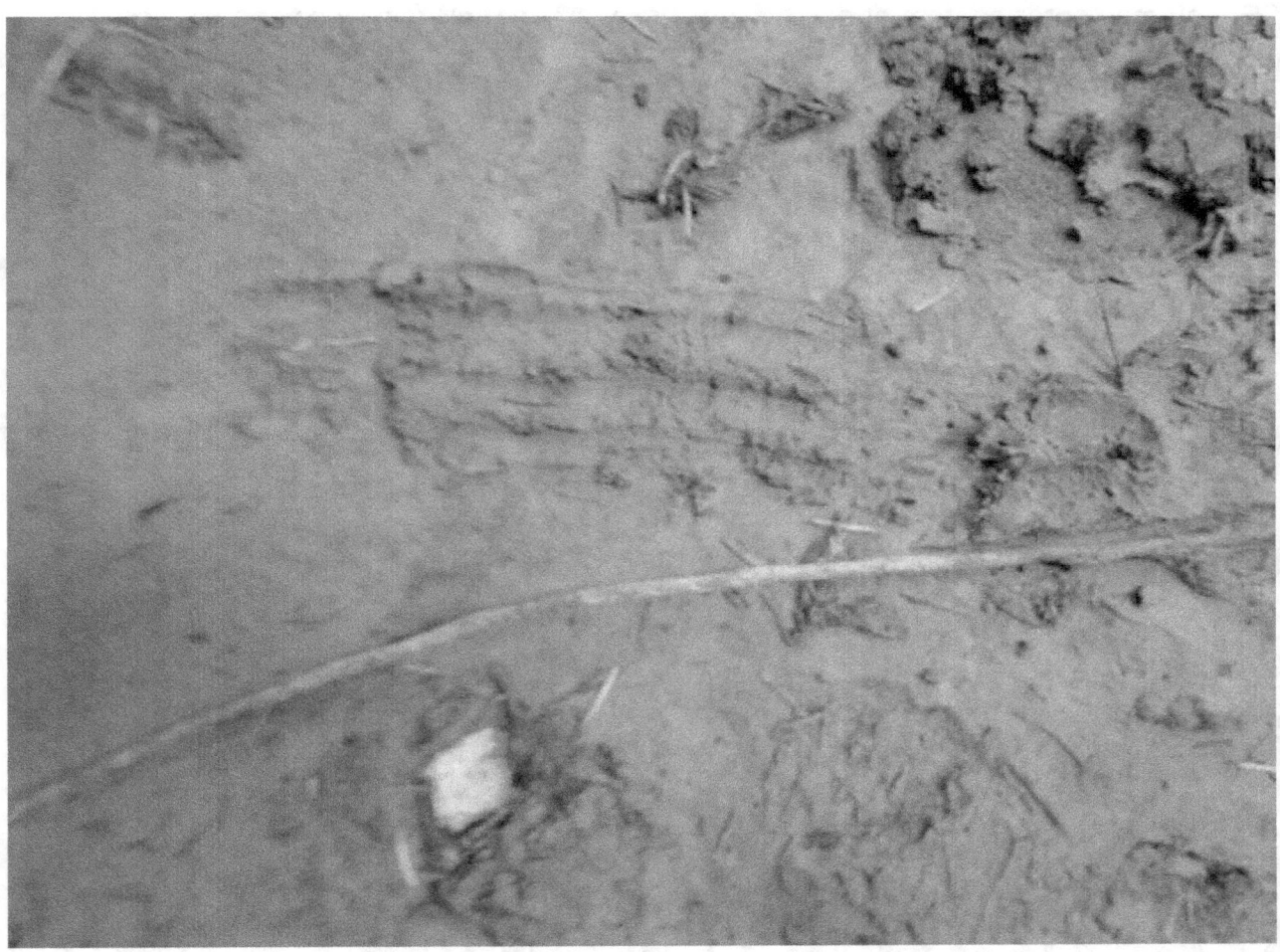

Different perspective of Sasquatch finger drag marks in soft clay, northern California.

PLAINTIFF: Your honor there are two last types of evidence to enter into the record, they are inconclusive as the first item regarding hair samples of the purported creatures cannot be accurately determined. DNA testing can only get as close as "unknown primate" which in scientific terms can mean many things. The second area of evidence is in regards to vocalizations of the creatures. This too cannot be accurately demonstrated however recordings do show a vocal range far above most known animals and humans on the North American continent.

JUDGE: You may enter an item of each, council may argue their relevance at a later time in the proceedings.

PLAINTIFF: Thank you your honor, I would like to enter the first item as item 22A and the second as Item 23A.

Item 22A

Hair sample of purported Sasquatch, often characterized as of different strand length and thick and coarse.

Item 23A

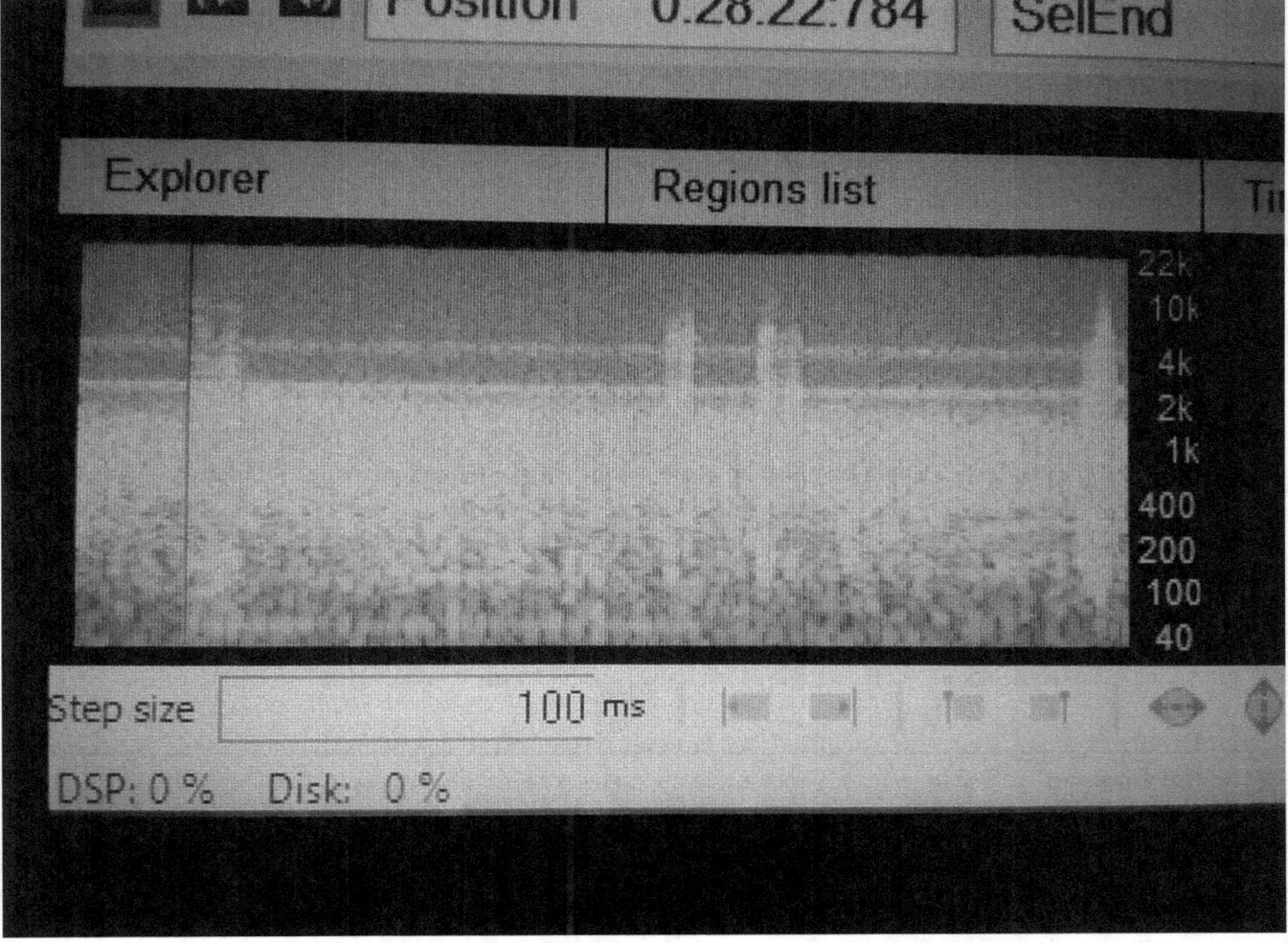

This audio graph is of a purported Sasquatch vocalization, its range on the chart is registered far above known animals and humans.

PLAINTIFF: Your honor I have one final item to enter into evidence, and this is in regard to legislative bodies establishing a precedent by recognition of the Sasquatch through legislation both recognizing and establishing laws to protect said species.

JUDGE: You may enter such documents as necessary into the court record.

PLAINTIFF: Thank you your honor. The documentation will be entered as items 24A and 24B.

Item 24A

ORDINANCE NO. 69-01

BE IT HEREBY ORDAINED BY THE BOARD OF COUNTY COMMISSIONERS OF SKAMANIA COUNTY:

WHEREAS, there is evidence to indicate the possible existence in Skamania County of a nocturnal primate mammal variously described as an ape-like creature or a sub-species of Homo Sapien; and

WHEREAS, both legend and purported recent sightings and spoor support this possibility, and

WHEREAS, this creature is generally and commonly known as a "Sasquatch", "Yeti","Bigfoot", or "Giant Hairy Ape", and

WHEREAS, publicity attendant upon such real or imagined sightings has resulted in an influx of scientific investigators as well as casual hunters, many armed with lethal weapons, and

WHEREAS, the absence of specific laws covering the taking of specimens encourages laxity in the use of firearms and other deadly devices and poses a clear and present threat to the safety and well – being of persons living or traveling within the borders of Skamania County as to the creatures themselves,

THEREFORE BE IT RESOLVED that any premeditated, willful and wanton slaying of any such creature shall be deemed a felony punishable by a fine not to exceed Ten Thousand Dollars ($10,000.00) and/or imprisonment in the county jail for a period not to exceed Five (5) years.

BE IT FURTHER RESOLVED that the situation existing constitutes an emergency and as such this ordinance is effective immediately.

ADOPTED this 1st day of April 1969.

BOARD OF COMMISSIONERS OF SKAMANIA COUNTY

Item 24B

ORDINANCE NO. 1984-2

PARTIALLY REPEALING AND AMENDING ORDINANCE NO. 1969-01

WHEREAS, evidence continues to accumulate indicating the possible existence within Skamania County of a nocturnal primate mammal variously described as an ape-like creature or sub-species of Homo sapiens;

WHEREAS, legend, purported recent findings, and spoor support this possibility; and

WHEREAS, this creature is generally and commonly known as "Sasquatch", "Yeti", "Bigfoot", or "Giant Hairy Ape", all of which terms may hereafter be used interchangeably; and

WHEREAS, publicity attendant upon such real or imagined findings and other evidence have resulted in an influx of scientific investigators as well as casual hunters, most of which are armed with lethal weapons; and

WHEREAS, the absence of specific national and state laws restricting the taking of specimens has created a dangerous state of affairs within this county with regard to firearms and other deadly devices used to hunt the Yeti and poses a clear and present danger to the safety and well being of persons living or traveling within the boundaries of this county as well as to the Giant Hairy Apes themselves; and

WHEREAS, previous county ordinance No. 1969-01 deemed the slaying of such a creature to be a felony (punishable by 5 years in prison) and may have exceeded the jurisdictional authority of that Board of County Commissioners; now, therefore

BE IT HEREBY ORDAINED BY THE BOARD OF COUNTY COMMISSIONERS OF SKAMANIA COUNTY that that portion of ordinance No. 1969-01, deeming the slaying of Bigfoot to be a felony and punishable by 5 years in prison is hereby repealed and in its stead the following sections are enacted:

SECTION 1. Sasquatch Refuge. The Sasquatch, Yeti, Bigfoot, or Giant Hairy Ape are declared to be endangered species of Skamania County and there is hereby created a Sasquatch Refuge, the boundaries of which shall be co-extensive with the boundaries of Skamania County.

SECTION 2. Crime – penalty. From and after the passage of this ordinance the premeditated, willful, or wanton slaying of Sasquatch shall be unlawful and shall be punishable as follows:

(a) If the actor is found to be guilty of such a crime with malice aforethought, such act shall be deemed a Gross Misdemeanor.

(b) If the act is found to be premeditated and willful or wanton but without malice aforethought, such act shall be deemed a Misdemeanor.

(c) A gross misdemeanor slaying of Sasquatch shall be punishable by 1 year in the county jail and a $1,000.00 fine, or both.

(c) The slaying of Sasquatch which is deemed a misdemeanor shall be punishable by a $500.00 fine and up to 6 months in the county jail, or both.

SECTION 3. Defense. In the prosecution and trial of any accused Sasquatch killer the fact that the actor is suffering from insane delusions, diminished capacity, or that the act was the product of a diseased mind, shall not be a defense.

SECTION 4. Humanoid/Anthropoid. Should the Skamania County coroner determine any victim/creature to have been humanoid the prosecuting attorney shall pursue the case under existing laws pertaining to homicide. Should the coroner determine the victim to have been an anthropoid (ape-like creature) the prosecuting attorney shall proceed under the terms of this ordinance.

BE IT FURTHER ORDAINED that the situation existing constitutes an emergency and as such this ordinance shall become effective immediately upon it's passage.

REVIEWED this 2nd day of April, 1984, and set for public hearing on the 16th day of April, 1984, at 10:30 o'clock a.m.

BOARD OF COUNTY COMMISSIONERS
Skamania County, Washington

PLAINTIFF: Counties are not allowed to make felony laws, only state and federal lawmakers have the authority to make felony laws. This is why in 1984 Skamania County had to revise the original ordinance and making offenses misdemeanors.

PLAINTIFF: Your honor, I am now prepared to make arguments with opposing council.

Author note: As I mentioned at the beginning of this book, my intent was not to get into a full fictional trial rather my intent was to demonstrate the various kinds of evidence as defined by the law (you the reader may return to how this is determined at the beginning of this book or research the Federal Rules of Evidence to learn more) and how various forms of evidence regarding the Sasquatch would fit into those categories. This has been a very loose trial setting, and of course in an actual trial the witness statements would be approached differently with very specific questions, and the same would be true of evidence. My overall intent with presenting this book in this perspective is an attempt to open minds and views. There is much more covered in the Federal Rules of Evidence, and no doubt attorneys would be able to add much to a legalistic approach to the problem of Sasquatch evidence. The subject of the Sasquatch has become mired in public opinion and should be looked at from more perspectives than personal opinions. You the reader are the jury, it is now up to you to decide

ABOUT THE AUTHOR

William Jevning is a two time witness in Sasquatch encounters. He is the author of books such as Notes From the Field, Tracking North Americas sasquatch, In Search of the Unknown, Haunted Valley, The Minnesota Iceman, Bigfoot Field Work 101 and Witness of the Unknown volume one. He has been on television shows such as the history channels Americas Book of Secrets, the mystery of Bigfoot and does many radio and podcasts. His website is williamjevning.com

www.ingramcontent.com/pod-product-compliance
Lightning Source LLC
Chambersburg PA
CBHW081345280526
45788CB00009B/2776